Christine Manfield's
Indian Cooking Class

Christine Manfield's

Indian Cooking Class

A JULIE GIBBS BOOK

for

SIMON & SCHUSTER
AUSTRALIA

Contents

Introduction

Think of this book as a personal masterclass. It's a guide, where I take you by the hand to explore the intoxicating world of spice and straightforward techniques that are the benchmark of Indian cooking. From popular snacks to tantalising salads, favourite curries, piquant pickles and enticing desserts, these modern and home-style recipes are simple to follow and easy to master.

With this collection of recipes, I am looking at the traditions and endless flavour compilations of Indian food through a contemporary Western lens to create an enriching sensory experience. These are recipes I have collected and adapted or invented myself, drawing on taste memories from my extensive travels through the regions of India over the past three decades. It is the abiding love I have for India and its diverse culinary heritage that I wish to share with you in these pages, so you, too, can discover the flavours that have come to define Indian food as we know it and to find pleasure and comfort in cooking it.

The Indian kitchen is a fragrant one defined by the masterful blending of spices and intriguing array of flavours with heady, captivating aromas. The Indian palate is adventurous and attuned to an extraordinary array of flavour combinations. Food is typically spiced up in the kitchen to varying degrees and the genius lies in using spice to enhance, rather than dominate. As you explore these recipes and develop confidence with their flavours and techniques, it's vital to learn to distinguish between spice and heat. These elements play different roles yet are often mistakenly confused. Chillies generally imply heat and, depending on type, can range from gentle to fiery, so you'll need to develop your palate to the nuances of chilli flavours and varieties, and use them accordingly.

Spicing food, on the other hand, is all about maximising and creating depth of flavour. Spices lie at the heart of Indian cooking and Ayurvedic practice (which ascribes specific attributes to each fruit, vegetable and spice), giving food its unique character. All spices are believed to have therapeutic properties and healing powers, so knowing how and what to blend is integral to balanced cooking.

It follows that learning to cook Indian food successfully demands an understanding of spice. The blending of spices gives a dish its character, complexity and distinctive flavour. It is a fascinating subject and practice, and one that provides constant challenges, while also helping to personalise your cooking through the countless nuances of taste and texture.

Experiment with the intricacies of spice chemistry until the blending becomes instinctive and know that a properly spiced dish should be awake, but not angry. Once this skill is mastered, you will enjoy one of the most pleasant culinary euphoria – the harmony of flavours. Spice blends are open to interpretation by the blender and blending is the essence of good cooking – it's akin to a sensual awakening. To indulge is to experience an intoxicating world, allowing us to enjoy aromatic, fragrant, pungent, mellow, fiery and delicious taste sensations. Spices are the words that come together to create the language of food. It's a little like writing a brilliant musical score. So when planning your menus, be it a simple family dinner or an extravagant, celebratory feast, be mindful to create a synergy of flavours, textures and cooking styles for harmony and balance. For the novice cook, there's a lot to learn.

India has always used outside influence and invasion to its advantage. This is manifest in its cultural diversity, religious complexity and geography, but is perhaps best displayed through its culinary traditions. The dominant Hindu and Muslim food habits and practices are complemented and influenced by Persian, English and Portuguese invaders, and the Jain, Parsi, Sikh, Buddhist and Christian religions, each with their own specific taboos. While the Mughal invaders from Persia gave India its grand architecture and extraordinary monuments, arguably their greatest legacy was the transformation of the country's culinary landscape by blending the refined cooking

of the royal courts with Indian spices and local ingredients. It was a union that led to some of the world's boldest and most exquisite recipes that still endure today. Layer that with regional differences and it's easy to see the extraordinary diversity in India's culinary make-up with foods that are specific to each region and religion, as well as those that are enjoyed for festivals and celebrations. I often say if you close your eyes and taste, you can identify where in the country you are by the flavour punctuations.

With this cookbook, my aim is to share my love for these distinctive flavours and to encourage intuitive, confident cooking. These approachable, everyday recipes have been inspired by my excitement for Indian flavours and traditions, yet are adapted to suit our modern lifestyles and tastes. They're relevant to the keen cook who respects long-held traditions, while also accommodating innovative changes to food culture. This collection sometimes takes familiar flavours and techniques in a new direction, but still remains true to origin. It also includes recipes where I have interpreted flavours and given them a more Western appearance. In both cases, the intention is to broaden your palate, and your appreciation and understanding of India's extraordinary culinary tapestry, then and now.

Inspired by the diverse culinary regions across the vast subcontinent, these recipes range from the northern plains where wheat, cereals, basmati rice, ghee and a generous use of cream and butter abound; to coastal regions accented by an abundance of seafood; onto the south, where coconuts, curry leaves, spices and rice dominate; to the desert states of the west – Rajasthan and Gujarat – where mustard, chickpeas, lentils and robust meat dishes reign supreme; and north to the broad Himalayan regions, where mountainous terrain and rivers determine farming practices, pork is a common meat, and the salting and fermentation of fruit and vegetables are defining characteristics. As is the common practice in all these regions, in your own cooking, be sure to use produce that's locally grown or harvested. Cooking in season when produce is at its peak with minimum travel miles is key to flavoursome fare, regardless of the cuisine.

Indian food isn't difficult to cook once you learn the basics. Start with simple steps and use my helpful tips along the way that make for organised and achievable preparation. Hopefully, as you cook your way through this book, you will be armed with a good knowledge of the essentials and an appreciation of spices, enabling you to conquer Indian cooking with confidence.

Now it's your turn to master the simple art of Indian cooking with recipes that are refreshing, vibrant, colourful and packed with flavour. It's all about sharing the love of good food – the common thread that lies at the heart of Indian cuisine.

Snacks

Think of Indian snacks in the same way you would Italian antipasti, Chinese dim sum or Spanish tapas. *Chaat* is the Indian name for savoury snacks and an integral part of the food culture. Exploring street food and snacks is a lesson in exploring colour, taste and aroma, with a never-ending list of visually thrilling morsels to sate the palate.

No matter where you are in India, snacking on street food is a daily ritual. More than an informal way of eating on-the-go, it's also a social exercise and a way of life. Snacks are sold by street vendors from their modest carts or makeshift kitchens, from tea stalls, on railway platforms and even aboard trains, with the vendors jumping on at one station and hawking their wares through the carriages before alighting at the next. You'll also find vendors at beachside hawker stalls, in temples and at *dhabas* (humble cafes).

Street food and snacks vary regionally and range from those commonly known in the west, such as kebabs, koftas, cutlets, samosas, pakoras, fritters, bhajias and momos, to the less familiar *kachoris* (deep-fried breads), *pani puri* (stuffed fried puffs), *papri chaat* (fried besan wafers tossed with potato, chickpeas, spices, chilli, chutney, yoghurt and sprinkled with sev puri), and stuffed *parathas* (flatbreads), all with flavours that range from delicately spiced to aromatic and fiery. Chaat is synonymous with Mumbai, but found across the country in every city, town and village with a plethora of snacks tempting with aromas that beckon you to eat.

The defining profile of snacks is their contrasting textures, encompassing both crunchy and soft with a flavour spectrum that ranges from sweet and salty to tangy and spicy. Street vendors are masters at producing snacks en masse, then packing up when stock is sold. Each vendor has a specialty, which draws customers in, and everyone has their favourite vendor for particular snacks. People in India are very friendly and they love nothing more than to strike up a conversation about food and to share their favourite places. It's the savvy traveller who seeks out this advice and local knowledge to take their curious palate for a flavourful adventure.

Depending on whom you talk to, Kolkata is widely regarded as being the most famous for its culture of street food. Although, I imagine a statement like this could be hotly contested by other cities in India. Growing to love the city more with every visit, I am astounded by the sheer inventiveness, thrift and skill displayed by the street vendors. It's a scene played out on the streets across India, the scope is so lively and invigorating. Essential tastes of this beguiling city include *jhaal muri* (spicy puffed rice); *singharas* (Bengali samosa); *kathi kebab rolls* (invented at Nizam's in Kolkata, spice-marinated beef, chicken or lamb kebabs cooked on a hotplate, rolled in an egg-coated

paratha with onions, chilli and garlic); *momos* (dumplings); *egg toast* (a masala omelette with bread filling); or sweet *sandesh* made with just milk and sugar.

Mumbai is home to the famous *bhel puri* (similar to jhaal muri, above), *vada pao* (potato burger), *pao bhaji* (vegetable curry in a soft bun), *bread pakora* (fried vegetable fritter), vegetable puffs and *bun maska* (a soft, buttery bun). While Gujarat is spoilt for choice with its repertoire of vegetarian snacks, such as the steamed *dhokla* (savoury lentil cakes), pani puri, *sev puri* (crisp crackers topped with potato, chutney and gram flour noodles), the widely known rice pancake *dosa* and the huge variety of salty, fried snacks or *farsan*. Varanasi is praised for its crispy *kachori* (deep-fried pastries), and you'll find the memorably sweet and sticky fried *jalebis* in Amritsar, Jaipur and Delhi. I will never forget the wickedly addictive butter dosa, the defining breakfast snack in Hyderabad; the *dal roti* (flatbread with lentil curry) in Kochi, the tandoor baked *kulcha* flatbreads in Amritsar; the creamy, rich yoghurt drink *lassi* in Jodhpur or the *aloo tikka* (potato fritters) in Jaipur. In Kerala, snacks are known as 'short eats' (a term also synonymous with Sri Lanka) or 'tea snacks', as they're usually served with tea. The term refers to a bite-size snack that is fried or stuffed and can include banana fritters, *vadas* (deep-fried lentil snack) or patties.

Namkeen or *bhujia* is the all-encompassing name given to salty and savoury snacks, such as sev, puri crackers, papdi, roasted chana, puffed rice, spiced nuts and fried peas, often seasoned with chaat masala. These are factory-made and packaged (like the Western potato chip) with much of their production centred around Delhi and Gujarat, but sold at Indian grocers the world over. *Walas* are vendors who ply their trade – tiffin wala, pakora wala, chai wala and, of course, the chaat wala. Think of them as mobile canteens that you'll find throughout India, carving out a living with their humble trade, which is essential to the backbone of society.

In this chapter, allow these recipes to bring a treasured travel memory to life or simply spruik up your repertoire with these jazzy snacks to stimulate the appetite. Being hand-held and convenient, they're ideal for casual grazing and perfect for serving with drinks.

Stuffed Potato Chops DF

Croquettes often take on the quaint name of chops in India, a popular and substantial snack found not only on the menus in the private clubs of Kolkata and Mumbai, but also with street food vendors. Spiced minced meat is enclosed in a mashed potato casing then coated with breadcrumbs and fried. This snack reminds me of a bite-size version of shepherd's pie, livened up with aromatic spices.

Makes 12

650 g potatoes, peeled
2 long green chillies, minced
½ teaspoon ground cumin
1 teaspoon ground coriander
½ teaspoon ground cardamom
½ teaspoon freshly ground black pepper
1 teaspoon sea salt flakes
2 tablespoons chopped coriander leaves
¼ cup fine semolina
2 eggs, beaten
200 g panko breadcrumbs
2 cups (500 ml) vegetable oil, for deep-frying
1 red onion, sliced into thin rings

LAMB FILLING
1 tablespoon vegetable oil
½ white onion, finely diced
1 tablespoon ginger garlic paste, see recipe
  page 436
200 g minced lamb
1 teaspoon ground coriander
1 teaspoon ground cumin
½ teaspoon Kashmiri chilli powder
½ teaspoon garam masala
1 teaspoon sea salt flakes
2 teaspoons lemon juice

To prepare the lamb filling, heat the oil in a frying pan over medium heat. Add the onion and cook for 4 minutes or until softened. Add the ginger garlic paste and cook a further 2 minutes or until fragrant. Add the lamb mince, stirring constantly to break up the mince, and cook for 4 minutes or until starting to colour. Add the ground spices, stir to combine and cook for a further 10 minutes or until lamb is tender. Stir through salt and lemon juice and cook for 5 minutes. Remove from heat and place the filling in a sieve over a bowl to allow excess liquid to drain. The meat shouldn't be too wet or you won't be able to roll it into the potato casing. Set aside to cool completely.

To prepare the potato, boil the potatoes in a pot of lightly salted water over medium–high heat for 10–12 minutes or until tender. Drain and allow potatoes to dry out for 10 minutes. Pass potatoes through a potato masher (do not puree in blender or food processor, as this will give a gluey texture).

Place the chilli, ground spices, salt and chopped coriander in a bowl with the mashed potato and mix to combine. While the potato is still warm, divide the mixture into 12 even-size portions and roll each portion into a ball in the palm of your hand. I find it helps to dampen your hands with water so the mixture doesn't stick. Using your finger, make a deep impression in the top of the ball and fill with a teaspoonful of the lamb filling. Carefully fold the potato over the filling to encase. Flatten the ball into a patty, dust with semolina, dip into the egg and roll to coat with the breadcrumbs. Place spaced apart in a single layer on a baking tray lined with baking paper.

Heat the oil in a wok or large saucepan over medium–high heat to 180°C. Fry the chops, in batches to maintain oil temperature and rolling in the oil for even cooking, for 4–5 minutes or until golden brown. Drain on paper towel. Serve topped with onion rings.

**Masterclass step-by-step
Stuffed Potato Chops →**

1 Heat the oil in a frying pan over medium heat.

2 Add the onion and cook for 4 minutes or until softened.

3 Add the ginger garlic paste and cook for a further 2 minutes.

4 Add the lamb mince, stirring to break up mince. Cook for 4 minutes.

5 Add the ground coriander and cumin and stir to combine.

6 Add the Kashmiri chilli powder and stir to combine.

7 Add the garam masala, stir and cook for 10 minutes.

8 Add the sea salt.

9 Add the lemon juice. Cook for 5 minutes.

10 Remove from heat. Place filling in a sieve over a bowl to drain.

11 Drain boiled potatoes.

12 Place on a tray to dry for 10 minutes.

13

Pass the potatoes through a potato masher into a bowl.

14

Add the chopped green chilli.

15

Add the ground spices.

16

Add the chopped coriander leaves and mix to combine.

17

While still warm, divide the mixture into 12 even-size portions. Roll into balls.

18

Dampen hands and flatten balls in the palm of your hand.

19

Place 1 teaspoon of the mince filling in the centre.

20

Carefully fold the potato over the filling to encase.

21

Dust each with semolina.

22

Dip in the egg.

23

Roll to coat with the breadcrumbs.

24

Fry, in batches, for 4–5 minutes or until

Potato and Pea Samosas ᵥ

Samosas are the perennial favourite snack all over India and known as *shingara* in Bengal. Handmade in the millions every day, everywhere, they're sold at tea stalls across the country and are a staple snack for workers, drivers and snack devotees. This version is based on the ones I ate in Ahmedabad. They can be made with various different fillings and Indians find it easier to buy them than make at home.

Makes 18

30 g ghee
250 g waxy potatoes, diced and par-boiled
1 teaspoon minced garlic
1 teaspoon minced ginger
2 small green chillies, minced
125 g shelled fresh peas, blanched
2 teaspoons chaat masala
2 tablespoons chopped coriander leaves
1 teaspoon sea salt flakes
½ teaspoon freshly ground black pepper
2 cups (500 ml) vegetable oil, for deep-frying
3 tablespoons mint chutney, to serve, see Pickles
    and Chutneys page 361

SAMOSA PASTRY
275 g plain flour
50 g chickpea (besan) flour
1 teaspoon sea salt flakes
100 g ghee, melted
75 ml warm water

To make the pastry, place all the ingredients in a food processor and blend until the dough forms into a ball. Turn out onto a bench and knead for 2 minutes. Wrap in plastic film and set aside to rest at room temperature for 2 hours.

Meanwhile, to make the filling, melt the ghee in a frying pan over medium heat. Add the potato, garlic, ginger and chilli for cook for 5 minutes or until softened and fragrant. Add the peas and toss to combine. Remove from heat and stir through the chaat masala, coriander, salt and pepper. Allow to cool completely.

To assemble the samosas, roll the pastry into a long, rope-like length. Cut into 18 even-size pieces and roll each piece out to a thin round (approximately 8 cm in diameter). Spoon the filling into the centre of each round, fold in half and fold in half again to make a triangle. Using your fingertips, press the edges together firmly to seal.

Heat the oil in a deep-fryer or wok to 180°C. Fry the samosas, a few at a time, for 5 minutes or until golden and crisp. Use a slotted spoon to keep the samosas submerged in the oil for even cooking. Drain on paper towel. Serve hot with mint chutney.

Potato and Tamarind Papdi DF, V

Contrasting textures with sweet and tangy flavours jumbled together makes *sev puri* one of my most enduring memories of street food snacks in India. Each papdi is a fried, bite-size puri disc, and if you don't have time to make them yourself, they are readily available in packets at Indian grocers. I think of this delectable snack as the Indian equivalent of a Thai *miang* (betel leaf snack).

Serves 6

50 g mashed potato
50 g finely diced red onion
50 g finely diced tomatoes
2 tablespoons boondi (puffed lentils),
   see Glossary
50 g sev (lentil batter), see Glossary
1 tablespoon chopped coriander leaves
2 teaspoons finely diced green mango, peeled
1 teaspoon chaat masala

SWEET TAMARIND CHUTNEY
½ cup (120 g) tamarind puree
4 dates, chopped
½ teaspoon ground cumin
50 g palm sugar

HOT CHUTNEY
½ cup coriander leaves, chopped
2 tablespoons mint leaves, chopped
3 small green chillies
2 garlic cloves
½ teaspoon ground cumin
½ teaspoon sea salt flakes

PAPDI
1 cup (150 g) plain flour
1 teaspoon sea salt flakes
½ teaspoon ajwain seeds, see Glossary
½ teaspoon cumin seeds
2 tablespoons melted ghee
2 cups (500 ml) vegetable oil

To make the papdi, sift the flour and salt into a bowl. Stir in the spices and ghee and use your hands to combine until mixture is crumbly and starting to come together. Add 2 tablespoons water and continue to knead the dough, adding a little more water as required. You should use about ⅓ cup (80 ml) to make the dough firm and pliable, but not sticky. It should be the same consistency as pasta dough. Cover the bowl with a cloth and set aside to rest for 20 minutes. Once rested, knead the dough again for a further 1 minute to loosen the glutens.

Divide the dough into 6 even-size pieces. Shape each piece into a ball and flatten between your hands. Roll out on a lightly floured surface to make a 2 mm-thick, 20 cm-diameter round. It should be just a little thicker than a pappadam. Prick the surface all over with a fork (this prevents the papdi from puffing up as they are fried). Cut smaller rounds using a 6 cm-round pastry cutter.

Heat the oil in wok or large saucepan over medium–high heat to 180°C. Fry the rounds, a few at a time, for 2 minutes or until golden. Turn over and cook on the other side for a further 2 minutes. Remove with a slotted spoon and drain on paper towel. Set aside to cool completely and store in an airtight container until ready to use. You will need approximately 30 (250 g) fried papdi for this recipe, any extra can be stored for later use.

To make the sweet tamarind chutney, place the tamarind, dates, cumin, sugar and 200 ml water in a saucepan over medium heat, bring to the boil and cook for 5–6 minutes. Pass the mixture through a coarse sieve and discard solids. The chutney should be of medium consistency, not too thick or thin. Set aside.

To make the hot chutney, place all the ingredients and 2 tablespoons of water (or enough to just loosen the mixture) in a mortar and pestle and grind to make a paste. Set aside.

Arrange the fried papdi in single layer on a flat plate without overlapping, this way they can be picked up individually. Top each papdi with mashed potato, chopped onion, tomato and boondi. Spoon over a little of each chutney to your taste and sprinkle liberally with sev to cover. Garnish with chopped coriander, diced green mango and a sprinkle of chaat masala.

Yoghurt and Chickpea Chaat v

Dahi papdi chaat is a snack originating in Delhi, but is widespread throughout India. It's similar to *sev puri* in its ingredient list and flavour profile, but with the addition of yoghurt. Rather than each papdi being garnished to serve as a single bite, they are bunched together in a single layer to form a base on a plate then everything is piled on top and eaten with a spoon. It's totally fine to use store-bought papdi to make it a quick fix snack, if you're not up to making your own. This snack is a real flavour bomb with every element complementing each other.

Serves 4

½ cup thick plain yoghurt
1 tablespoon caster sugar
1½ teaspoons sea salt flakes
1 cup diced boiled potato
1 cup cooked chickpeas
½ cup mung bean sprouts
2 tablespoons pomegranate seeds
½ teaspoon ground cumin
½ teaspoon Kashmiri chilli powder
¼ teaspoon chaat masala
20 store-bought or homemade papdi discs,
    see Potato and Tamarind Papdi recipe left
2 tablespoons sweet tamarind chutney,
    see Potato and Tamarind Papdi recipe left
1 tablespoon green chilli chutney, to serve,
    see Pickles and Chutneys page 364
2 tablespoons chopped coriander leaves
2 tablespoons sev (lentil batter), see Glossary

Place the yoghurt, sugar, ½ teaspoon salt and 2 tablespoons water in a bowl and whisk until smooth.

Place the diced potato, chickpeas, mung bean sprouts, pomegranate seeds, remaining 1 teaspoon salt and the ground spices in a bowl. Add to the yoghurt mixture and stir to combine.

To serve, arrange 5 papdi on each plate to form a base for the topping. Spoon over the potato mixture to cover and drizzle generously with the tamarind chutney and green chilli chutney. Garnish with the chopped coriander and sev.

Spicy Puffed Rice DF, GF, V

Jhaal muri is a popular Bengali street food snack I became enamoured with in Kolkata. Prepared by street vendors from their modest kerb-side carts, each bite of this savoury snack is a revelation of textures and flavours and is the Bengali version of Mumbai's *bhel puri*. *Muri* is the Hindi word for 'puffed rice', hence the snack's name. Traditionally served in cones made from newspaper or small bowls made from dried neem leaves when consumed on the street, I also serve it as a salad to accompany grilled fish or roasted vegetables. Once you have all the ingredients prepared, the assembly is very quick and it's excellent to serve with welcome drinks at a dinner or party. The only trick is to make sure you serve it as soon as you've mixed the ingredients together, as this keeps all the textures intact.

Serves 6

1 cup fried rice flakes
1 cup puffed brown rice
¼ teaspoon garam masala
½ teaspoon chaat masala
¼ teaspoon ground cumin
½ teaspoon Kashmiri chilli powder
¼ teaspoon ground black salt
½ red onion, finely diced
1 long green chilli, finely diced
½ small cucumber, peeled, seeded and finely diced
1 tomato, quartered, seeded and finely diced
2 small boiled chat (or new) potatoes, peeled and finely diced
1 tablespoon chopped coriander leaves
½ teaspoon minced ginger
3 tablespoons roasted peanuts, roughly chopped
3 tablespoons sev (lentil batter), see Glossary
1 tablespoon shredded coconut
2 teaspoons lime juice
2 teaspoons mustard oil
1 teaspoon sea salt flakes

Heat a frying pan over low heat, add the rice flakes and puffed brown rice and cook, stirring to keep an even heat, for 2–3 minutes or until crisp and crunchy. Add the ground spices and black salt and toss until rice is evenly coated. Remove from heat and allow to cool.

Place the onion, chilli, cucumber, tomato and potato in a bowl with the coriander and ginger and mix to combine. Add the toasted puffed rice mixture, peanut, sev and coconut and mix to combine. Add the lime juice, mustard oil and salt and toss to combine. Serve immediately.

Potato Puri Puffs, Tamarind and Mint Water DF, GF, V

Pani puri is one of India's most common street foods, consisting of a round or ball-shaped hollow puri, known as *golgappa* in Varanasi and Delhi and *puchkar* in Kolkata. They're stuffed with spiced potato and chickpeas, filled with *khatta meetha pani*, or 'sweet tangy water', and eaten on the spot.

Serves 6

PURI PUFFS
1 cup (160 g) fine semolina
2 tablespoons plain flour
½ teaspoon sea salt flakes
1 teaspoon baking powder
2 tablespoons vegetable oil
2 cups (500 ml) vegetable oil, extra,
    for deep-frying
1 tablespoon chopped mint

POTATO STUFFING
2 tablespoons vegetable oil
100 g cooked potato, peeled and finely diced
2 tablespoons cooked black chickpeas, slightly
    mashed
½ teaspoon sea salt flakes
2 teaspoons chaat masala
½ teaspoon chilli powder
2 tablespoons chopped coriander leaves

TAMARIND MINT WATER
1 cup (250 ml) mint leaves
½ cup coriander leaves
2 small green chillies, chopped
1 tablespoon lime juice
2 teaspoons minced ginger
1 teaspoon chaat masala
¼ cup (60 ml) tamarind puree
3 tablespoons caster sugar
½ teaspoon ground black salt
2 teaspoons ground cumin
½ teaspoon ground fennel seeds
½ teaspoon freshly ground black pepper
3 tablespoons boondi (puffed lentils),
    see Glossary

To make the puri puffs, place the semolina, flour, salt, baking powder and oil in a bowl and, using your hands, work the mixture until it is crumbly. Add ¼ cup (60 ml) hot water, turn the dough out onto and knead for 2 minutes or until it comes together. Add another ¼ cup (60 ml) hot water and continue to knead for a further 3 minutes or until a smooth dough forms. Add a little extra water if it feels too firm. You're kneading the dough long enough to soften the glutens, but not overwork it.

Roll the dough into a ball, place in a bowl, cover with a cloth and set aside to rest for 30 minutes. Turn the dough out onto a bench and knead for 2 minutes, the dough should feel quite elastic. Divide into 3 even-size pieces and roll each piece into a 4 mm-thick round, keeping the sheet of dough in one piece without any cracks. The dough must be even and thin, otherwise the puris won't puff up when fried. Use a 4 cm-round pastry cutter to cut out rounds.

Heat the oil in wok or large saucepan over medium–high heat to 180°C. Fry the puri rounds, a few at a time, for 1 minute or until they puff up. Turn over in the oil and continue to cook, flipping a couple more times, for 5 minutes or until crisp and golden. The puris need to cook in the oil until crisp and golden inside and out – if they're not cooked through, they will be too soft in the centre. Remove puri puffs from the oil with a slotted spoon and drain on paper towel. Allow to cool. Store in an airtight container for up to 1 week.

To make the potato stuffing, heat the oil in a frying pan over medium heat. Add the potato and chickpeas and cook, tossing, for 2 minutes. Season with salt, chaat masala and chilli powder and stir through chopped coriander. Set aside.

To make the tamarind mint water, place all the ingredients, except the boondi, in a food processor with 2 cups (500 ml) water and a few ice cubes and blend until smooth. Stir in the boondi just as you are ready to serve.

To serve, using the tip of a sharp knife, make a hole in the centre of each puri puff. The hole needs to be big enough to drop the filling into the centre without breaking the puff – it's a fine balance. Carefully spoon the potato stuffing into the centre of each puri to half-fill and sprinkle with chopped mint. Arrange on plates and serve tamarind mint water separately, to be poured into each puri puff just as it's ready to be eaten.

Dal-stuffed Pastries v

Who doesn't love a fried pastry? I make it my mission when travelling throughout India to sample as many different versions as possible. I find them utterly addictive. *Kachoris* are fried pastries with a spicy dal stuffing that varies from region to region. They're a roadside snack apparently invented in Rajasthan for busy traders. I tasted them for the first time in Kolkata with urad dal and mashed green pea stuffing, which has led to this recipe. I've also had them with a black dal stuffing at a Bihari restaurant in Delhi and with mung dal stuffing (the most common) in Jaipur and Jodphur. The dal stuffing can be made ahead of time, making the final preparation much faster.

Makes 18

100 g plain flour
100 g wholemeal flour
1 teaspoon sea salt flakes
3 teaspoons ghee
1 teaspoon finely shredded curry leaves
1 teaspoon nigella seeds
2 cups (500 ml) vegetable oil, for deep-frying
mint chutney, to serve, see Pickles and Chutneys
    page 361

DAL STUFFING
100 g split urad dal (white lentils), washed and
    soaked in cold water for 2 hours, drained
2 tablespoons vegetable oil
1 teaspoon cumin seeds
¼ teaspoon ground turmeric
¼ teaspoon asafoetida
2 small green chillies, minced
1 tablespoon minced ginger
50 g peas, blanched and mashed to a rough paste
1 teaspoon sea salt flakes
½ teaspoon freshly ground black pepper

To make the dal stuffing, place the dal in a food processor and blend to make a rough paste. Set aside.

Heat the oil in a frying pan over medium heat. Add the cumin seeds and cook for 30 seconds or until they start to pop. Add the turmeric, asafoetida, chilli and ginger and cook, stirring to combine, for a further 30 seconds. Add the dal paste to the pan and stir to coat with the spices. Reduce heat to low, add ½ cup (125 ml) water and cook for 15 minutes or until the water has been absorbed and the mixture has thickened.

Stir through the mashed peas, salt and pepper and set aside to cool.

To make the pastry, sift both the flours and salt into a bowl. Add the ghee, curry leaves and nigella seeds and, using your hands, knead into the flour until the mixture resembles breadcrumbs. Add ½ cup (125 ml) water and continue to work the dough until it is soft and pliable. You may need to add a little extra water. Turn the dough out onto a lightly floured surface and knead for a further 5 minutes (to stretch the glutens) or until shiny and smooth. Cover with a clean cloth and set aside to rest for 30 minutes at room temperature.

Divide the dough into 18 even-size pieces and roll each piece into a ball. Roll each ball out to a 10 cm-diameter flat round, resembling a pancake. Place a spoonful of dal stuffing in the centre of each round and fold the dough over to make a half-moon shape. Press the edges to seal and flatten slightly with a rolling pin, don't press too hard or the filling will spill out.

Heat the oil in a kadhai or wok over high heat to 180°C. To test the temperature of the oil, sprinkle in some flour, if the flour sizzles, the oil is ready. Fry the pastries, a few at a time, for 2 minutes or until golden and crisp. Turn and cook on the other side for a further 1 minute. Using a large, mesh spoon, keep the pastries submerged in the oil so they puff up. Drain on paper towel and serve warm with mint chutney.

Beetroot, Spinach and Cheese Parcels GF, V

Palak paneer is a classic Indian vegetable dish, a slow simmered stew of spinach and fresh cheese. Adding beetroot gives a sweet earthiness and depth of flavour to the mix and makes an intriguing combination. I have taken this up a notch by blanching large beetroot leaves, removing the central stem, to use as a wrapper for the filling, in the exact same way as making a Greek dolmade. This way you have neat little parcels to serve as a snack, far less messy for eating. If that doesn't appeal or sounds like too much fuss, you can fill small pastry shells for serving as a snack to have with drinks. Easier still, place the beetroot mix in a bowl next to a stack of fried pappadams on the table so guests can assemble their own.

Serves 8

2 tablespoons vegetable oil
1 red onion, finely diced
1 tablespoon ginger garlic paste, see recipe
  page 436
1 tablespoon fresh curry leaves
1 teaspoon ground cumin
1 teaspoon ground turmeric
1 bunch English spinach, finely chopped
1 teaspoon sea salt flakes
300 g tomatoes, peeled, seeded and diced
2 small red chillies, minced
2 medium beetroots, roasted, peeled and cut into
  1 cm dice
300 g paneer, cut into 1 cm cubes
¼ teaspoon garam masala
3 tablespoons thick plain yoghurt
1 tablespoon chopped dill
16 large beetroot (or spinach) leaves, central
  stems removed, blanched
1 punnet red chard cress, snipped

Heat the oil in a large, deep frying pan over medium heat. Add the onion and cook for 4 minutes or until softened. Add the ginger garlic paste and curry leaves and cook for 2 minutes or until softened. Add the cumin and turmeric and cook for 1–2 minutes or until aromatic. Add the spinach, stir to coat with the spiced onion and cook for 2 minutes or until wilted. Season with salt, add the tomato and chilli, increase heat to high and bring to the boil. Add the beetroot, cover with a lid, reduce heat to low and simmer gently for 15 minutes. Add the paneer and garam masala, stir to combine and cook for 1 minute or until heated through. Whisk the yoghurt in bowl with 1 tablespoon water to loosen and stir through the mixture with the dill to combine.

To serve, place the blanched leaves on a bench, spoon the mixture onto one end of each leaf and roll up, folding in the sides as you go, to enclose the filling. Arrange rolls on a plate, seam-side down, and scatter with cress to serve.

Green Pea and Onion Fritters GF, V

This is another riff on a pakora, a delectable fried vegetable snack.

Serves 4

1 cup (150 g) chickpea (besan) flour
80 g thick plain yogurt
1 cup fresh or frozen green peas
1 large red onion, sliced into thin rings
1 garlic clove, crushed
2 teaspoons minced ginger
1 tablespoon fresh curry leaves
2 tablespoons chopped coriander leaves
½ teaspoon brown mustard seeds
½ teaspoon ground cumin
½ teaspoon ground turmeric
½ teaspoon chilli powder
½ teaspoon garam masala
1 teaspoon sea salt flakes
2 cups (500 ml) vegetable oil, for deep-frying
mint chutney, to serve, see Pickles and Chutneys
    page 361

Place the flour and yoghurt in a bowl with 100 ml water and whisk to make a thick, smooth batter. Add the remaining ingredients, except the oil and chutney, and stir to combine.

Heat the vegetable oil in a deep-fryer or saucepan over medium–high heat to 180°C. Drop teaspoonfuls of the batter into the oil, in batches, to make small clusters, stirring each time to ensure they don't stick together. Take care they're not too big or thick, or they won't cook evenly. Fry, turning over in the oil with a spoon as they cook, for 3–4 minutes or until golden and crisp. Remove from oil with a slotted spoon and drain on paper towel. Serve hot with the mint chutney.

Sweet Corn Fritters DF, GF, V

This fritter is inspired by a pakora snack I've enjoyed on my travels in Rajasthan, where corn plays a starring role in many recipes. I like to serve these fritters with tomato kasundi pickle. They also make a great addition to a picnic hamper.

Serves 6

1 cup (140 g) rice flour
1 teaspoon baking powder
2 eggs, lightly beaten
½ cup (125 ml) coconut cream
3 corn cobs, kernels removed
3 green shallots, finely sliced
2 tablespoons minced ginger
2 garlic cloves, crushed
1 cup coriander leaves, chopped
½ teaspoon sea salt flakes
½ teaspoon freshly ground black pepper
75 ml vegetable oil
3 tablespoons chopped coriander, extra, to serve
1 long red chilli, thinly sliced diagonally

Place the flour, baking powder, egg and coconut cream in a bowl and whisk to combine. Add the corn kernels, shallot, ginger, garlic, coriander, salt and pepper and stir to combine. The mixture should be a thick batter. If necessary, add a little extra flour.

Heat the oil in a large frying pan over medium heat. Drop teaspoonfuls of the batter into the hot oil and fry for 2 minutes or until crisp. Turn and cook on the other side for a further 2 minutes or until golden. Drain on paper towel over a wire rack. Serve topped with chopped coriander and sliced chilli while hot and crisp.

Cauliflower Pakoras DF, GF, V

Pakoras are the Indian name for fried fritters, where vegetables or fish are coated in a spiced chickpea batter and deep-fried. They're another popular and versatile fried snack that you'll find at roadside vendors, in restaurants and in home kitchens alike. The batter responds better if it has been allowed to rest in the fridge for 30 minutes before cooking. If it thickens up, simply add a splash more water. You're looking for the consistency of pancake batter, so it sticks to the cauliflower when dropped into the hot oil. These are a handy snack to have in your repertoire when cooking for gluten-free friends.

Serves 4

2 cups (500 ml) vegetable oil, for deep-frying
½ cauliflower, cut into small florets
mint yoghurt chutney to serve, see Pickles
    and Chutneys page 362

PAKORA BATTER
100 g chickpea (besan) flour
1 teaspoon baking powder
1 teaspoon garam masala
½ teaspoon ground turmeric
1 teaspoon Kashmiri chilli powder
2 teaspoons white vinegar
1 teaspoon sea salt flakes

To make the pakora batter, place all the pakora ingredients together in a food processor and pulse to combine. Pour in 275 ml water and blend until a pancake-like batter forms. If it looks a bit thick, add a little extra water, but it shouldn't be too thin or it won't coat the cauliflower.

Heat the oil in large saucepan or wok over high heat to 180°C. Dip the cauliflower into the batter to coat and fry, in batches, for 4 minutes or until crisp and golden. Drain on paper towel, serve hot with mint yoghurt chutney.

Onion Bhajias DF, GF, V

A seemingly endless list of *farsan* (salty snacks) are the hallmark of Gujarati food held in reverence, and *bhajias* are among their repertoire. These have a thinner batter that acts as a light glue to keep the onion slices together in a jumbled ball. I've tasted different bhajia using fresh tea leaves in the Darjeeling region, while small spinach leaves or other leafy greens work equally well. Think of it as Indian-style tempura, with the obligatory spicing.

Serves 6

3 red onions, sliced into thin rings
1 teaspoon ground turmeric
1½ teaspoons ground coriander seeds
2 small green chillies, finely chopped
½ teaspoon sea salt flakes
1⅓ cup (200 g) chickpea (besan) flour
1 teaspoon baking powder
2 cups (500 ml) vegetable oil, for deep-frying
mint yoghurt chutney or cucumber raita, to serve, see Pickles and Chutneys page 343

Knead the onion rings to extract any excess liquid and squeeze to discard. Place the onion rings, turmeric, coriander, green chilli and salt in a bowl and mix to combine. Sprinkle over the chickpea flour and baking powder with 2 tablespoons water and continue to knead to combine. If the mixture is too dry, add a little more water, 1 tablespoon at a time. It shouldn't look like a batter, but more like mayonnaise sticking to shredded cabbage.

Heat the oil in a kadhai or wok over medium–high heat to 180°C. To test the temperature of the oil, sprinkle in some flour, if the flour sizzles, the oil is ready. Loosely drop tablespoonfuls of the onion batter into the oil in batches (this is to maintain the oil temperature). Fry for 2 minutes or until crisp and golden. Turn and cook for a further 2 minutes. Remove from the oil with a slotted spoon and drain on paper towel. Serve immediately with mint yoghurt chutney or cucumber raita.

Deep-fried Okra Sticks DF, GF, V

Okra can be an undervalued vegetable, but this recipe of *kurkuri bhindi* is the best way to eat okra in my books. It's an utterly addictive snack. If you have been hesitant to try okra, then this is the recipe for you. Apart from making a great go-to snack that takes no time to prepare, you can also serve them with a simple vegetable dal and curd rice for contrasting textures and flavours to complete a meal.

Serves 6–8

500 g small okra, washed in cold water, dried
1 teaspoon sea salt flakes
2 teaspoons hot chilli powder
100 g chickpea (besan) flour
2 cups (500 ml) vegetable oil, for deep-frying
1 teaspoon chaat masala

Cut the okra lengthwise into thin strips and sprinkle with the salt and chilli powder. Dust with the flour and mix well to ensure the flour sticks to the okra. Heat the oil in a wok or large saucepan over medium–high heat to 170°C. To test the temperature of the oil, sprinkle in some flour, if the flour sizzles, the oil is ready. Fry the okra sticks, in small batches, for 2–3 minutes or until crisp and golden. Remove from oil with a slotted spoon and drain on paper towel. Sprinkle with chaat masala and serve while hot and crisp.

Spiced Potato Burger v

Vada pao (or *pav*) is one of the definitive street snacks of Mumbai. It's called a 'Bombay sandwich' in local dialect and is served from humble food carts across the city, often as a breakfast-on-the go for busy commuters. It's a total carb hit, essentially a soft milk bun split in half with a fried potato patty and coriander chutney sandwiched in between – exactly like a Western-style burger.

Serves 6

300 g potato, peeled, boiled and mashed
1 white onion, finely diced
1 tablespoon ginger garlic paste, see recipe
   page 436
2 small green chillies, minced
½ teaspoon black mustard seeds
2 pinches of asafoetida
½ cup chopped coriander leaves
2 teaspoons sea salt flakes
1 cup (150 g) chickpea (besan) flour
1 teaspoon ground turmeric
1 teaspoon chilli powder
2 cups (500 ml) vegetable oil
6 soft white milk buns or bread rolls, halved
2 tablespoons unsalted butter, softened
coriander coconut chutney, see Pickles and
   Chutneys page 358

Place the potato, onion, ginger garlic paste, green chilli, mustard seeds, asafoetida, coriander and 1 teaspoon salt in a bowl and mix well to combine. Divide the mixture into 6 even-size portions, roll each into a ball and flatten to make a patty.

In a separate bowl, mix the chickpea flour with the remaining 1 teaspoon salt, turmeric and chilli powder. Gradually stir in enough water, about ½ cup (125 ml), to make a medium-thick paste. Add a little extra water if mixture is too dry.

Heat the oil in wok or saucepan over medium–high heat to 180°C. Dip each patty into the chickpea batter to thoroughly coat and slide 3 patties at a time into the hot oil. Fry for 3 minutes, turn and fry for a further 3 minutes or until crisp and golden. Remove from the oil with a slotted spoon and drain on paper towel.

To assemble, spread both sides of the buns generously with the butter. Place a fried potato patty on one side of each bun, spread with coriander chutney and sandwich with remaining bun halves.

Steamed Lentil Cakes GF, V

Steamed lentil sponge cakes with a feathery-light texture, *dhoklas* are a signature of Gujarati cuisine. The chickpea batter is left to ferment with yoghurt before being steamed. They are like biting into a cloud and a welcome change to the plethora of snacks that are deep-fried. The *tarka* is the final seasoning that is poured hot over the cakes as you are about to serve, releasing their aromas and flavour.

Serves 4

2 cups (300 g) chickpea (besan) flour, sifted
1 cup thick plain yoghurt, whisked until smooth
1 teaspoon sea salt flakes
2 tablespoons vegetable oil, plus extra,
   for greasing
½ teaspoon ground turmeric
2 small green chillies, minced
1 teaspoon minced ginger
1 tablespoon lemon juice
1 teaspoon bicarbonate of soda
1 teaspoon brown mustard seeds
1 long green chilli, sliced into rounds
1 tablespoon fresh curry leaves
3 tablespoons chopped coriander leaves
½ cup shredded fresh coconut

Place the chickpea flour and yoghurt in a bowl with 200 ml warm water and whisk until well combined and smooth. Stir in the salt, cover with a clean cloth and set aside on a bench for 4 hours or until bubbles appear on the surface.

Grease a 20 cm-square, non-stick baking tin with extra oil. Add the turmeric, chilli and ginger to the fermented mixture and whisk vigorously, this allows the air to be incorporated into the batter, giving it lightness when cooked. Place the lemon juice, bicarbonate soda and 1 teaspoon of oil in a bowl and whisk to combine. Add to the batter and whisk until incorporated. Pour batter into the prepared tin and place in a steamer tray over boiling water. Cover steamer with a lid and steam for 25 minutes or until cake is just set in the centre. Allow to cool for 30 minutes on a wire rack before cutting into 3 cm squares. Arrange squares on a serving plate.

To make the tarka seasoning, heat the remaining oil in a small frying pan over low–medium heat. Add the mustard seeds, green chilli and curry leaves and cook for 30 seconds or until they start to pop. Remove from heat immediately and pour the tempered oil over the dhoklas. Garnish with chopped coriander leaves and shredded coconut to serve.

Fried Lentil Patties DF, GF, V

Dal vada is a classic Indian snack that harks back to ancient times. These spiced lentil patties are often served from breakfast throughout the day, particularly in south India and Gujarat.

Makes 18

110 g split mung dal (green lentils)
110 g split urad dal (white lentils)
3 tablespoons vegetable oil
3 red shallots, finely diced
2 small green chillies, minced
3 tablespoons curry leaves, shredded
1 tablespoon minced ginger
½ teaspoon ground fennel
½ teaspoon garam masala
½ teaspoon ground turmeric
½ teaspoon ground cumin
½ teaspoon Kashmiri chilli powder
3 tablespoons grated fresh coconut
3 tablespoons chopped coriander leaves
1 teaspoon sea salt flakes
2 tablespoons urad flour, see Glossary
¼ teaspoon baking powder
2 cups (500 ml) vegetable oil, extra,
    for deep-frying
1 small red onion, sliced into thin rings
mint chutney, to serve, see Pickles and Chutneys
    page 361

To prepare the vada, place the dals together in cold water and soak for 5 hours. Drain and rinse.

Place the softened dal and 3 tablespoons water in a blender or food processor and blend to form a thick paste. Leave the texture a little coarse, not smooth. Set aside.

Heat the oil in a frying pan over low–medium heat. Add the shallot, chilli, curry leaves and ginger and cook for 1 minute or until fragrant. Add the ground spices, coconut, coriander and salt and stir to combine. Allow to cool.

Add the cooled spiced shallot mixture to the dal paste and mix to combine. Add the urad flour and baking powder and, using your fingers, knead until the dough comes together. If the dough feels a little firm, add a splash of water.

Shape the dough into small, walnut-size balls and flatten slightly to make patties. Heat the extra vegetable oil in a large wok or saucepan over medium–high heat to 180°C. Fry the vadas, in batches, turning halfway for even cooking, for 5 minutes or until golden and crisp. Drain on paper towel. Scatter over onion rings and serve with either mint chutney or hot chilli sauce.

Coconut Crab Pakoras DF, GF

I made these bite-size snacks when staying with friends on the Konkan coast south of Mumbai, purchasing crabs from the morning fish market and extracting the meat to make these little beauties. It's a riff on a pakora or fried fritter, lushed up with sweet crabmeat. Luckily in Australia we have the convenience of buying fresh-picked crabmeat from our fishmongers, taking away the time-consuming and tedious work of extracting the meat from the shell. If crabmeat doesn't appeal, you can replace it with finely minced raw prawn meat to achieve the same result. Another way of serving them is to dip the crab balls into egg then coat in panko breadcrumbs and deep-fry. Either way, they need to be deep-fried to get that deliciously crunchy shell with a soft, steamed centre.

Serves 6

250 g raw spanner crabmeat
200 g cooked mashed potato
2 tablespoons chopped mint
2 small red chillies, minced
1 teaspoon minced ginger
2 tablespoons grated fresh coconut
1 teaspoon ground coriander
1 teaspoon sea salt flakes
½ teaspoon freshly ground white pepper
½ cup (90 g) rice flour
1 litre vegetable oil, for deep-frying
mint yoghurt chutney, to serve, see Pickles
     and Chutneys page 362

PAKORA BATTER
100 g chickpea (besan) flour
1 teaspoon baking powder
1 teaspoon garam masala
½ teaspoon ground turmeric
1 teaspoon Kashmiri chilli powder
2 teaspoon white vinegar
1 teaspoon sea salt flakes

To make the pakora batter, place all the ingredients in a food processor and pulse to combine. Add 1 cup (250 ml) water and blend until a batter forms. If it looks a little thick, add extra water, but it shouldn't be too watery or it won't coat the crab. Refrigerate for 1 hour before using.

Place the crabmeat, mashed potato, mint, chilli, ginger, coconut, ground coriander, salt and pepper in a bowl and mix thoroughly to combine. Roll tablespoonfuls of the mixture into balls and roll in the rice flour to lightly coat.

Heat the oil in a large saucepan or wok over medium–high heat to 180°C. Dip the crab balls in the batter, one at a time to coat, shake off excess batter and fry, in batches, for 3–4 minutes or until golden. Remove with a slotted spoon and drain on paper towel. Serve with mint yoghurt chutney.

Masala Pappads GF, V

Think of this as an Indian take on pizza, where the crisp pappadam acts as a base for the topping. It's an easy-to-prepare snack to enjoy with drinks. A simple raw salsa has been pimped up with a splash of spice and scattered over the fried pappadams with a swirl of thin yoghurt. What's not to love?

Makes 8

4 tablespoons diced tomato
2 tablespoons diced white onion
1 long green chilli, finely diced
1 tablespoon chopped mint
1 tablespoon chopped coriander
1 teaspoon ground cumin
½ teaspoon sea salt flakes
2 cups (500 ml) vegetable oil, for deep-frying
8 large black pepper pappadams (I use the Patak's brand)
2 tablespoons thick plain yoghurt

Place the tomato, onion, chilli, mint and coriander, cumin and salt in a bowl and mix to combine. Heat the oil in a large saucepan or wok over medium–high heat to 170°C. Fry the pappadams, one at a time, for 45 seconds or until crisp. Drain on paper towel.

Mix the yoghurt and 1 tablespoon water in a bowl to dilute to a thin consistency. Arrange the pappadams on a serving plate and spoon a little tomato salsa on top to lightly cover surface. Drizzle with the yoghurt to serve.

Spiced Eggplant Yoghurt Dip GF, V

An all-time favourite and highly sought-after by everyone who tastes it, this recipe has been part of my repertoire for decades. But it has taken until now to appear in any of my books. You can serve it with a stack of pappadams as a snack and it also makes an ideal partner to lamb or chicken kebabs cooked over hot coals.

Serves 6

1 cup (250 g) fresh curd (hung yoghurt), stirred, see Eggs and Dairy page 110
½ cup (125 g) eggplant pickle, see Pickles and Chutneys page 346
½ teaspoon sea salt flakes
1 x 300 g purple eggplant, cut into 2 cm dice and deep-fried
3 tablespoons chopped coriander leaves, plus extra, to serve
pappadams, to serve

Place the curd, eggplant pickle and salt in a bowl and mix to combine. Fold through the fried eggplant and coriander leaves until well combined. This is best eaten the day it is made. Don't place it in the fridge as this dulls the flavours. Cut the pappadams in half and fry to make crisps. Top eggplant dip with extra coriander leaves and serve with pappadam crisps.

Fried Fish Nuggets GF

This fish snack finds its roots in Amritsar, where a firm-textured fish is cut into chunks, bathed in a spicy coating and deep-fried until crisp. Known as Amritsari fish on any menu, it typically uses freshwater fish. I like to use either ling or flathead fillets, as both hold together perfectly during cooking and retain moisture and texture with the fish almost steaming under its crunchy, spicy coating. Serve it with green chilli chutney (page 364) and you're onto a total winner.

Serves 6

750 g fish fillets, skin and bones removed
½ teaspoon ground turmeric
100 ml malt vinegar
250 g fresh curd (hung yoghurt), see recipe
  page 110
1 cup (150 g) chickpea (besan) flour
3 tablespoons ginger garlic paste, see recipe
  page 436
1 egg, beaten
1 tablespoon lemon juice
2 teaspoons ajwain seeds, see Glossary
2 teaspoons chilli powder
1 teaspoon sea salt flakes
1 litre vegetable oil, for deep-frying
½ teaspoon chaat masala
1 tablespoon fried curry leaves
green chilli chutney, to serve, see Pickles and
  Chutneys page 364

Cut the fish into 10 cm-long, 3 cm-thick slices to make even-size pieces. Place on a flat tray in a single layer. Place the turmeric and vinegar in a bowl to combine and sprinkle over the fish. Set aside for 15 minutes. Blot the fish slices dry with paper towel to remove excess moisture.

Place the curd, chickpea flour, ginger garlic paste, egg, lemon juice, ajwain seeds, chilli powder and salt in a bowl and stir to combine. Add the fish and use your hands to toss gently to thoroughly coat each piece. Set aside to marinate for 20 minutes.

Heat the oil in a wok or large pot to 180°C. Fry the fish, in batches, for 5–6 minutes or until crisp and golden. Drain on paper towel. Sprinkle with chaat masala and fried curry leaves and serve with green chilli chutney.

Beef Dumplings DF

Momos are steamed savoury dumplings of the Himalayan region with Tibetan and Nepalese heritage. They're very similar in look and preparation to the Chinese *jiaozi* dumpling and are also popular in Kolkata with its close proximity to mountain communities and their unique food culture. You can substitute chicken or pork mince for the beef, if you prefer – all these meats are interchangeable and consumed by the Buddhist and Muslim communities of the Himalayas. Steaming the dumplings over a pot of simmering chicken or meat stock enhances the flavour no end, so I recommend trying that to taste the difference.

Makes 25

3 cups (450 g) plain flour
pinch of sea salt flakes

FILLING
300 g minced beef
½ small white onion, finely diced
2 teaspoons sea salt flakes
2 teaspoons ginger garlic paste, see recipe
    page 436
½ small carrot, finely grated
2 tablespoons chopped coriander leaves

CHILLI RELISH
1 tomato, charred over hot coals
6 garlic cloves, chopped
2 teaspoons chilli powder
½ teaspoon sea salt flakes
1 tablespoon finely chopped green shallot tops
2 teaspoons chopped coriander leaves

To make the chilli relish, place the charred tomato, garlic, chilli and salt in a food processor and blend to make a puree. Stir through the shallot and coriander. Set aside until ready to serve.

To make the filling, mix all ingredients together in bowl until combined. Set aside.

To make the dumpling dough, mix the flour and salt in a bowl and gradually add approximately 300 ml water, mixing with your hands until a stiff paste forms. Cover and set aside to rest for 30 minutes.

Divide the dough into 25 even-size pieces and roll into balls. Roll each ball out on a lightly floured surface to an 8 cm round (use a pastry cutter or the rim of a glass or teacup). Place a teaspoonful of the filling into the centre of each pastry round and fold over to make a half-moon. Gather the edges and crimp together using a little water to help them stick. Brush a sheet of baking paper with oil (this is to prevent sticking) and place the baking paper on a steamer tray over a pot of simmering meat stock. In batches, add momos, spaced apart, then cover with a lid and steam for 25 minutes. You will have to do this in 2 or 3 batches, depending on the size of your steamer. Serve warm with the chilli relish.

Soups

Dating back to early Sanskrit texts, soups have had their place in India for centuries. A food for convalescing and to aid in recovery, many soups have medical or therapeutic properties. They're nutritious and sustaining, thickened with lentils or based on rice, wheat or vegetables, often without spice and sometimes with meat. The Hindi word for soup is *shorba*, meaning 'broth', which is traditionally served with the other main dishes as part of a banquet, not as a separate course beforehand, a practice more typical in the West. During British colonial rule, traditions changed and soup came to be served as a first course in Indian restaurants. Many soups are given an Indian makeover with the addition of spice and these are the dishes I turn to when seeking comfort and easy cooking.

In the south, the light, tamarind-based *rasam* translates as 'pepper water' and is the most well-known soup. It can be based on cereals, rice or lentils, depending on regional variations. A staple of the Hindu repertoire, rasam is made with *toor dal* (yellow split lentils), it's thinner and lighter than *sambar*, which also originates in the south, and gets its tangy piquancy from tomatoes, tamarind and lemon. *Sambar*, on the other hand, is a thick, lentil-based soup, more like a vegetable stew. It's also cooked with tamarind and seasoned with a spice mix blended purposely for this soup. A blend of cumin, coriander, fenugreek, mustard seeds and black pepper, you can find this sambar spice blend ready-made at Indian grocers.

Muslims, who are genial hosts, often start their meal with a light meat broth. I have shared the table with Bohra Muslims in Gujarat and been served a smooth almond and lentil soup. I've sat with traders in Chor Bazaar (Thieves Market) in Mumbai and eaten a hearty bowl of *nalli nihari* – lamb trotters rendered tender through slow cooking and flavoured with marrow and heady spices, it's served with crisp roti to mop up the juices. And going to Kashmir means visiting one of the humble, hole-in-the-wall shops to eat harisa soup, which is cooked only during the winter months. This is a rich, unctuous lamb soup with a high fat content, where the lamb is cooked in a *handva* pot overnight over glowing coals until the meat becomes paste-like. Served with *chuot*, a Kashmiri-style dense winter flatbread, it demands a good appetite and offers warmth and sustenance against the frigid weather.

Then there are the soups that have become part of the everyday vernacular, such as the colonial *mulligatawny* and the Burmese *khao swe*, and if you're travelling in the north through the Himalayas, the Buddhist communities cook *thukpa* as a mainstay. This Tibetan noodle soup is austere in its simplicity with thick, rope-like noodles and slow-simmered meat (usually yak, goat or chicken), seasoned with *dalle paste*, the fiery chilli condiment beloved in this region – it's a whack of heat that brings everything to life.

Buttermilk Sambar GF, V

A soothing vegetable soup with the gentle tang of yoghurt and buttermilk and an underlying fiery heat, *mor sambar* is typical of southern cooking. It's good for gut health and easy to digest, a great one to prepare for restorative nourishment. Okra, choko or eggplant can be used as a substitute for the gourd and potato.

Serves 6

3 tablespoons ghee
2 teaspoons split urad dal (white lentils), washed and drained
2 teaspoons toor dal (yellow split lentils), washed and drained
1½ teaspoons fenugreek seeds
1 teaspoon coriander seeds
½ teaspoon asafoetida
4 small dried chillies, crushed
½ cup shredded fresh coconut
2 teaspoons minced ginger
1 cup (250 ml) buttermilk
1 cup thick plain yoghurt
½ teaspoon ground turmeric
1 teaspoon sea salt flakes
1 teaspoon black mustard seeds
1 teaspoon cumin seeds
1 long red chilli, finely sliced
2 tablespoons fresh curry leaves
1 cup diced ash (winter) gourd or choko
1 potato, peeled and cut into 1 cm dice
100 g masoor dal (red lentils), washed, boiled for 15 minutes and drained
1 tablespoon fried curry leaves

Heat 1 tablespoon ghee in a frying pan over medium heat. Add the urad and toor dals and stir to combine. Add 1 teaspoon of fenugreek seeds and the coriander seeds and asafoetida. Add the chilli and cook, taking care not to burn, for 1 minute or until fragrant and spices are starting to pop. Transfer to a blender or food processor with the coconut, ginger and half the buttermilk and blend to make a coarse paste. Place the yoghurt, remaining buttermilk, turmeric and salt in a bowl and mix to combine. Add the coconut paste to the yoghurt mixture and stir to combine.

Heat the remaining 2 tablespoons ghee in a saucepan over medium heat. Add the mustard, cumin and remaining ½ teaspoon fenugreek seeds, red chilli and curry leaves and cook for 45 seconds or until they start to pop. Add the gourd and potato and cook for 1 minute, stirring to coat the vegetables with the spice base. Add just enough water (about 300 ml) to cover the vegetables and cook for 10 minutes or until soft but not mushy, it should be simmering not boiling rapidly. Add the boiled masoor dal and stir through the buttermilk mixture. Once the soup begins to simmer, remove from heat to ensure it doesn't split or curdle. Top with fried curry leaves to serve.

Masterclass step-by-step
Buttermilk Sambar ➜

1

Heat 1 tablespoon ghee in a frying pan over medium heat.

2

Add the urad and toor dals.

3

Add 1 teaspoon fenugreek seeds, the coriander seeds, and asafoetida.

4

Add the chilli and cook for 1 minute.

5

Place in a food processor or blender.

6

Add the shredded coconut and ginger.

7

Add half the buttermilk and blend to make a coarse paste.

8

Place the yoghurt, remaining buttermilk, turmeric and salt in a bowl.

9

Stir to combine.

10

Add the coconut paste.

11

Stir to combine.

12

Heat the remaining 2 tablespoons ghee in a saucepan over medium heat.

13

Add the mustard seeds, cumin seeds and remaining fenugreek seeds.

14

Add the red chilli and curry leaves. Cook for 45 seconds or until they pop.

15

Add the gourd and potato and cook, stirring, for 1 minute.

16

Add just enough water to cover

17

Add the cooked masoor dal.

18

Stir through the buttermilk mixture and

Tomato Rasam DF, GF, V

This is the quintessential comfort food of southern India. A tangy and light peppery broth famous for its rejuvenating and digestive properties, it's ideal to serve in any season for its refreshing flavour.

Serves 6

1 cup toor dal (yellow split lentils), soaked in
    cold water for 30 minutes and drained
8 ripe tomatoes, roughly chopped
2 tablespoons tinned tomato puree
    (not to be confused with paste)
1 tablespoon vegetable oil
2 teaspoons black mustard seeds
2 teaspoons cumin seeds
12 fresh curry leaves
1 teaspoon sea salt flakes
1 teaspoon ground turmeric
½ teaspoon asafoetida
2 teaspoons jaggery or palm sugar, shaved
2 teaspoons minced ginger
1 tablespoon lime juice
3 tablespoons coriander leaves, roughly chopped

RASAM POWDER
2 teaspoons black pepper
1 teaspoon cumin seeds
2 teaspoons coriander seeds
4 small dried chillies
2 teaspoons toor dal (yellow split lentils)

To make the rasam powder, place all the ingredients in a spice grinder and grind to make a fine powder. Set aside. You will only need 2 tablespoons of the powder for this recipe. Store the remainder in an airtight container.

Cook the soaked dal in a pot of salted boiling water for 15 minutes or until soft. Drain and set aside.

Place the tomatoes in a food processor and blend to make a puree. Pass through a sieve to remove seeds and skins. Add the tinned tomato puree to the fresh puree and stir to combine. Set aside.

Heat the oil in a large saucepan over medium heat. Add the mustard and cumin seeds and curry leaves and cook for 30 seconds or until fragrant, being careful not to burn. Add the tomato puree, salt, turmeric, asafoetida, palm sugar, ginger and 2 tablespoons of rasam powder and stir to combine. Bring to the boil and cook for 10 minutes. Add the cooked dal and lime juice, stir to combine, and cook for a further 1 minute. Remove from heat, check seasoning and adjust with salt, if necessary. Top with chopped coriander to serve.

Beetroot and Coconut Soup GF, V

This soup embodies the deep and satisfying flavours of Kerala with the earthy sweetness of beetroot partnered with coconut for a silken texture. It's a delicious cold soup that's ideal for serving in summer. Make sure you cook your beetroot before making this soup – you can either boil or steam them whole before peeling them.

Serves 4

600 g cooked beetroot, peeled
60 g celery stalk, chopped
handful of celery leaves (the pale ones from the inner stalk)
200 ml coconut milk
⅓ cup (80 ml) pouring cream
2 teaspoons sea salt flakes
2 tablespoons caster sugar

Place all the ingredients together with a good handful of ice cubes in a food processor or high-performance blender and blend to a smooth puree. Taste and adjust seasoning, if necessary. Serve chilled with paratha or appam.

Green Mango Rasam DF, GF, V

Sour and pungent, this rejuvenating rasam is a delicious variation to its tomato cousin. It's equally fiery with the tempered spices floating on the top and is delicious served simply with steamed rice. The pureed pulp gives the required body to this soup. It's best to try this during mango season when green unripe fruit are in abundance.

Serves 6

4 x 250 g green (unripe) mangoes, peeled
3 teaspoons black peppercorns
3 teaspoons cumin seeds
3 tablespoons vegetable oil
5 small green chillies, minced
1 teaspoons sea salt flakes
2 tablespoons shaved palm sugar
1 teaspoon black mustard seeds
12 fresh curry leaves
4 small dried chillies
1 teaspoon chopped coriander leaves

Place the mangoes in a saucepan of boiling water and cook for 25 minutes or until softened. Cut the softened pulp from the seeds and blend or pass through a sieve until smooth. Set aside.

Place the peppercorns and cumin in a frying pan over low heat and cook for 30 seconds or until fragrant. Remove from heat, place in a spice grinder and grind to a powder. Heat 2 tablespoons of the oil in a frying pan over medium heat. Add the chilli and cook for 30 seconds. Add the ground spices and combine. Remove from heat.

Place the mango pulp in a saucepan over medium heat with 6 cups (1½ litres) water and bring to the boil. Stir through the spiced chilli, salt and sugar and cook, stirring, for 3 minutes or until boiling. Remove from heat and ladle into bowls.

Place the mustard seeds, curry leaves, dried chilli and remaining oil in a frying pan over medium heat and cook for 30 seconds or until fragrant. Spoon over the rasam and garnish with coriander.

Tomato Shorba DF, GF

Shorba is the Hindi word for soup and this is an Indian version of the classic tomato soup. Light in body and gently spiced, I find using a stock gives it infinitely more flavour. You can use chicken (as I have) or meat stock, or to keep it vegetarian, use vegetable stock. Many restaurants throughout India, modest or grand, will serve this soup at the start of a meal.

Serves 6

3 cups (750 ml) chicken (or other) stock
3 ripe tomatoes, chopped
200 ml tomato passata
1 red onion, chopped
4 garlic cloves, sliced
2 teaspoons chopped ginger
2 bay leaves
1 teaspoon Kashmiri chilli powder
1 black cardamom pod, cracked slightly
2 mace blades
2 teaspoons coriander seeds
1 teaspoon cumin seeds
1 teaspoon fennel seeds
1 teaspoon black peppercorns
2 teaspoons sea salt flakes
2 tablespoons chopped coriander leaves

FINISHING SPICE
¼ teaspoon black cardamom seeds
½ teaspoon cumin seeds
½ teaspoon coriander seeds
¼ teaspoon fennel seeds
¼ teaspoon black peppercorns

To make the finishing spice, place all the spices together in a spice grinder and grind to a powder. Set aside.

Place the stock in large saucepan over medium heat with the tomatoes, passata, onion, garlic, ginger, bay leaves, chilli powder and whole spices and bring to the boil. Reduce heat to medium–low and simmer gently for 45 minutes. Remove from heat and pass the soup through a sieve, pushing down with the back of a spoon to extract as much liquid and flavour as possible. Discard solids. Return the soup to the saucepan and bring back to the boil. Season with salt and remove from heat. Stir through a little of the finishing spice (to your own taste), ladle into serving bowls and top with chopped coriander.

Yellow Dal and Coconut Yoghurt Soup DF, GF, V

A bowl of this soup on a wintry day is richly rewarding. Its soothing qualities hit the spot, plus it's so easy to prepare, making it an ideal one-pot number for when you're after maximum reward for minimum effort using only pantry staples. Don't stress if you can't get hold of coconut yoghurt, which I have used to keep this recipe dairy-free, just use regular thick, plain yoghurt – the end result will be just as delicious.

Serves 6

3 tomatoes, chopped
2 tablespoons coconut oil
¼ teaspoon black mustard seeds
2 tablespoons fresh curry leaves
3 red shallots, diced
1 tablespoon ginger garlic paste, see recipe
　　page 436
2 small red chillies, finely sliced
¼ teaspoon ground fenugreek
1 teaspoon ground cumin
1 teaspoon ground coriander
1 teaspoon ground turmeric
1 teaspoon Kashmiri chilli powder
400 ml coconut milk
200 g chana dal (split chickpeas), soaked
　　for 30 minutes and drained
150 g baby spinach leaves
3 tablespoons coconut yoghurt
3 teaspoons sea salt flakes
12 oven-roasted cherry tomatoes, see Glossary
1 long red chilli, seeded and julienned

Place the tomatoes in a blender and blend to make a puree. Strain to remove seeds. Set aside.

Heat the coconut oil in a heavy-based saucepan over medium heat. Add the mustard seeds and cook for 40 seconds or until they start to pop. Add the curry leaves, shallot, ginger garlic paste and chilli and cook for 3 minutes or until softened and starting to colour. Add the ground spices, stir to combine, and cook for a further 1 minute or until fragrant. Add the tomato puree, coconut milk and dal with 3 cups (750 ml) water and bring to the boil. Simmer for 45 minutes or until dal are tender.

Ladle 1 cup (250 ml) soup into a jug and use a stick blender to puree. Return to the saucepan with the soup and stir to combine. This helps to thicken the soup's texture. Add the spinach leaves, yoghurt and salt and stir until the spinach is wilted. Ladle into bowls and garnish with roasted cherry tomatoes and red chilli to serve.

Vegetable Sambar DF, GF, V

Dal and vegetables create the texture or body for this soup and the taste of the sambar is reliant on the blend of spices or sambar powder, which you can make yourself or buy from an Indian grocer. It's traditionally served as a first course for a south Indian meal, along with steamed idli or boiled rice and pappadams. It's important to not overcook the vegetables; they should hold their shape. The final balance of flavour comes with the addition of tamarind, palm sugar and the tempered spices or *tadka*.

Serves 4

½ cup toor dal (yellow split lentils), washed and drained
2 tablespoons vegetable oil
1 teaspoon black mustard seeds
½ teaspoon fenugreek seeds
½ teaspoon cumin seeds
½ teaspoon asafoetida
½ teaspoon chilli flakes
12 fresh curry leaves
2 small green chillies, sliced
1 cup diced mixed vegetables (such as red onion, okra, red capsicum, potato and green beans or peas), cut into 1 cm dice
1 tomato, finely chopped
200 ml tamarind puree
1 tablespoon shaved palm sugar
2 teaspoons sea salt flakes
½ teaspoon ground turmeric
2 tablespoons chopped coriander leaves
1 tablespoon fried curry leaves

SAMBAR POWDER
2 teaspoons chana dal (split chickpeas)
2 teaspoons coriander seeds
1 small dried chilli
¼ teaspoon cumin seeds
¼ teaspoon mustard seeds
1 clove

To make the sambar powder, heat a small pan over low heat, add the chana dal and all the spices and cook for 1 minute or until toasted and fragrant. Allow to cool before grinding to a powder. Set aside. You will only need 1 tablespoon of the powder for this recipe. Store the remainder in an airtight container.

Place the dal and 2 cups (500 ml) water in a saucepan over medium heat. Cook, stirring occasionally, for 1 hour or until lentils are soft and mushy. Remove from heat and set aside. Do not strain, as you need the cooked dal and its liquid for the sambar.

Heat the oil in a heavy-based saucepan over medium heat. Add the mustard, fenugreek and cumin seeds, asafoetida, chilli flakes and curry leaves and cook for 30 seconds or until they start to pop. Add the green chilli and diced vegetables and stir to combine. Increase heat to high, add the tomato, tamarind, palm sugar, salt, turmeric and 1 tablespoon sambar powder with 1 cup (250 ml) water, bring to the boil and simmer for 10–15 minutes or until vegetables are soft. Add the cooked dal with its liquid and stir to combine. Cook for a further 5 minutes or until soft and tender. Top with coriander and fried curry leaves to serve.

Vegetable Noodle Soup DF, V

With its Tibetan heritage, *thukpa* is an everyday soup in the northern and eastern Himalayan regions. Fragrant, wholesome and simple to prepare, this soup reflects its close proximity to China with the use of noodles and Sichuan pepper, both commonly available in this region. If you can't find dried Hakka noodles, you can substitute with chow mein, Hokkien, fresh egg noodles or rice stick noodles (if you wanted to keep it gluten-free). Traditionally, some salted or fermented cabbage water is added with the starchy noodle water in the soup base, but I have taken the liberty of using Korean kimchi, which gives the soup extra tang and pungency. You can just as easily use Chinese pickled cabbage or bamboo shoots, readily available at Asian grocers. This soup is traditionally served with a hot chilli relish or chutney.

Serves 4

4 teaspoons sea salt flakes
200 g dried Hakka (or chow mein) noodles
2 tablespoons vegetable oil
1 tablespoon finely chopped ginger
1 white onion, finely sliced
1 long red chilli, finely sliced
1 large carrot, peeled and julienned
1 cup shredded wombok (Chinese cabbage)
2 ripe tomatoes, finely chopped
2 teaspoons red chilli paste (or momo chilli chutney)
2 teaspoons ginger garlic paste, see recipe page 436
1 teaspoon garam masala
1 teaspoon ground turmeric
1 teaspoon freshly ground black pepper
½ teaspoon ground Sichuan pepper
1 teaspoon mild curry powder
pinch of asafoetida
2 teaspoons tamari soy sauce
3 tablespoons finely shredded kimchi (with liquid)
2 large Swiss chard (silver beet) leaves, finely shredded
2 teaspoons lemon juice
3 tablespoons chopped coriander leaves

Place 6 cups (1½ litres) of water in a saucepan over high heat and bring to the boil. When it reaches a rapid boil, add 2 teaspoons salt and the noodles and boil for 4 minutes or until the noodles are cooked. Drain the noodles and reserve the cooking water for making the soup. Refresh noodles under cold, running water to stop further cooking. Strain again and set aside.

Heat a wok over medium–high heat. Add the oil, stir in the ginger and cook for 20 seconds. Add the onion and chilli, and cook, stirring constantly, for a further 2 minutes or until softened. Add the carrot and cabbage and stir to combine. Immediately stir through the remaining 2 teaspoons salt, tomato, chilli paste, ginger garlic paste, ground spices and tamari and cook for 1 minute. Add the kimchi with its liquid and the reserved 6 cups (1½ litres) noodle cooking water and bring to the boil. Add the shredded Swiss chard and cook for 3 minutes. Add the lemon juice, check for seasoning, and add a little extra salt, if required. Remove from heat and stir through the coriander. Divide the cooked noodles between serving bowls and ladle over the soup.

Spiced Chickpea and Spinach Soup v

One of the essential pulses of the Indian pantry, chickpeas are used in myriad preparations throughout the country, from everyday dishes to celebratory feasts. For the best texture, it is ideal to use dried peas. Soak and cook them yourself as the tinned variety tend to be softer and lack the right texture. In India, I've cooked this with fresh fenugreek leaves, which are sadly not available here, so I have substituted spinach leaves with a little kasoori methi powder, available at Indian grocers. If you happen to have purslane growing in your garden, this makes a great addition to the soup instead of spinach.

Serves 6

200 g dried chickpeas, soaked in cold water
    overnight and drained
2 tablespoons ghee
2 teaspoons brown mustard seeds
1 teaspoon fenugreek seeds
2 teaspoons fresh curry leaves
1 brown onion, finely diced
2 small red chillies, minced
2 garlic cloves, minced
1 teaspoon minced fresh turmeric
1 teaspoon ground turmeric
2 cups (500 ml) coconut milk
300 ml vegetable stock (or water)
3 teaspoons sea salt flakes
1 tablespoon lime juice, strained
3 tomatoes, peeled, seeded and finely diced
120 g baby spinach leaves, roughly chopped
1 tablespoon kasoori methi (dried fenugreek
    leaves) powder
12 green beans, cut into 50 mm rounds
1 tablespoon mint yoghurt chutney, to serve,
    see Pickles and Chutneys page 362
2 teaspoons fried curry leaves

TURMERIC SPINACH FRITTERS
⅓ cup (50 g) chickpea (besan) flour
⅓ cup (50 g) plain flour
1 teaspoon ground turmeric
1 teaspoon ground cumin
1 teaspoon sea salt flakes
vegetable oil, for deep-frying
24 baby spinach leaves

To make the soup, place the soaked chickpeas in a large pot and cover with cold water. Bring to the boil over medium heat and cook, skimming surface occasionally, for 1 hour or until softened to al dente texture. If necessary, top up water to ensure the chickpeas remain submerged during cooking. Drain and set aside.

Melt the ghee in a large saucepan over medium–high heat. Add the mustard seeds, fenugreek seeds and curry leaves and cook for 30 seconds or until they start to pop. Add the onion, chilli, garlic and fresh turmeric and cook for 3 minutes or until softened. Add the ground turmeric and cook for 2 minutes or until fragrant. Add the coconut milk, bring to the boil, reduce heat to low and simmer for 5 minutes. Add the stock and simmer for a further 20 minutes. Season with salt and lime juice.

While the soup is simmering, make the turmeric spinach fritters. Place the chickpea and plain flours, spices, salt and 50 ml water in a bowl and mix to make a thin batter. Heat the oil in a wok or large saucepan to 180°C. Dip the spinach leaves, one at a time, in the batter to lightly coat and fry for 2 minutes or until golden and crisp. Drain on paper towel.

Stir the tomato, chopped spinach, kasoori methi and beans through the soup and cook for a further 1 minute or until spinach has wilted. Ladle into bowls, add a dollop of mint yoghurt chutney and sprinkle over the fried curry leaves. Place the turmeric spinach fritters on top of the soup and serve immediately.

Crab, Ginger and Coconut Soup DF, GF

A recipe I developed for my restaurant repertoire, this refined soup combines the essential flavours of India with the more elaborate technique of making a stock. The stock is made by roasting crab shells to give a greater depth of flavour. Of course, this can be done ahead of time and the stock frozen until required, making the final preparation that much faster.

Serves 8

1 tablespoon vegetable oil
1 tablespoon brown mustard seeds
2 teaspoons ground fennel seeds
2 tablespoons fresh curry leaves
2 tablespoons finely diced red shallot
600 g fresh-picked mud crabmeat
1 cup shredded fresh coconut
2 tablespoons diced tomato, peeled and seeded
4 small red chillies, sliced into fine rounds
1 tablespoon minced ginger
2 tablespoons shredded coriander leaves
sea salt flakes, to taste

CRAB AND COCONUT BROTH
1 tablespoon vegetable oil
2 teaspoons brown mustard seeds
1 teaspoon fenugreek seeds
3 red shallots, diced
4 small green chillies
½ teaspoon ground turmeric
1 ripe tomato, diced
1 tablespoon fresh curry leaves
2 tablespoons minced ginger
400 ml coconut milk
400 ml crab stock, see Glossary
1 tablespoon sea salt flakes
⅓ cup (80 ml) lime juice

To make the crab and coconut broth, heat the oil in a frying pan over medium heat. Add the mustard seeds and cook for 30 seconds or until they start to pop. Add the fenugreek seeds and cook for 20 seconds. Add the shallot and chilli and cook for 4 minutes or until translucent. Add the turmeric, tomato, curry leaves and ginger and cook, stirring, until fragrant. Reduce heat to low, stir through the coconut milk and simmer for 10 minutes before adding the crab stock. Increase heat to high and bring to the boil. Once boiling, reduce heat to low and simmer gently for 5 minutes. Remove from heat and season to taste with salt and lime juice. Strain through a fine sieve and discard solids. Set aside and keep warm.

To prepare the crab, heat the oil in a frying pan over medium heat. Add the mustard and fennel seeds and when they start to pop, add the curry leaves and shallots and stir to combine. Cook for 1 minute or until softened. Add the crabmeat, toss to combine and cook for 2 minutes for flavours to mingle. Remove pan from heat and add the shredded coconut, tomato, red chilli, ginger, coriander and salt to taste. Arrange crab in bowls and ladle over the broth to serve.

Turmeric and Mustard Fish Soup DF, GF

Machher jhol is a traditional spicy fish stew found in the Bengali and Odia cuisines of the east coast. Typically, a curried fish stew served with rice and liberally seasoned with turmeric, garlic and ginger, I have added extra liquid to make it into a flavoursome soup. Freshwater (river) fish is the preferred option here, so I would suggest wild barramundi, estuary perch, Murray cod or rainbow trout. I've had equal success, flavour-wise, with Australian farmed groper as its texture is similar to that of the cod. Cooking the fish on the bone is ideal for this – so it's best to buy a whole fish that's gutted and scaled (get your fishmonger to do this for you) and then cut crosswise to yield 4 even-size cutlets on the bone, each weighing approximately 150 g. This will depend entirely on the type and size of fish you choose. If the fish is smaller, it will be better to buy a couple and slice 8 cutlets (2 per serve). If you can't source the small angled gourds, you could substitute with apple eggplant, cut into quarters. To lush this soup up even further, use fish stock instead of water for an added depth of flavour.

Serves 4

5 teaspoons sea salt flakes
1 teaspoon ground turmeric
2 teaspoons ground coriander
½ teaspoon Kashmiri chilli powder
1 tablespoon lemon juice
4 x 150g Murray cod cutlets (or other freshwater fish, see above)
100 ml mustard oil
1 cup cauliflower florets
2 teaspoons panch phoran, see Glossary
3 red shallots, finely diced
2 small green chillies, minced
2 teaspoons ginger garlic paste, see recipe page 436
3 ripe tomatoes, chopped
1 teaspoon ground turmeric, extra
1 teaspoon ground coriander, extra
1 teaspoon Kashmiri chilli powder, extra
1 teaspoon ground cumin
3 small Asian angled (luffa) gourds, sliced into thin rounds (choose ones that are no bigger than 10 cm-long)
2 tablespoons chopped coriander leaves

Place 2 teaspoons of the salt, ground spices and lemon juice in a large tray and stir to combine. Add the fish and rub the spice mixture into both sides of the fish. Set aside to marinate for 10 minutes.

Heat a large frying pan over medium–high heat and add 2 tablespoons of the mustard oil. Once it starts to smoke, add the fish and cook for 2 minutes. Turn and cook fish on the other side for 1 minute only. The fish should start to firm up but not cook through. Remove and drain on paper towel.

Add the cauliflower to the same frying pan and cook for 2 minutes or until brown all over. Remove and place in a bowl. Cover with plastic wrap and set aside to sweat.

Heat a large, heavy-based saucepan over medium heat. Add the remaining mustard oil and panch phoran and cook for 20 seconds or until fragrant. Add the shallot, chilli and ginger garlic paste and cook for 3 minutes or until softened. Add the tomato and cook for 2–3 minutes or until broken down. Add the extra ground spices and ground cumin and cook for a further 1 minute before adding 6 cups (1½ litres) water. Bring to the boil and simmer for 5 minutes. Add the gourd and fried cauliflower, reduce heat to low and simmer gently for 5 minutes. Add the fish cutlets and cook for a further 5 minutes or until heated through. Season with remaining salt to taste. Ladle into bowls and sprinkle with chopped coriander to serve.

Chicken Mulligatawny DF, GF

This spicy lentil soup, a colonial derivative of *rasam* or pepper water (*milagu thanni* in Tamil), is perhaps the most well-known Anglo-Indian dish from the days of the Raj. Modified to include meat (chicken or lamb), this nourishing soup has woven its way into the everyday vernacular of India's cuisine and is served across the country in homes and restaurants. A dish that defines its mixed-race heritage, you can expect to see it on any club menu. For a vegetarian version, it can be made without chicken, but I do find the addition of shredded chicken gives this soup that extra dimension of flavour and it's a great way of using up leftover roast chicken. Either way, you need to start with a reliable curry powder if you aren't making your own. Traditionally, it's served with boiled or steamed rice, which you spoon into the soup in small quantities as you eat.

Serves 4

2 tablespoons vegetable oil
6 golden shallots, diced
2 tablespoons curry leaves
250 g masoor dal (red lentils), rinsed under cold water
1.2 litres chicken stock (or water)
2 tablespoons ginger garlic paste, see recipe page 436
3 small green chillies, minced
½ teaspoon freshly ground black pepper
1 tablespoon hot curry powder
1 teaspoon ground turmeric
½ teaspoon chilli powder
½ teaspoon garam masala
2 potatoes, peeled and diced
3 teaspoons sea salt flakes
2 teaspoons caster sugar
1 tablespoon lime juice
250 g cooked chicken, shredded
steamed rice, to serve

Heat the oil in a heavy-based pot over medium heat. Add the shallots and curry leaves and cook for 3 minutes or until softened. Add the lentils, stock, ginger garlic paste, chilli, spices and potato and bring to the boil. Cover with a lid, reduce heat slightly and simmer for 30 minutes or until lentils and potato are soft. Remove from heat and allow to cool for 10 minutes before placing in a food processor. Blend to make a thick puree, if the puree is too thick, dilute it with a little extra stock or water for the right consistency. Return soup to the pot over low heat with the salt, sugar and lime juice and stir to combine. Adjust seasoning if necessary, it may require a little extra salt. Stir through the shredded cooked chicken and cook for 2 minutes. Ladle into bowls and serve with steamed rice.

Chicken Khao Swe DF, GF

Introduced to Kolkata by the Burmese traders who plied the waters between both countries, these soupy noodles with their mildly spiced coconut gravy is the definition of comfort food. It's a popular breakfast or lunch dish and sometimes served when convalescing. It can also be made with beef shanks, where the meat is slowly braised before being added to the broth and noodles for an even richer flavour. Traditionally, wheat flour noodles are used for their spring and slight chewiness, but I have used the Thai rice stick noodles here, as I enjoy their slippery texture. An essential element to the soup is the garnish of fried noodles, eggs and fried shallots, which provides both contrast and depth of flavour.

Serves 8

3 teaspoons ground turmeric
1 teaspoon sea salt flakes
4 x 160 g chicken marylands
1 teaspoon coriander seeds
1 teaspoon cumin seeds
½ teaspoon fennel seeds
½ teaspoon fenugreek seeds
4 small dried chillies
2 white onions, chopped
5 cm piece ginger, chopped
4 garlic cloves
4 small red chillies, chopped
2 tablespoons vegetable oil
1 tablespoon chickpea (besan) flour
400 ml coconut milk
400 g cooked rice stick noodles

GARNISH
2 cups (500 ml) vegetable oil, for deep-frying
60 g dried vermicelli (seviyan)
2 tablespoons chopped coriander leaves
3 green shallots, finely sliced
4 small green chillies, finely sliced
4 hard-boiled eggs, peeled and halved
3 small dried chillies, dry-roasted and crushed
3 tablespoons fried shallot slices, see Glossary
2 limes, quartered

To cook the chicken, mix together 2 teaspoons of the turmeric and the salt and rub all over the chicken to coat. Arrange chicken in a large pot or saucepan and place over medium heat. Pour in enough water to just cover the chicken and bring to the boil. Reduce heat to low, cover, and cook for 30 minutes or until meat is tender. Remove chicken from pot and set aside to cool slightly. Strain the broth and reserve 600 ml. When chicken is cool enough to handle (but not cold), shred the meat, discarding the skin and bones. Set aside until ready to serve.

To make the soup, place the whole spices and dried chilli in a frying pan over low heat and cook for 30 seconds or until fragrant, being careful not to burn. Allow to cool before using a spice grinder to finely grind. Place the onion, ginger, garlic and chilli in a food processor or blender and process until smooth.

Heat the oil in a heavy-based pot over medium heat. Add the onion puree and cook for 5–6 minutes or until softened and starting to colour. Add the ground spices and the remaining ground turmeric, stir to combine and cook for 2 minutes or until fragrant. Add the reserved 600 ml cooking broth and bring to a simmer. Mix to combine the chickpea flour with the coconut milk and pour into the broth, stirring continuously until combined. Reduce heat to low and simmer for a further 10 minutes. Season.

While the soup is cooking, fry the vermicelli for the garnish. Heat the oil in wok or small saucepan to 160°C. Make a nest of vermicelli in a metal sieve, lower into the hot oil and fry for 2 minutes or until golden and crisp, loosening the strands with a fork for even cooking. Drain on paper towel.

To serve, divide the cooked rice stick noodles between bowls, add the shredded chicken and ladle over the hot soup. Top with the fried vermicelli, coriander, green shallot, green chilli, eggs, dried chilli, fried shallot and lime wedges.

Home-style Nourishing Lamb Soup GF

Nadan aadu is a staple of Kerala and cooked for anyone convalescing. Its nourishing and rejuvenating properties offer the comfort of humble home cooking and care. It's important to cook meat on the bone to extract maximum nutrients and flavour. Small shanks work brilliantly for this as they're more tender. Ideally you want to cook eight, allowing two per serve. Larger shanks will take longer to cook, so adjust the cooking time.

Serves 4

3 tablespoons ghee
100 g finely diced onion
2 teaspoons cornflour
½ teaspoon sea salt flakes
1 teaspoon freshly ground black pepper
25 g red shallots, finely sliced
1 small red chilli, finely sliced

SOUP BASE
1.2 kg small lamb shanks, halved crosswise
    (ask your butcher to do this for you)
1 small red onion, sliced
1 tablespoon ginger garlic paste, see recipe
    page 436
10 fresh curry leaves
2 cloves
1 cinnamon stick
½ teaspoon fennel seeds
½ teaspoon cumin seeds
½ teaspoon ground turmeric
½ teaspoon black peppercorns
2 teaspoons sea salt flakes
3 litres water

To make the soup base, place all ingredients together in a large pot over high heat and bring to the boil. Reduce heat to low and cook, skimming the surface, for 1 hour 45 minutes or until reduced by a third and the meat is very tender. Remove from heat and strain the stock into a pot, reserving the lamb but discarding other solids. Set aside and skim off any fat that rises to the surface of the stock.

Heat 2 tablespoons of ghee in a large pot over high heat. Add the onion and cook for 10 minutes or until golden brown. Mix the cornflour with a little water to make a paste and stir into the onion. Cook for 2–3 minutes or until browned. Season with salt and pepper. Add the strained lamb stock and reserved lamb shanks to the pot and bring to the boil. Cook for 5 minutes before removing from heat.

Meanwhile, heat the remaining ghee in a frying pan over medium heat. Add the shallot and cook for 5 minutes or until brown. Stir the fried shallots and chilli through the soup and ladle into bowls to serve.

Salads

As a general rule, most food in India is cooked, including salads. It's not as common to find raw ingredients put together in the way we're accustomed to eating salads. Vegetables are usually cooked (often a little too thoroughly), rendering them soft and mushy and forgoing the crisp textural contrasts we associate with a raw salad. Although there are salads in India, they are not considered a main dish and are never served alone, but rather as an optional side dish. They're an accompaniment to other dishes on the shared table and considered vital for the balance they bring when enjoyed as part of a meal. It must be said, though, that keen cooks and chefs in modern India have adopted, adapted and incorporated salads into their repertoire resulting in some inspired creations.

Salads add balance, variety, colour, texture, freshness and diversity to the cook's range and the ingredients must be at their sparkling best. No limp leaves or over-ripe, soggy vegetables or fruit – texture is of paramount importance. Salads are all about crunch, moisture, mouth-feel and flavour, so it's in the home kitchen where we can most enjoy them, particularly for those who are reticent to eat them when travelling in India.

Salads are personal interpretations of what's fresh, in season and readily available, with combinations of flavours and textures based on your own imagination. Expand your repertoire to include salads embellished with nuts, sprouted lentils, puffed rice, lentils or rice flakes, raw onion seasoned with black salt and cumin, and other textural elements that bring contrast and layered flavours that bounce on your tastebuds. Having a couple of excellent salad dressings in the fridge means you can easily put together a salad quickly and with minimal cooking – perfect for long summer days or when you're short on time.

Spiced Green Tomatoes DF, GF, V

A simple vegetable dish I collected from a country cook in Rajasthan, this recipe is perfect for using green tomatoes as they hold their shape and texture better than ripe ones in this instance. I think of this dish more as a salad than anything else, so make sure you buy firm, green and totally unripe tomatoes to get the right texture and flavour. If you can get them, or grow them, green ox heart tomatoes have the best texture. You can serve this with other vegetable salads or as an accompaniment to a meat curry.

Serves 4

600 g green tomatoes, blanched and peeled
75 ml vegetable oil
1 teaspoon cumin seeds
½ teaspoon black mustard seeds
2 teaspoons sea salt flakes
1 teaspoon ground turmeric
1 teaspoon chilli powder
50 g caster sugar

Cut the tomatoes into thick, round slices. Heat the oil in a saucepan over medium heat. Add the cumin and mustard seeds and cook for 30 seconds or until fragrant. Add the tomato and cook, stirring occasionally, for 5 minutes or until tomatoes are soft but still holding their shape. Add the salt, turmeric and chilli powder and toss to combine. Add 100 ml water and the sugar to the pan and cook for 10 minutes or until water has evaporated. Adjust seasoning, if necessary, and serve warm.

Kashmiri Tomato Salad DF, GF, V

Kashmiri in origin, this salad makes a great addition to a thali plate or served as an accompaniment to grilled fish or meat. Naturally, it's best during the summer when tomatoes are picked ripe from the vine and full of flavour. Sometimes I use different types of tomatoes together, such as truss, cocktail and kumato or ox heart tomatoes.

Serves 4

¼ cup (60 ml) vegetable oil
1 teaspoon mustard oil
1 teaspoon black mustard seeds
2 teaspoons nigella seeds
1 tablespoon finely shredded ginger
2 small green chillies, minced
1 teaspoon caster sugar
1 teaspoon ground turmeric
½ teaspoon ground chilli
1 teaspoon sea salt flakes, plus extra, to taste
8 ripe tomatoes, unpeeled, cut into eighths

Heat both the oils in a frying pan over medium heat. Add the mustard and nigella seeds and cook until they start to pop. Add the ginger, green chilli and sugar and cook for 30 seconds or until softened. Stir in the turmeric, ground chilli and salt and stir to combine. Add the tomato and cook for 5 minutes or until tomato is just softened without breaking down. Remove from the heat and allow to stand for 15 minutes or until the juices emerge. Season with extra salt to taste and serve warm.

**Masterclass step-by-step
Kashmiri Tomato Salad ➜**

1

Heat the oils in a frying pan over medium heat.
Add the mustard and nigella seeds.

2

Cook the seeds until they start to pop.

3

Add the ginger, green chilli and sugar
and cook for 30 seconds.

4

Add the turmeric, ground chilli and salt
and stir to combine.

5

Add the tomato and stir to combine.

6

Cook for 5 minutes or until the tomato is just softened.

7

Remove from heat and allow to stand

8

Season with salt to taste and serve warm.

Roadside Chickpea Salad DF, V

Chana chaat is a favourite salad from my travels in Mumbai, where it's commonly known as *bhel puri*. Packed with distinctive fresh and vibrant flavours and contrasting textures, this salad is such a funky, moreish combination – it's a party for the palate. Assembled on the spot as a snack from roadside vendors or local cafes, I have embellished this slightly to make it a stand-alone salad to serve with your preferred flatbread or as an accompaniment to a simple grill.

Serves 6

100 g sprouted mung bean sprouts
   (or mixed grains)
300 g cooked chickpeas (canned is fine)
75 g cooked freekeh (green wheat)
4 tablespoons fresh pomegranate seeds
2 tablespoons sultanas
150 g cooked potato, cut into 5 mm dice
2 ripe tomatoes, seeded and diced
2 small green chillies, finely sliced
1 small red onion, finely diced
2 tablespoons shredded coriander leaves
2 tablespoons pumpkin seeds
1 tablespoon toasted white sesame seeds
1 tablespoon roasted peanuts, roughly chopped
1 teaspoon sea salt flakes
1 tablespoon lime juice
¼ cup (60 ml) grapeseed oil
3 tablespoons green mango chutney, see
   Pickles and Chutneys page 361
3 pappadams, cut into thin strips and deep-fried

Place the mung bean sprouts, chickpeas, freekeh, pomegranate seeds, sultanas, potato, tomato, chilli, onion and coriander in a bowl and stir to combine. Set aside.

Place the pumpkin seeds in a frying pan over low heat and cook until toasted, taking care not to burn. Add to the salad with the sesame seeds, peanuts and salt. Mix the lime juice and grapeseed oil together and stir through the salad. Add the chutney and stir thoroughly to combine. Top with the fried pappadam strips and serve immediately.

Sweet and Sour Beetroot Salad DF, GF, V

Pineapple brings a subtle sweetness to this intriguingly simple salad, which showcases another of my favourite vegetables – beetroot. This recipe also ticks the boxes for its Ayurvedic and wellness properties.

Serves 4

2 teaspoons coconut oil
1 teaspoon black mustard seeds
1 pinch asafoetida
250 g grated beetroot
1 cup mung bean sprouts
2 tablespoons shredded fresh coconut
200 g pineapple, cut into 1 cm dice
2 tablespoons shredded coriander leaves
½ teaspoon sea salt flakes
1 tablespoon lime juice

Heat the oil in small frying pan over low heat. Add the mustard seeds and once they start to pop, add the asafoetida. Remove from heat and set aside.

Mix to combine the beetroot with remaining ingredients in a bowl. Stir through the cooled tempered mustard seeds and serve immediately.

Coconut Beetroot Salad GF, V

Pachadi is something I discovered and fell in love with on my travels through Kerala, where it's commonly served as a side dish or condiment. Seasonal vegetables (cucumber, beetroot or ash gourd, also known as winter melon) or fruit are grated, shredded or pounded and cooked with curry leaves and coconut before being folded through yoghurt. It makes a truly luscious salad to serve alongside other vegetable dishes or as an accompaniment to grilled fish. Every time I cook this for friends, it leaves them swooning.

Serves 4

2 tablespoons organic coconut oil
3 small green chillies, minced
2 tablespoons fresh curry leaves
2 medium-size beetroots, peeled and grated
3 tablespoons grated fresh coconut
1 teaspoon brown mustard seeds
sea salt flakes
80 g thick plain yoghurt

Heat the oil in a frying pan over medium heat. Add the green chilli and curry leaves and cook for 30 seconds or until fragrant, taking care not to burn. Add the beetroot and cook, stirring, until softened.

Meanwhile, blend the coconut and mustard seeds in food processor to make a paste and add to the beetroot. Cook until the mixture starts to froth and bubble. Season with salt, remove from heat and allow to cool for 15 minutes. Stir through the yoghurt and serve at room temperature.

Kachumber Salad DF, V

This is my ramped-up version of the classic Indian chopped salad. It's one of the few in their repertoire that requires no cooking. The addition of toasted flatbread adds a great textural contrast to the salad. To make it gluten-free, simply use a flatbread made with non-gluten flour. It makes a great accompaniment to a curry, fried fish or barbecued lamb chops.

Serves 4–6

1 chapati flatbread, torn into 2 cm pieces
2 large ripe tomatoes, seeded and diced
1 cucumber, peeled, seeded and diced
1 red onion, finely diced
2 long green chillies, seeded and finely diced
3 tablespoons pomegranate seeds
30 ml lemon juice
1 teaspoon sea salt flakes
1 teaspoon cumin seeds, roasted and ground
½ teaspoon chaat masala
¼ teaspoon Kashmiri chilli powder
3 tablespoons shredded coriander leaves

Preheat oven to 160°C. Place the bread pieces on baking tray in single layer and toast until crisp. Set aside.

Make sure the tomato, cucumber and onion are cut into uniform dice. Place in a bowl with the green chilli, pomegranate seeds, lemon juice, salt and spices and toss to combine. Place in the fridge until ready to serve. Toss the toasted chapati and shredded coriander through the salad to serve.

Cucumber Peanut Salad DF, GF, V

This fragrant salad was served to me at a cafe in Goa years ago. Its contrasting textures resonated with me, so I've re-created it from my taste memories and, whenever I make it, I'm transported straight back to that place on the beach. Peanuts are grown and used in many regions of India and make a tasty snack when roasted and sprinkled with salt or added to rice or curry for textural contrast.

Serves 4

2 telegraph cucumbers, peeled
2 small green chillies, minced
60 g shredded fresh coconut
2 tablespoons shredded coriander leaves
1 tablespoon shredded mint leaves
1 tablespoon lime juice
¼ teaspoon dried chilli flakes
60 g roasted peanuts, roughly chopped
1 tablespoon sunflower oil
1 teaspoon black mustard seeds
2 tablespoons fresh curry leaves
½ teaspoon caster sugar
1 teaspoon sea salt flakes

Split the cucumbers in half lengthwise and scoop out the seeds. Cut each piece in half again lengthwise, then cut crosswise into uniform 1 cm dice. Place the cucumber, green chilli, coconut and herbs in a bowl with the lime juice, chilli flakes and peanut and stir to combine. Heat the oil in a small frying pan over medium heat. Add the mustard seeds and cook for 30 seconds or until they start to pop. Add the curry leaves and cook for 20 seconds or until crisp. Pour the spiced oil over the salad, season with sugar and salt and stir to combine. Serve immediately.

Banana Blossom Salad DF, GF, V

Bale hoovu palya is an intriguing salad I first tasted when staying in Hampi. This recipe brings the flavours of the south to the fore and is ideal to make if you happen to have flowering banana trees in your backyard or access to fresh banana blossoms. It's important to remember, the sliced blossom will turn black if soaked in vinegar, so make sure you always acidulate the water with lemon juice to prevent discolouration of the flowers.

Serves 4

2 banana blossoms, see Glossary
½ cup (125 ml) lemon juice
⅓ cup (80 ml) vegetable oil
1 teaspoon black mustard seeds
½ cup channa dal (split yellow chickpeas)
4 small green chillies, minced
½ cup fresh curry leaves
½ teaspoon asafoetida
2 teaspoons sea salt flakes
100 g shredded fresh coconut
½ cup coriander leaves, roughly chopped

Remove all the outer leaves of each blossom, until you're left with the pale, soft inner core. Add 4 tablespoons lemon juice to a large bowl of cold water. Thinly slice the blossoms crosswise and add to the lemon water. Allow to soak for 30 minutes. Drain blossom in a colander and rinse under cold, running water until water runs clear. Return the blossom to a bowl of water and set aside to soak for a further 20 minutes. Drain again and squeeze to remove excess water.

Heat the oil in large frying pan over medium heat. Add the mustard seeds and cook for 30 seconds or until they start to pop. Add the dal, chilli, curry leaves and asafoetida and cook, tossing in the pan, for 90 seconds or until the dal becomes golden. Add the blossom slices and stir to combine. Add the salt and the coconut and cook for 2 minutes. Remove from heat and stir through the remaining 2 tablespoons of lemon juice and the coriander leaves to serve.

Masala Broad Bean, Lentil and Asparagus Salad DF, GF, V

This is a wonderful salad to celebrate the spring season when broad beans and asparagus come into their own. The salad leaves are interchangeable, depending what's available. I look out for small leaves with peppery notes, such as land cress, dandelion, mustard cress or wild rocket.

Serves 6

150 g broad beans (peeled weight)
12 spears green asparagus
120 g cooked brown (or black beluga) lentils
6 green onions, finely sliced
6 breakfast radish, finely sliced into rounds
1 cup mint leaves, shredded
50 g salad leaves (landcress, baby cos, elk), stems removed
6 tablespoons fried rice flakes
3 tablespoons fried garlic slices

GARAM MASALA DRESSING
2 small red chillies, minced
2 garlic cloves, crushed
¼ teaspoon ground ginger
½ teaspoon garam masala
2 teaspoons sea salt flakes
2 tablespoons brown sugar
30 ml rice vinegar
30 ml lime juice
¼ cup (60 ml) grapeseed oil

To make the garam masala dressing, place all ingredients in a jug and mix with a stick blender until emulsified. Check for balance of flavours and seasoning, adjust with salt if necessary.

To prepare the salad, cook the broad beans and asparagus in boiling water for 2 minutes or until al dente. Drain and plunge into iced water to cool. Drain again. Peel the broad beans. Place the broad beans and asparagus in a bowl with the lentils, onion, radish, mint and salad leaves. Add enough garam masala dressing to lightly coat the salad and toss to combine. Scatter over the fried rice flakes and garlic slices to serve.

Smoked Eggplant Salad DF, GF, VF

A perennial favourite, this salad is best consumed soon after it's made to capture its smoky vibrancy and silken texture. The flavours will become dull and muted once refrigerated.

Serves 4

½ teaspoon cumin seeds
2 eggplants
¼ cup (60 ml) olive oil
2 tablespoons diced brown onion
5 cloves garlic, minced
2 tablespoons coriander leaves, chopped
1 teaspoon minced ginger
1 teaspoon sea salt flakes
½ teaspoon freshly ground black pepper
25 ml strained lemon juice

Place the cumin seeds in a non-stick pan over low heat and dry-roast until fragrant. Allow to cool before grinding to a fine powder.

Carefully holding the eggplant with tongs, char over a direct flame until blackened and blistered on all sides. Peel, squeeze to remove any bitter juices from the flesh and chop finely. Heat a frying pan over medium heat. Add the oil, onion and garlic and cook for 4–5 minutes or until pale and golden. Place the onion and garlic in a bowl with the eggplant and remaining ingredients and mix to combine. Taste and adjust seasoning, if necessary. Serve immediately or at room temperature.

Green Bean, Pea and Coconut Poriyal DF, GF, V

Poriyal is technically regarded as a dry curry, but I use and think of it more as a warm salad. This preparation is typical of the south, where the vegetables are subtly spiced and balanced with fresh coconut. Other vegetables, such as cabbage or potato, red capsicum, yams or plantains, are also popular cooked in this manner. Snake beans, broad beans or cluster beans can be used instead of round green beans, if you prefer.

Serves 4

2 tablespoons coconut oil
1 teaspoon black mustard seeds
1 teaspoon cumin seeds
1 teaspoon split urad dal (white lentils), rinsed
2 tablespoons fresh curry leaves
1 long red chilli, finely sliced diagonally
½ teaspoon ground turmeric
½ teaspoon asafoetida
3 red shallots, finely diced
400 g green beans, trimmed and cut into
    5 mm lengths
200 g shelled green peas
3 tablespoons shredded fresh coconut

Heat the oil in a wok or large frying pan over medium heat. Add the mustard seeds, cumin, dal, curry leaves and chilli and cook for 45 seconds or until seeds start to pop. Add the turmeric, asafoetida, and shallot and cook, stirring to combine, for 4 minutes or until softened and shallot is beginning to colour. Stir through the beans and peas, season with salt and cook for 2 minutes or until just softened. Remove from heat and stir through the shredded coconut. Serve warm or at room temperature. Don't refrigerate, as this dulls the flavours.

Cabbage and Coconut Thoran DF, GF, V

A *thoran* is a versatile dry vegetable salad that I've seen prepared by home cooks from Kerala to Rajasthan. The shredded vegetables are flash fried in a pan over high heat with just enough warmth to wilt but without cooking through and softening. The textures remain crisp and fresh, and the spicing is subtle yet apparent, making a refreshing change from the usual array of cooked dishes.

Serves 6

2 tablespoons vegetable oil
1 tablespoon black mustard seeds
20 fresh curry leaves
1 tablespoon finely shredded ginger
½ teaspoons dried chilli flakes
10 white cabbage leaves, finely shredded
½ cup shredded fresh coconut
2 teaspoons sea salt flakes
4 tablespoons coriander leaves, chopped

Heat the oil in a frying pan or wok over medium heat. Add the mustard seeds and curry leaves and cook for 30 seconds or until they start to pop. Add the ginger, chilli flakes and shredded cabbage, stir to coat with the spices, and cook for 30 seconds or until cabbage is just wilted. Remove pan from heat, add the coconut, salt and coriander leaves and toss to combine. Serve immediately.

Spiced Potato and Green Pea Salad GF, V

Like eggplant, potatoes play a starring role in Indian cooking. Their versatility lends them to myriad preparations, partnering with spices and herbs to create memorable flavour combinations.

Serves 4

600 g small new potatoes (chats or kipfler), scrubbed
2 tablespoons vegetable oil
1 teaspoon brown mustard seeds
1 tablespoon fresh curry leaves
2 golden shallots, finely diced
3 garlic cloves, crushed
½ teaspoon ground turmeric
½ teaspoon ground cumin
½ teaspoon dried chilli flakes
1 teaspoon sea salt flakes
125 g fresh or frozen green peas
½ cup shredded coriander leaves
2 tablespoons thick plain yoghurt

Cook the potatoes in a pot of salted, boiling water until tender but still holding their shape. Drain and allow to dry. When cool enough to handle, peel and discard skins and halve or quarter, depending on their size. Set aside.

Heat the oil in frying pan over medium heat. Add the mustard seeds and curry leaves and cook for 30 seconds or until they start to pop. Add the shallot and garlic and cook for 1 minute. Reduce heat to low, add the spices and salt and cook for 2 minutes or until aromatic.

Meanwhile, cook the peas in boiling water for 2 minutes for fresh or 1 minute for frozen or until al dente. Drain.

Add the potato and peas to the frying pan, toss to combine and cook for a further 1 minute. Remove from heat, check seasoning and add more salt, if necessary. Allow to cool for 15 minutes before stirring through the coriander leaves and yoghurt to serve.

Tamarind Potato Salad GF, V

This recipe is perfect for when new potatoes are in season. I like to use waxy potatoes for this salad, such as kipfler, Dutch creams, Jersey royals, nicola or bintje (to name a few). The tamarind and yoghurt add a delicious tanginess to the creamy texture of the potatoes.

Serves 6

1 kg baby (new) potatoes, washed
2 tablespoons tamarind puree
1 tablespoon ground cumin
2 teaspoons ground coriander
2½ tablespoons brown sugar
1 teaspoon sea salt flakes
2 tablespoons shredded fresh ginger
2 tablespoons thick plain yoghurt
4 tablespoons chopped coriander leaves

Cook the potatoes in large pot of lightly salted boiling water for 12–15 minutes or until tender. While the potatoes are cooking, prepare the dressing. Place the tamarind, ground spices, sugar, salt, ginger and 100 ml water in small saucepan over medium heat and simmer gently, stirring occasionally, for 10 minutes or until slightly thickened and syrupy.

When potatoes are cooked, drain and cut or break in half and toss through the tamarind dressing. Mix the yoghurt with 2 tablespoons water to dilute its texture slightly. Place potatoes in a serving dish, drizzle with the yoghurt and top with the chopped coriander to serve.

Curry Fish Salad DF, GF

This fish salad with its layers of flavour and textural contrasts is the bomb! I developed this dish for my restaurant menus – it's fresh and light with a dressing that captures the essence of a mild curry sauce. The fish is cooked, but the salad ingredients are raw to create contrast. Then the dressing binds it all together in perfect harmony. It's the flavour of curry without any heaviness on the palate – transformed into a refreshing, vibrant salad. The best fish to choose for this salad would be snapper, mulloway, trumpeter, pearl perch, blue-eye trevalla, Spanish mackerel or other fleshy, white fish.

Serves 4

400 g white fish fillet, skin removed
1 tablespoon vegetable oil
1 teaspoon ground turmeric
1 teaspoon sea salt flakes
½ teaspoon freshly ground black pepper
1 small cucumber, peeled and shaved into fine ribbons
½ small green mango, sliced and shredded
1 celery stick, finely sliced
½ red onion, finely sliced
½ avocado, diced
8 green beans, sliced diagonally and blanched
½ cup coriander leaves
1 tablespoon shredded mint leaves
2 handfuls watercress sprigs
2 tablespoons boondi (puffed lentils)
2 tablespoons fried curry leaves

CURRY DRESSING
40 ml lime juice
25 ml coconut vinegar
1 tablespoon caster sugar
2 teaspoons sea salt flakes
1 garlic clove, minced
1 teaspoon ground ginger
2 teaspoons mild curry powder
½ teaspoon freshly ground black pepper
185 ml grapeseed oil

To make the curry dressing, place all ingredients in a bowl and blend with a stick blender until emulsified. Taste and adjust seasoning and balance, if necessary.

To prepare the fish, cut fillets crosswise into 2 cm-thick slices. Place the oil, turmeric, salt and pepper in a bowl and mix to combine. Rub over the fish to season and place on a flat baking tray. Cook under a preheated grill for 4–5 minutes or until fish is just cooked. Allow to cool for few minutes while you prepare the salad.

Place the cucumber, mango, celery, onion, avocado, beans, coriander and mint leaves, watercress and boondi in a bowl and toss to combine. Flake the fish into small pieces and add to the salad. Pour over enough curry dressing to lightly coat and toss to combine. Arrange salad on plates and scatter with fried curry leaves to serve.

Oyster, Cucumber and Yoghurt Salad GF

The addition of freshly shucked oysters gives a traditional Indian raita an ethereal quality and transforms it into a refined salad that references the sea. My preferred yoghurt for this recipe is buffalo milk; its silken, creamy texture and tanginess makes the perfect partner for the brininess of oysters. Light and smooth, this salad is perfect for summer and a different way of serving oysters, or raita, for that matter.

Serves 6

250 g buffalo yoghurt
18 rock (or native angasi) oysters, in their shells
1 tablespoon chopped dill
½ teaspoon minced ginger
1 teaspoon minced red shallot
2 teaspoons sea salt flakes
½ teaspoon freshly ground white pepper
2 tablespoons lime juice
½ teaspoon nigella seeds
2 tablespoons finely diced cucumber
2 green shallots, finely sliced
1 punnet red mustard or radish cress, snipped
1 cucumber, peeled and shaved into fine ribbons

Hang the yoghurt in a muslin-lined sieve set over a large bowl so the excess whey drips out and place in the fridge overnight to thicken into a curd.

Shuck the oysters and remove from their shells. Do not wash the oysters as this diminishes their flavour. Wipe off any shell grit with paper towel.

Place the hung yoghurt, dill, ginger, shallot, salt, pepper and half the lime juice in a bowl and mix to combine. Add the nigella seeds and half the diced cucumber and stir to combine. In a separate bowl, mix together the oysters and their juices with the green shallot, mustard cress, and remaining diced cucumber and lime juice. Arrange the cucumber ribbons in serving bowls and spoon over some of the yoghurt salad. Arrange the oysters on top to serve.

Ginger Crab Salad DF, GF

The pungency of fresh ginger is a natural partner for the sweetness of crabmeat, underpinned with aromatic spicy tones that bring a gentle warmth to the palate. This is a warm salad that positively bounces with flavour.

Serves 4

2 tablespoons organic coconut oil
1 teaspoon brown mustard seeds
½ teaspoon fennel seeds
2 cm piece fresh ginger, peeled and cut into fine julienne
4 garlic cloves, finely sliced
3 red shallots, finely sliced
3 small green chillies, finely sliced
½ teaspoon ground turmeric
½ teaspoon garam masala
3 tablespoons fresh curry leaves
1 teaspoon freshly ground black pepper
400 g raw spanner crabmeat
1 ripe tomato, diced
1 cup watercress leaves, stalks removed
1 tablespoon lemon juice
1 tablespoon fresh ginger juice, see Glossary
1 teaspoon sea salt flakes
2 tablespoons coriander leaves
2 tablespoons fried ginger slices

Heat the oil in a frying pan over medium heat. Add the mustard and fennel seeds and cook for 30 seconds or until they start to pop. Add the ginger, garlic, shallot and green chilli and cook, stirring, for 2 minutes or until softened and fragrant. Add the ground turmeric, garam masala, curry leaves and black pepper and stir to combine. Add the crabmeat and tomato and toss to coat with the spice mixture. Don't overwork the crabmeat or it will become mashed. Cook for 30 seconds or just long enough to heat the crab through. Add the watercress leaves and toss to combine. Remove from heat, stir through the lemon and ginger juices, salt and coriander leaves. Scatter with fried ginger to serve.

Watermelon, Turmeric Squid and Mint Salad DF, GF

This recipe uses ingredients that reference India without being a traditional salad in any sense, but this warm dish is a magical combination of flavours and textures. With cooling watermelon and mint, a gentle spicy heat and tender squid, it's my interpretation of bringing common flavours together through a different lens.

Serves 4

50 ml watermelon juice
40 ml lime juice
1 tablespoon caster sugar
2 teaspoons sea salt flakes
1 tablespoon vegetable oil
½ teaspoon cumin seeds
2 teaspoons garlic, minced
1 red bird's eye chilli, minced
2 teaspoons ground chilli
½ teaspoon ground coriander
½ teaspoon ground turmeric
200 g cleaned squid tubes, cut in half and scored
200 g watermelon, rind removed and cut into 3 cm dice
1 watermelon radish, peeled and sliced into thin rounds
4 tablespoons mint leaves, roughly chopped
2 tablespoons fried shallot slices, see Glossary

Mix to combine the watermelon juice, lime juice, sugar and salt. Set aside.

Heat the oil in a frying pan over low–medium heat. Add the cumin seeds and cook for 30 seconds or until fragrant. Add the garlic and minced chilli and cook for 45 seconds or until softened. Add the ground spices and stir to combine. Increase heat to medium, add the squid and cook, stirring for 1 minute or until squid begins to curl and is coated with the spices. Add the diced watermelon and cook for 30 seconds or until warmed through. Add the radish and toss to combine. Remove from heat, pour over the watermelon lime dressing and toss to coat squid and watermelon. Arrange salad on plates. Sprinkle with the mint and fried shallot to serve.

Lamb and Eggplant Yoghurt Salad GF

This is a great flavour-packed summer salad inspired by Indian flavours. The spiced yoghurt seasons and tenderises the meat during cooking, while the yoghurt dressing offers contrast to a regular vinaigrette. You can also wrap the salad in hot naan or roti bread as a delicious alternative to a sandwich for a quick lunch.

Serves 4

2 x 200 g lamb backstrap fillets, trimmed
1 tablespoon ghee
1 small cucumber, peeled
16 cherry tomatoes, halved
1 tablespoon shredded ginger
2 golden shallots, peeled and finely sliced
1 x 250 g purple eggplant, peeled, cut into
    1 cm dice and deep-fried
150 g thick plain yoghurt
2 tablespoons eggplant pickle, see Pickles and
    Chutneys page 346
1 teaspoon sea salt flakes
50 ml lemon juice, strained
2 tablespoons shredded mint leaves
2 tablespoons shredded coriander leaves
2 handfuls mâche (lamb's lettuce) leaves or small
    rocket leaves

SPICED YOGHURT MARINADE
½ teaspoon coriander seeds
½ teaspoon cumin seeds
½ teaspoon black mustard seeds
½ teaspoon garam masala
½ teaspoon ground turmeric
½ teaspoon nigella seeds
1 teaspoon sea salt flakes
½ teaspoon freshly ground black pepper
2 teaspoons ginger garlic paste, see recipe
    page 436
60 g thick plain yoghurt

To make the spiced yoghurt marinade, place the coriander, cumin and mustard seeds in a frying pan over low heat and cook for 30 seconds or until fragrant. Allow to cool before grinding in a spice grinder or mortar and pestle. Place in a bowl with the remaining marinade ingredients and mix to combine. Set aside.

Cut each lamb backstrap in half crosswise to yield 4 portions. Add to the marinade and toss to combine. Set aside to marinate for 30 minutes at room temperature.

Melt the ghee in a frying pan or flat grill plate over medium–high heat. Add the lamb and cook for 2–3 minutes each side or until browned but still pink in the centre. Allow the lamb to rest for 2–3 minutes before cutting crosswise into thin slices.

To make the salad, cut the cucumber in half lengthwise and scoop out the seeds. Cut into thin half-moon slices. Place in a bowl with the tomato, ginger, shallot and fried eggplant and toss to combine. Place the yoghurt, eggplant pickle, salt and lemon juice in a separate bowl and stir to combine. Add to the salad and stir to combine. When ready to serve, add the mint, coriander and mâche leaves to the salad and toss to combine. Arrange lamb on plates and top with the salad to serve.

Eggs and Dairy

India is the leading milk-producing country in the world and this shines through in each of the regional cuisines. From milk we get cream, yoghurt, curd, butter, ghee and buttermilk, making it one of the most valuable and appreciated food sources. An Indian diet without any of these essential and nourishing ingredients is nigh on inconceivable. Milk is nothing short of a gift from nature.

Considered a pure food because an animal does not have to be killed to obtain the product, milk holds religious and spiritual significance. Many dishes cooked with milk are considered auspicious. It also plays a pivotal role in the Ayurvedic diet and, in a country where nearly half the population are vegetarian, milk products are the principle source of protein and energy. Milk is a beverage of high prestige and the importance of dairy in Indian cooking serves to add essential moisture, protein and nutrition to the daily diet.

Playing a key role in the creation of many of India's finest dishes, dairy imparts richness and a desirable additional layer of flavour. When thickened by being reduced over simmering heat without stirring, it magically transforms into *rabri*, a popular dessert where the milk is usually sweetened slightly before being cooked. *Khoa* is the thick, creamy layer that forms on the surface of milk and is carefully skimmed off – this naturally occurs with milk that is raw, unadulterated and fresh from the cow. This khoa is often added to a lassi to give an added richness to the drink – my personal favourite. Adding milk to a bread dough results in a softer texture, a typical practice in Gujarat when making roti, and one that I tend to follow myself.

Yoghurt (*dahi*) makes its presence felt in myriad marinades, gravies and sauces for meats and fish. It plays a starring role in vegetarian dishes, raita condiments and some chutneys, as well as adding creaminess when stirred into a sauce before serving. Foods cooked in the tandoor oven are reliant on their yoghurt marinade to maintain moisture and succulence during cooking. More often than not, Indian households make their own yoghurt every morning after purchasing fresh milk at the market. It's one of the daily rhythms of kitchen life.

Paneer is a fresh cheese made from bountiful milk supplies across the country. It's a dairy product that provides sustenance to vegetarian dishes with the cheese replacing meat or fish proteins in many preparations. *Ghee* is an Indian version of clarified butter (different to the Western version in the way it is cooked), where fresh butter is melted and simmered over low heat until the milk solids and moisture have evaporated, yielding a clear, golden liquid with a characteristic nutty aroma. It is one of the most common fats used in cooking throughout the country. Ghee should be kept refrigerated and because it is a pure fat (the milk solids in butter that normally burn at

a certain point have been removed) this means it can be heated to a high temperature without spoiling or burning. It's also common practice for adults and children to swallow a spoonful of warm ghee every day, as it's said to enhance intelligence and purify the digestive system.

There are daily milk markets in cities, rural towns and villages across the country, where vendors collect milk from local farmers and producers. They come together at daybreak to fill people's urns, jugs and buckets with enough to take home for their daily cooking rituals. This ritual is played out every day in every region but, of course, is not the only way to purchase milk. Modern living has seen a shift to store-bought ingredients, milk being one of them, and the locals have their preferred reliable brands. However, the tradition of supporting the local milkmen is a strong one that lives on.

I have seen shops in many different cities and towns that specialise in ghee or yoghurt. They're often a modest shopfront in a local market with their wares on display. Clever household cooks know that the best time to buy these fresh products is first thing in the morning when they are in peak condition. Although cow's milk is the most commonly used, buffalo and goat milk also play a part, as these animals are integral to India's animal husbandry and farming practices. Generous amounts of butter and cream underpin the cooking of the dairy-rich Punjab region, in particular, and most Indian sweets are based on milk, sugar and ghee.

A common sight when driving on any road is a motorbike or bicycle rider carrying an enormous, precariously balanced stack of eggs packed into crates. They look like they'll topple over at any minute, but somehow they never do. Eggs are another essential ingredient to the Indian repertoire, even though they're not eaten by Brahmin and Jain Hindus, who maintain a strict vegetarian diet and eschew all meat products for religious reasons. For the rest of the country, eggs provide essential protein and are consumed in vast quantities. They're easy to prepare, appearing in countless savoury preparations, from boiled in their shells, peeled and added to a curry or rice, to scrambled or baked to make a wonderful breakfast dish. Eggs are the ultimate comfort food.

As such, it is likely already apparent that this is not the chapter to refer to for vegan (non-dairy) cooking.

How to make paneer GF, V

A fresh, unripened cheese and a staple in the Indian kitchen, paneer has a texture like tofu and a mild taste that allows it to take on the flavours of the spices and aromatics with which it is cooked. Some Western recipes suggest substituting cottage cheese or a firm ricotta and, although the texture and consistency are not quite the same, it's the closest approximation. Paneer is made with full-cream milk (no excuses), as the fat content is essential for flavour and creaminess. The heated milk is coagulated using lemon juice and vinegar, allowing curds to form, in the same way you'd make any fresh cheese. Do remember, for any of the recipes in this chapter, If you're using store-bought paneer and not making your own, soak it in warm water for 30 minutes before using.

Makes approximately 750 g

2 litres full-cream milk
200 ml pouring cream
100 ml buttermilk
120 ml white vinegar

Line a round sieve with a double layer of muslin and stand over a bowl, ensuring there is space between the sieve and the base of the bowl.

Pour the milk into a heavy-based saucepan over low heat and bring to a simmer. As the milk starts to bubble and break the surface, stir in the cream followed by the buttermilk. Once it starts to boil again, stir through the vinegar. Stir continuously until the milk starts to curdle and lumps begin to form. Remove from heat and set aside for 5 minutes.

When it has cooled slightly and the lumps are quite large, use a sieve spoon to gently place the curds into the muslin, reserving the whey. Fold the muslin over the curds and refrigerate for 3 hours. At this stage, the curds will be creamy and soft. Place a plate on the curds to weigh down and cover the strainer and bowl with plastic wrap and refrigerate for a further 2 hours. The excess whey will drip through the muslin and the curd inside will become firm. The reserved whey can be used for cooking rice or in a curry gravy, it's full of valuable nutrients and shouldn't be discarded.

Remove plate and refrigerate for a further 2 hours to compress and allow it to become firm. Cover and leave, in the fridge, for a final 2 hours. The paneer is now ready to use. It will keep covered and sealed in the fridge for 5 days.

**Masterclass step-by-step
Paneer ➡**

1 Pour the milk into a heavy-based saucepan over low heat and bring to a simmer.

2 As the milk starts to bubble and break the surface, stir in the cream.

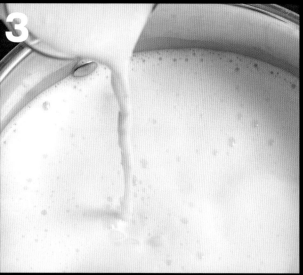

3 Stir in the buttermilk.

4 Once the milk starts to boil again, stir in the vinegar.

5 Stir continuously until the milk starts to curdle and lumps begin to form.

6 Remove from heat and leave to sit for 5 minutes.

7

Use a sieve spoon to gently place the curds in the muslin, reserving the whey.

8

Fold the muslin over the curds.

9

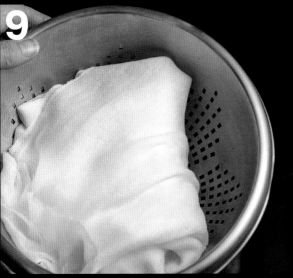

Cover and refrigerate for 3 hours.

10

Place a plate on the curds to weigh down, cover with plastic wrap and refrigerate for a further 2 hours.

11

Remove plate, cover and refrigerate for a final 2 hours.

12

The paneer is ready to use and will keep for up to 5 days in the fridge.

How to make yoghurt GF, V

Yoghurt is fermented milk and indispensable to Indian cooking. When making yoghurt, be sure to use full-cream milk from a reputable local farmer, rather than a generic industrial product that lacks in flavour and texture. It's the same principle with the yoghurt starter; use an artisanal brand from a small producer, one that has live yeasts that acts as the mother culture for making the yoghurt. Don't waste your time with an industrial product. As with any cooking, starting with the very best ingredients gives immeasurable rewards and superior flavour.

Makes 1 kg

1 litre full-cream milk
½ cup thick plain yoghurt

Pour 2 tablespoons water into a saucepan, this prevents the milk from sticking to the base of the pan. Add the milk and heat gently over low heat until it reaches 90°C. You will need an accurate thermometer to gauge this. This process should take anything up to 40 minutes before the temperature is reached.

Remove milk from heat and set aside on the bench to cool to 45°C. It should be cool enough so as not to kill the culture in the yoghurt, yet warm enough to activate the culture. Gently stir in the yoghurt until combined. Pour into sterilised glass jars and seal with lids. Wrap the jars in a towel and sit on a flat tray. This helps to provide a stable warmth. Set aside in the warmest spot in your kitchen or in the oven, not turned on, and away from any draught for 12 hours or overnight.

Unwrap the jars of yoghurt and refrigerate. The yoghurt will keep for 2 weeks. When you're ready to make another batch, keep ½ cup of the yoghurt as the base for the next batch. This is the mother culture you'll need to feed your yoghurt each time.

Masterclass step-by-step
Yoghurt ➜

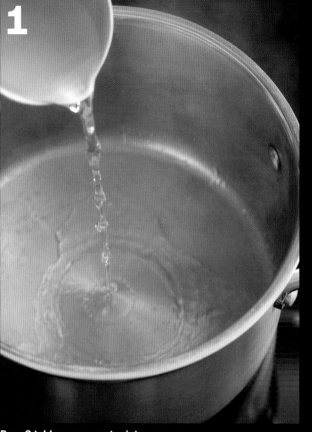

1

Pour 2 tablespoons water into a saucepan.

2

Add the milk and heat gently over low heat until it reaches 90°C.

3

You will need an accurate thermometer to gauge this. It may take up to 40 minutes.

4

Remove from heat and set aside to cool to 45°C. Add the yoghurt.

5

Stir gently until combined.

6

Pour into sterilised glass jars and seal with lids.

7

Wrap the jars in a towel and sit on a flat tray.

8

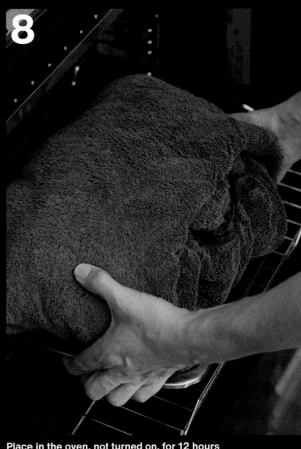

Place in the oven, not turned on, for 12 hours or overnight.

Sweet Yoghurt Cream GF, V

Shrikhand is a sweetened whipped yoghurt made during the hot summer months to cool the palate. It's served as a refreshing finale to a thali in Gujarati restaurants or as a dip for crisp *puris* (deep-fried bread) in Mumbai. The recipe for this silky, smooth treat dates back to ancient Sanskrit texts, but is very straightforward to make with the curd (hung yoghurt) being whipped with the sugar and flavourings until smooth. It can be flavoured with lemon, saffron or cardamom. I liken it to Chantilly cream for its feather-light texture and simplicity.

Serves 4

1 tablespoon pouring cream
½ teaspoon saffron threads
400 g fresh curd (hung yoghurt), see recipe right
1 teaspoon ground cardamom
80 g caster sugar
1 tablespoon flaked almonds, lightly toasted

Place the cream and saffron in small bowl over low heat and cook until it starts to simmer, taking care not to burn. Remove from heat and set aside to infuse and cool for 10 minutes. Place the curd in a large bowl with the saffron cream, cardamom and sugar and, using a stick blender with whisk attachment, whisk until combined and smooth. Divide between 4 serving glasses or small bowls, cover and refrigerate for 2 hours. Sprinkle with flaked almonds to serve.

How to make fresh curd (hung yoghurt) GF, V

Indian recipes call for curd or hung yoghurt – both terms are interchangeable and both are correct. The yield is generally a little more than half of the quantity of yoghurt you start with.

Makes approximately 600 g

1 kg yoghurt
1 teaspoon table salt

Line a colander with a double layer of muslin cloth. Stir the salt into the yoghurt and pour into the muslin-lined colander. Fold the muslin over to cover the yoghurt and sit the colander over a deep bowl or pot. You want to ensure there is space between the base of the colander and the base of the bowl. Refrigerate for 6 hours to thicken the yoghurt. During this time, the whey will have dripped through the muslin, reserve the whey for another use (I use it in place of water when cooking rice). Don't hang the yoghurt for too long, as it will become too firm. Lift the colander from the bowl and unwrap the muslin. Place a flat plate over the colander and invert the curd onto the plate. Lift the colander from the curd and gently remove the muslin. The curd is ready to use.

**Masterclass step-by-step
Fresh Curd (Hung Yoghurt)** ➜

1 Line a colander with a double layer of muslin cloth.

2 Stir the salt into the yoghurt.

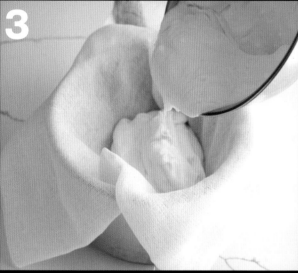

3 Pour the yoghurt into the muslin-lined colander.

4 Fold the muslin over to cover the yoghurt.

5 Sit the colander over a bowl and refrigerate for 6 hours.

6 Lift the colander from the bowl.

7

Unwrap the muslin.

8

Place a flat plate over the colander.

9

Invert the curd onto the plate.

10

Lift the colander from the curd.

11

Remove the muslin.

12

The curd is ready to use.

Spinach and Cheese GF, V

Saag paneer is a classic vegetarian dish of Punjabi origin (hence the addition of cream) found on restaurant menus and in home kitchens across India and beyond. This is comfort food at its best, where cubes of fresh paneer and spinach are simmered together in a light sauce.

Serves 4

500 g English spinach leaves, stalks removed
100 ml vegetable oil
250 g paneer, cut into 2 cm cubes
1 tablespoon ghee
1 tablespoon ginger garlic paste, see recipe
    page 436
2 small green chillies, minced
½ teaspoon ground cumin
½ teaspoon chilli powder
1 teaspoon ground fenugreek seeds
2 tomatoes, seeded and diced
1 tablespoon sea salt flakes
2 tablespoon cream
1 teaspoon garam masala

Blanch the spinach leaves in a saucepan of boiling water for 30 seconds. Drain and refresh in iced water. Drain again and squeeze to remove any excess water. Place the cooked spinach in a food processor and blend to make a rough paste. Set aside.

Heat the oil in a frying pan over medium heat. Add the paneer cubes and cook, turning, for 2–3 minutes or until golden. Drain on paper towel and set aside.

In the same frying pan, melt the ghee over medium heat. Add the ginger garlic paste and green chilli and cook for 2 minutes or until softened. Add the cumin, chilli powder and fenugreek seeds and cook for a further 90 seconds or until fragrant. Add the tomato, salt and spinach puree and cook for 6–8 minutes or until liquid has evaporated. Fold the fried paneer gently into the spinach and simmer for a further 5 minutes. Add the cream and stir to combine. Sprinkle with garam masala to serve.

Baked Curd GF, V

Marwadi kadhi is a Rajasthani dish of the Marwadi traders (sometimes spelled Marwari) in and around Jodhpur, where curd (hung yoghurt) is cooked in a *kadhai* (a cooking vessel similar in shape to a wok). This is an excellent example of how to use chickpea (besan) flour and yoghurt, two staple ingredients in desert cooking. This spiced curd sauce is traditionally served with roti or rice seasoned with cumin during summer.

Serves 4

2 cups (300 g) chickpea (besan) flour
560 g curd (hung yoghurt), see recipe on
    previous page
1 tablespoon ghee
½ teaspoon coriander seeds
¼ teaspoon cumin seeds
1 teaspoon minced green chilli
4 fresh curry leaves
1 teaspoon chilli powder
1 teaspoon ground turmeric
1 teaspoon sea salt flakes
1 tablespoon vegetable oil
2 long dried chillies
2 tablespoons freshly chopped coriander leaves

Place the flour and curd in bowl and mix until combined. Melt the ghee in a kadhai or deep-sided frying pan over medium heat. Add the coriander and cumin seeds, green chilli and curry leaves and cook for 30 seconds or until fragrant. Add the curd mixture, stirring continuously, and reduce heat to low. Add the chilli powder and turmeric and cook, stirring continuously, for 3–4 minutes or until smooth – use a whisk at this stage if you find it easier. Add ½ cup (125 ml) water and salt and cook for 5 minutes or until the mixture thickens. Transfer the curd to a serving bowl and set aside at room temperature while you cook the chillies.

Heat the vegetable oil in a separate small frying pan over medium heat. Add the dried chillies and cook for 90 seconds or until they start to change colour. Remove from oil. Garnish the baked curd with the fresh coriander and fried chillies to serve.

Scrambled Cheese GF, V

In India, this popular dish of the north is often served at roadside food stalls or *dhabas* (canteens). Known as *paneer bhurji*, meaning 'scrambled', the crumbled cheese is cooked with spices and aromatics in the same way as scrambled eggs. It's a very easy, heart-warming dish to make. If you don't have time to make paneer, you can use fresh ricotta or cottage cheese with equal success. Serve with roti, chapati or toast.

Serves 4

2 tablespoons vegetable oil
1 teaspoon cumin seeds
2 teaspoons minced ginger
4 small green chillies, minced
1 red onion, finely diced
1 teaspoon ground coriander
½ teaspoon chilli powder
1 teaspoon ground turmeric
½ teaspoon ground fennel seeds
¼ teaspoon ground cardamom
½ teaspoon ground cinnamon
1 teaspoon freshly ground black pepper
1 teaspoon sea salt flakes
12 cherry tomatoes, halved
1 red capsicum, seeded and cut into 1 cm dice
1 yellow capsicum, seeded and cut into 1 cm dice
400 g paneer, coarsely crumbled
1 tablespoon lime juice
2 tablespoons chopped coriander leaves
½ teaspoon garam masala

Heat the oil in a frying pan over medium heat. Add the cumin seeds and cook for 30 seconds or until they start to pop. Add the ginger and green chilli, stir to combine and cook for 1 minute or until fragrant. Add the onion and cook, stirring frequently, for 4 minutes or until starting to colour. Add the ground spices and salt and cook a further 2 minutes. Add the tomato and capsicum and cook for 10 minutes or until tomatoes break down and a sauce forms. Add the crumbled paneer and cook for 2 minutes, stirring but taking care not to mash the cheese or overcook it so it breaks down, until warmed through. Remove pan from heat and stir through the lime juice and coriander. Spoon onto plates and sprinkle with garam masala to serve.

Mango Lassi GF, V

Lassi is a popular drink made by whisking curd with water, salt and sometimes ginger or lemon. It can be made richer by floating a layer of thick cream on top. Make sure the mango and the yoghurt are chilled before blending.

Serves 4

1 ripe mango, peeled and diced
1 cup thick plain yoghurt
½ cup (125 ml) full-cream milk
1 tablespoon caster sugar
½ teaspoon chaat masala

Place all ingredients together in a blender with a few ice cubes and blend until combined and smooth. Pour into glasses and serve chilled.

Spiced Buttermilk Lassi GF, V

Masala chaas is a popular summer drink that aids digestion, the buttermilk giving a tangy flavour and the black salt (*kala namak*) adding a unique pungency, which can be polarising for palates not accustomed to its taste. It is often served after a rich meal or banquet. When making this, buy buttermilk from a small-scale, artisanal producer, the mass-produced version lacks authenticity of flavour and texture.

Serves 4

1 cup (250 ml) buttermilk
1 green chilli, chopped
2 teaspoons chopped ginger
1 tablespoon chopped mint leaves
½ teaspoon cumin powder
½ teaspoon ground black salt
¼ teaspoon sea salt flakes
¼ teaspoon chaat masala
1 tablespoon chopped mint, extra, to garnish

Pour the buttermilk into a blender with 2 cups (500 ml) water, 6 ice cubes and all remaining ingredients except the extra mint. Blend until combined and smooth. Pour into serving glasses and garnish with the extra mint to serve.

Rice and Egg Fritters DF, GF, V

Typical of the Malabar coastal region, *mutta surka* are crispy golden fritters I've had cooked for me by Faiza Moosa at her guesthouse in Thalassery. They are wickedly good and the type of snack that disappears in an instant, leaving you hungry for more. Serve them with a spicy chutney, a vegetable curry or mutton stew.

Makes 12

200 g parboiled white rice
2 eggs
1 teaspoon sea salt flakes
2 cups (500 ml) vegetable oil, for frying

Soak the rice in water for 5 hours. Wash, drain and place in a food processor with the eggs, salt and a little water and blend to make a smooth paste of pouring consistency.

Heat the oil in a wok or deep saucepan to 170°C. Using a ladle, pour ¼ cup (60 ml) of the batter into the hot oil and fry, in batches, for 2 minutes or until fritters puff up. Turn and fry on the other side for a further 2 minutes or until golden. Remove from oil with a mesh spoon and drain on paper towel. Repeat until all fritters are cooked. Serve with chutney of your choice.

Paneer Fritters V

A flavoursome cheese patty, this mix is pressed into small, round cakes in the same manner as a fish cake or patty. A firm ricotta or feta can be used in place of the paneer, if you have trouble sourcing it or can't make it ahead of time. Just be mindful of the saltiness, you may need to adjust the seasoning.

Serves 4

250 g firm paneer, coarsely grated
½ cup chopped coriander leaves
¼ cup chopped mint leaves
2 green shallots, finely sliced
1 small green chilli, minced
2 teaspoons ginger garlic paste, see recipe page 436
1 teaspoon lemon juice
2 eggs, beaten
2 tablespoons plain flour
1 teaspoon ground cumin
1 teaspoon sea salt flakes
½ teaspoon freshly ground black pepper
600 ml vegetable oil, for deep-frying
green chilli chutney, to serve, see Pickles and Chutneys page 364

Place all ingredients except the oil and chutney in a bowl and mix well until thoroughly combined.

Using wet hands, take spoonfuls of the mixture and roll into small balls. Press into flat patty shapes and place in a single layer on a flat tray lined with baking paper. Cover and refrigerate for 1 hour before cooking.

Heat the oil in a large saucepan or wok to 180°C. Cook the patties, in batches, for 2 minutes. Turn and fry on the other side for a further 2 minutes or until golden. Remove from oil with a mesh spoon and drain on paper towel. Repeat until all fritters are cooked. Serve with green chilli chutney.

Cucumber Raita GF, V

This is a cooling and refreshing salad that is essential on any Indian table. I like to serve it alongside grilled or barbecued meats or fish. If you're making a wrap using a flatbread, spread this onto the bread with a spicy vegetable filling and some tangy chutney to make a delicious lunch. Use tender, young cucumbers to avoid any bitter taste in the yoghurt.

Serves 6

2 cups thick plain yoghurt, stirred
2 small cucumbers, peeled, seeded and finely diced
1 tablespoon finely diced red onion
1 small green chilli, minced
1 tomato, seeded and finely diced
2 teaspoons caster sugar
1 teaspoon sea salt flakes
1 teaspoon cumin seeds, roasted and ground
1 teaspoon nigella seeds
1 tablespoon chopped mint

Place the yoghurt, cucumber, onion, chilli, tomato, sugar and salt in a bowl and stir well to combine. When ready to serve, sprinkle with the cumin, nigella seeds and mint.

Pomegranate and Apple Raita GF, V

Any manner of vegetables, fruits and herbs can be used to make raita, and this fruit-based yoghurt salad makes a wonderful accompaniment to biryani and pulao or served with grilled fish and myriad vegetable dishes. You can substitute finely diced cucumber for the mung sprouts, if you wish.

Serve 6

500 g thick plain yoghurt
1 red shallot, finely diced
1 teaspoon minced ginger
1 apple, peeled and finely diced
2 tablespoons mung sprouts
½ cup (80 g) pomegranate seeds
2 tablespoons shredded mint leaves
1 teaspoon sea salt flakes
2 teaspoons caster sugar
1 teaspoon ground cumin

Place the yoghurt in a bowl and whisk until smooth. Gently stir in the shallot, ginger, apple, sprouts, half the pomegranate seeds, mint, salt, sugar and cumin until combined. Garnish with remaining pomegranate seeds to serve.

Yoghurt Kebabs with Beetroot Sauce v

Dahi ke kabab comes from the Gujarati repertoire and is a popular dish on vegetarian menus in many Indian restaurants. This particular recipe was given to me by Jessi Singh, a well-known Indian restaurateur in Australia. I prefer to use panko crumbs to coat the kebabs, as I find they give a more interesting textural coating than dried fine breadcrumbs. Easy to prepare and very moreish, these soft and creamy croquette-style kebabs make for a great starter.

Serves 4

30 g ginger
4 garlic cloves
4 small green chillies
400 g fresh curd (hung yoghurt), see recipe
  page 110
1 teaspoon ground cardamom
2 teaspoons sea salt flakes
2 tablespoons caster sugar
50 g panko breadcrumbs
100 ml vegetable oil, for frying
2 tablespoons fried curry leaves

BEETROOT SAUCE
200 g beetroot, peeled and cut into small dice
1 teaspoon chopped ginger
2 small green chillies
1 teaspoon sea salt flakes
2 teaspoons caster sugar
200 g fresh curd (hung yoghurt), see recipe
  page 110

To make the beetroot sauce, place the beetroot, ginger, chilli, salt and sugar in a food processor or blender and blend to a fine puree. Stir the beetroot puree into the curd to combine. Set aside. The sauce will keep in an airtight container in the fridge for 2 days.

To make the kebabs, place the ginger, garlic and chilli in a food processor and blend to make a paste. In a large bowl, gently mix the curd with the ginger chilli paste, cardamom, salt and sugar to combine. Roll tablespoonfuls of the mixture into small balls and flatten the top gently with your fingers, so the shape resembles a croquette or patty. Roll in the breadcrumbs to coat.

Heat the oil in a frying pan over medium heat. Fry the kebabs, in batches, taking care not to overload the pan, for 2 minutes or until golden and crisp. Turn and fry on the other side for a further 2 minutes. Remove from pan with a slotted spoon and drain on paper towel. Spoon beetroot sauce onto plates, arrange kebabs on top and garnish with fried curry leaves to serve.

Egg Curry GF, V

Reliant on kitchen staples and thrifty cooking, this curry is an easy one to prepare and an ideal comfort dish for any time of the day. To save time, have the dal curry made ahead then simply reheat and add the fried eggs to serve. I like it with a buttery naan or toasted sourdough.

Serves 4

2 teaspoons ground turmeric
2 teaspoons Kashmiri chilli powder
2 teaspoons sea salt flakes
1 tablespoon chickpea (besan) flour
6 large eggs, hard-boiled and peeled
2 tablespoons mustard oil
400 g split mung dal (green lentils), washed, soaked for 1 hour
1 long green chilli, chopped
1 tablespoon ginger garlic paste, see recipe page 436
1 tablespoon vegetable oil
1 teaspoon black mustard seeds
1 teaspoon cumin seeds
1 brown onion, thinly sliced lengthwise
1 tablespoon fresh curry leaves
2 tablespoons thick plain yoghurt
1 teaspoon caster sugar
2 tablespoons chopped coriander leaves
½ teaspoon garam masala

Place half the turmeric, chilli powder and salt with the chickpea flour in a bowl and mix to combine. Rub water over the peeled eggs to moisten and rub over the spiced salt to coat the eggs.

Heat the mustard oil in a small frying pan over medium–high heat. When it starts to smoke, add the eggs and fry for 4 minutes, turning with a spoon for even colour, or until golden. Drain on paper towel and reserve oil.

Drain the water from the dal and rinse again. Place the softened dal in a food processor with the green chilli, ginger garlic paste and just enough water (about 50 ml) to form a coarse paste and pulse briefly. Don't overwork the dal as you want to retain some of its texture, not make it smooth.

Heat the reserved mustard oil and the vegetable oil in a deep-sided frying pan over medium heat. Add the mustard and cumin seeds and when they start to pop, add the onion and curry leaves and stir to combine. Cook for 5 minutes or until onion starts to brown. Add the remaining turmeric and chilli powder with the yoghurt and cook, stirring constantly, for 2 minutes. Reduce heat to low, add the dal puree and stir to combine. Cook gently for 10 minutes or until the dal is soft and comes away from the base of the pan. Add just enough water (about 200 ml) to loosen the sauce without it being too runny. Add the sugar and remaining salt and stir to combine. Increase heat to medium and bring to a simmer. Cut the fried eggs in half lengthwise and add to the curry, stirring to coat the eggs. Top with coriander leaves and garam masala and serve hot.

Masala Scrambled Eggs GF, V

Akoori is a Parsi breakfast dish served at Irani cafes in Mumbai and a dead easy one to make at home. It just gives that extra dimension to regular scrambled eggs. If I have the time, I like to make chapati, served hot straight from the pan, with these eggs.

Serves 4

40 g unsalted butter
1 small red onion, finely diced
1 teaspoon ground turmeric
½ teaspoon Kashmiri chilli powder
½ teaspoon garam masala
2 garlic cloves, crushed
2 small green chillies, minced
2 tomatoes, seeded and finely diced
1 teaspoon sea salt flakes
8 large eggs, whisked
2 tablespoons chopped coriander leaves

Melt the butter in a frying pan over medium heat. Add the onion and cook for 2–3 minutes or until softened. Add the ground spices and stir to combine. Add the garlic and chilli and cook for a further 1 minute. Add the tomato and salt and cook for 1 minute before pouring the beaten egg into the pan. Reduce heat to low and cook for 2 minutes, stirring the eggs gently to scramble as they cook. The eggs should be soft and runny, not firm. Stir through the coriander and remove pan from heat. By this time the eggs should be just set. Serve immediately.

Egg Roast DF, GF, V

A prized breakfast dish I came across in northern Kerala, *mutta kakkathil* is typically served with appams or hoppers and is a wonderful dish to showcase the beauty of eggs, especially if you can get organically harvested ones. The eggs are boiled and fried before being pan-roasted in a spicy sauce to glaze them.

Serves 4

4 hard-boiled eggs, peeled
2 teaspoons chilli powder
¼ teaspoon ground turmeric
1 teaspoon sea salt flakes
¼ cup (60 ml) vegetable oil
250 g onion, finely diced
1 teaspoon ginger garlic paste, see recipe
    page 436
3 small green chillies, minced
1 teaspoon ground coriander seeds
¼ teaspoon ground fennel seed
1 tablespoon chopped curry leaves
¼ cup (60 ml) coconut cream
1 tablespoon chopped coriander leaves

Make a few shallow slits in the eggs, taking care not to cut into the yolks. Place ¼ teaspoon of the chilli powder, a pinch of the turmeric powder and a pinch of the salt in a bowl and mix to make a paste. Rub spice paste all over the eggs and set aside.

Heat the oil in a frying pan over medium heat. Add the eggs and fry for 4 minutes or until golden. Remove from pan and set aside.

In the same pan, add the onion and cook for 4 minutes or until softened. Add the ginger garlic paste and green chilli and cook for 4 minutes or until it starts to colour. Stir in the remaining chilli powder, turmeric and salt with the coriander, fennel and curry leaves and cook for 2–3 minutes. Stir in the coconut cream and simmer for 10 minutes or until thickened. Return the fried eggs to the pan and spoon over the masala sauce to coat. Reduce heat to low and cook for 4 minutes. Sprinkle with coriander to serve.

Green Masala Eggs DF, GF, V

Here, eggs are bathed in a gently spiced curry sauce, which is given a tangy kick of flavour with the addition of green chilli chutney. If you don't have this chutney made and don't have time to, you can dip into your pantry and use another ready-made chutney, such as mango or lime.

Serves 4

¼ cup (60 ml) vegetable oil
1 brown onion, finely diced
1 tablespoon ginger garlic paste, see recipe
  page 436
1 teaspoon ground turmeric
1 teaspoon Kashmiri chilli powder
1 teaspoon ground coriander
400 ml coconut milk
2 long green chillies, finely sliced
1 tablespoon green chilli chutney, see Pickles
  and Chutneys page 364
1 teaspoon sea salt flakes
4 large hard-boiled eggs
2 tablespoons chopped mint leaves
2 tablespoons chopped coriander leaves

Heat half the oil in a frying pan over medium heat. Add the onion and cook, stirring occasionally, for 4 minutes or until softened. Add the ginger garlic paste and cook for 1 minute. Stir through the ground spices and cook for a further 1–2 minutes or until fragrant. Add the coconut milk, chilli and chutney, bring to a simmer and cook for 5 minutes. Season with salt.

While the sauce is cooking, heat the remaining oil in a small frying pan over medium heat. Add the eggs and cook, stirring in the hot oil, until browned and starting to become crisp. Using a slotted spoon, carefully remove eggs from the pan and cut in half lengthwise. Add the egg to the sauce and stir through the mint and coriander. Serve with steamed basmati rice or rice appams.

Masala Omelette GF, V

Cooked like a traditional omelette, this Indian version adds a splash of spice to the mix. Serve with toast or chapati and some mint chutney for an indulgent breakfast or snack.

Serves 2

6 large eggs
2 green shallots, finely sliced
2 teaspoons minced ginger
2 small green chillies, minced
1 teaspoon ground cumin
½ teaspoon ground turmeric
1 tomato, seeded and diced
2 tablespoons chopped coriander leaves
1 teaspoon sea salt flakes
2 tablespoons ghee

Crack the eggs into a large bowl and whisk together until fluffy. Add all the remaining ingredients except the ghee and whisk to combine.

Cooking one omelette at a time, heat half the ghee in a shallow, non-stick frying pan over medium heat. Pour in half the egg mixture and cook for 1 minute, stirring and pulling the egg toward the centre of the pan so it covers the base. Cook for a further 1 minute, without stirring, until most of the egg is cooked. Fold the omelette in half or carefully roll over onto itself. Using an egg slide, gently remove from the pan and slide onto a plate. Repeat with remaining ghee and omelette mix. Serve immediately.

Masala Chai GF, V

This gently spiced milky tea is ubiquitous throughout India and is a wonderful ritual to share with locals. There are tea vendors, *chai walas*, at every corner in every city and town, who deliver tea to offices and shops, and there are tea stalls along every road and highway. More often than not, the tea is served in small, single-use clay cups that are smashed on the ground afterwards. I use Assam tea leaves to make this chai for the required strength of flavour. Milk is an essential element to masala chai and low-fat skim or alternative milks just don't cut it. Some sugar is used for sweetness, but the quantity is at your own discretion.

Serves 4

1 tablespoon black tea leaves
8 green cardamom pods, cracked
1 teaspoon black peppercorns
3 cloves
1 cinnamon stick
1 tablespoon chopped ginger
400 ml full-cream milk
1½ tablespoon caster sugar

Place 400 ml water, tea leaves, spices and ginger in a saucepan over medium heat and gently bring to the boil. Simmer for 2 minutes. Add the milk and sugar and simmer for a further 5 minutes. Strain through a fine sieve into a jug and pour the chai into small cups or glasses. To achieve the frothy effect, pour from 1 metre above the cup, moving the jug up and down as you pour – it's quite a dramatic effect.

Vegetables

ndia is a country where the majority of the population is vegetarian, be it for moral, economic or religious reasons. So it's only natural that much of its food centres around enviable and infinite vegetable preparations.

Vegetable dishes are the cornerstone of Indian cooking. The central practice of vegetarianism in India is highly complex and varied, depending on levels of strictness in the diet, but never monotonous. Menus are divided into vegetables (includes eggs, onion and garlic), pure vegetables (without eggs) and non-vegetable (with meat or fish). For me, personally, cooking with vegetables rather than being strictly vegetarian is enlightening and adds adventure and diversity to my ever-expanding repertoire.

During my frequent travels to India, I turn with curiosity and desire to the plethora of vegetarian dishes on offer. It's the best country to travel through as a vegetarian, as you're blessed with so much choice and regional diversity. Encompassing everything from street food snacks to pastries, salads, braises and curries, vegetables bring a distinctive flavour and texture to a dish. Add to that the different elements of sweet, sour, salty, pungent, bitter and astringent at play when cooking and combining ingredients, each with a direct connection to balancing flavours and wellbeing, and vegetables along with spices play a pivotal and transformative role.

When travelling through rural India, you'll see fields ablaze with the colourful saris of women harvesting their crops, those very colours imitated in their food. Blessed with the largest variety of vegetables and grains, the vegetable markets are bursting with an astonishing array of plant life. Visit one and you'll witness market vendors hunched over their booty, which is often displayed spread out on cloth or piled in baskets, hawking whatever is fresh and grown locally. Indians shop daily and cook with what's local and in season. It's a mantra we'd all do well to live by wherever we are in the world. Being connected to our food source and knowing the provenance of what we eat is becoming increasingly important. When growing your own or shopping for vegetables at farmers markets, pick them young and small. Avoid those giant specimens you'll find on the supermarket shelves that are smothered in plastic with an indeterminate shelf life and lacking real flavour. Big is not always best and vegetables prepared as soon after harvesting as possible are imminently more flavoursome and nutritious.

Allowing vegetables to play a starring role in a dish is liberating and expands the scope of your culinary repertoire. These recipes are packed with fragrance and flavour and are immensely inviting. The beauty of Indian cuisine is that it invites us to embrace the vegetable world, where we may discover endless combinations to delight and inspire. What's more, vegetarian recipes are largely straightforward to prepare – a bonus for the home cook.

Spinach Koftas GF, V

Palak kofta is a classic dish of north Indian heritage, where the koftas are fried in oil before being simmered in a spicy sauce. Adding fresh cheese (ricotta or paneer) and cooked potato gives a creaminess and a firmer body to the spinach mixture, making the koftas less likely to fall apart when fried. The mix can be made ahead of time and stored overnight, making the final cooking a lot quicker.

Serves 4

1 tablespoon vegetable oil
½ white onion, finely diced
1 tablespoon ginger garlic paste, see recipe
    page 436
1 small green chilli, minced
300 g English spinach leaves, washed and
    chopped (weight after stems removed)
100 g firm ricotta, grated
200 g mashed potato (about 1 large potato
    to yield ½ cup)
180 g chickpea (besan) flour
1 tablespoon raw cashews, ground
1 teaspoon garam masala
1 teaspoon sea salt flakes
½ teaspoon freshly ground black pepper
¼ cup (45 g) rice flour
1 litre vegetable oil, extra, for deep-frying
1 long green chilli, seeds removed, finely diced

KOFTA SAUCE
2 tablespoons vegetable oil
½ teaspoon cumin seeds
1 red onion, finely diced
2 teaspoons ginger garlic paste, see recipe
    page 436
1 tablespoon raw cashews, ground
½ teaspoon ground turmeric
1 teaspoon ground coriander
½ teaspoon ground cumin
½ teaspoon garam masala
½ teaspoon chilli powder
1 teaspoon sea salt flakes
2 tomatoes, finely diced

To make the kofta sauce, heat the oil in a frying pan over medium heat. Add the cumin seeds and cook for 30 seconds. Add the onion and cook for 4 minutes or until starting to colour. Add the ginger garlic paste and ground cashew and cook for 1 minute. Add the ground spices and salt and stir to combine. Add the tomato with 4 tablespoons of water and cook for 10 minutes. Remove from heat and allow to cool for 10 minutes. Transfer sauce to a food processor or blender and process until smooth. Check seasoning and adjust, if necessary. Set aside.

To make the koftas, heat the oil in a frying pan over medium heat. Add the onion and cook for 3 minutes or until starting to soften. Add the ginger garlic paste, chilli and chopped spinach, stir to combine and cook for 2 minutes or until spinach has wilted. Remove from heat and set aside to cool for 15 minutes.

Place spinach mixture in a food processor and process until smooth. Add the ricotta, potato, chickpea flour, ground cashew, garam masala, salt and pepper and pulse until the mixture comes together to form a dough. Using lightly floured hands, shape spoonfuls of the kofta mixture into quenelles. Roll in the rice flour to lightly coat and press gently to flatten.

Heat the extra oil in a deep saucepan to 170°C. Fry the koftas, in batches (don't fry too many at once or the oil temperature will drop, making the koftas soggy), for 4–5 minutes or until golden and crisp. Drain on paper towel.

Reheat the sauce over medium heat until simmering, spoon onto plate and arrange the koftas on top. Garnish with diced green chilli and serve hot with roti or steamed rice.

Masterclass step-by-step
Spinach Koftas →

1 Heat the oil in a frying pan over medium heat, add the onion and cook for 3 minutes.

2 Add the ginger garlic paste.

3 Add the green chilli.

4 Add the chopped spinach.

5 Stir to combine and cook for 2 minutes or until spinach has wilted.

6 Set aside to cool for 15 minutes. Process until smooth.

7

Add the ricotta.

8

Add the potato, chickpea flour, ground cashew, garam masala, salt and pepper.

9

Pulse until the mixture comes together to form a dough.

10

Using lightly floured hands, shape spoonfuls into quenelles.

11

Roll in the rice flour to lightly coat and press gently to flatten.

12

Fry the koftas, in batches, for 4–5 minutes or until golden. Drain on paper towel.

Okra Masala DF, GF, V

A common summer vegetable, *bhindi* is Hindi for okra. It's sometimes called 'lady's finger', which in India, is picked when green, young and small and well before it develops that slimy characteristic. You could substitute with small eggplant – just cut it into chunks and deep-fry before adding. Any vegetable preparation that is rather dry like this one (not swimming in sauce) is an ideal accompaniment to dal and rice.

Serves 4

500 g small okra, washed
50 ml vegetable oil
1 teaspoon mustard oil
1 teaspoon black mustard seeds
12 fresh curry leaves
1 small red onion, finely diced
1 teaspoon ground cumin
1 teaspoon ground coriander
2 teaspoons garam masala
1 teaspoon ground turmeric
4 garlic cloves, minced
3 small green chillies, sliced
1 teaspoon sea salt flakes
1 tablespoon chopped coriander leaves

Trim the tops off the okra and cut into 6 mm-round slices. Heat both the oils in a wide-based pan or wok over medium heat. Add the mustard seeds and cook for 30 seconds or until they start to pop. Add the curry leaves and cook for 20 seconds or until crisp. Add the onion and cook, stirring constantly, for 4 minutes or until it begins to colour. Stir in the ground spices and cook, stirring, for 1 minute or until fragrant. Add the sliced okra, garlic and chilli and cook for 5 minutes or until the okra is soft. The sauce should be quite thick (not soupy) and coat the okra. Season with salt and stir through the chopped coriander to serve.

Sweet Corn and Tomato GF, V

This is my take on a dish served to me in a Jaipur restaurant years ago. Both these vegetables are staples in the Rajasthani region, where crops grow prolifically under the hot desert sun. This punchy, light stew makes a great lunch snack served with roti, and equally makes a terrific vegetable partner to barbecued sausages. Make when both vegetables are in season and at their peak flavour.

Serves 4

3 teaspoons ghee
3 sweet corn cobs, husks and silks removed
pinch of ajwain seeds, see Glossary
3 red shallots, diced
2 teaspoons minced ginger
2 tomatoes, peeled and blended to make a puree
2 teaspoons tomato paste
½ teaspoons ground turmeric
1 teaspoons ground coriander
½ teaspoons Kashmiri chilli powder
1 teaspoons ground kasoori methi (dried fenugreek leaves), see Glossary
1 teaspoons sea salt flakes
12 oven-roasted cherry tomatoes, see Glossary
2 tablespoons chopped coriander

Preheat hot coals or barbecue to high heat. Melt 1 tablespoon of ghee in a small saucepan. Brush the corn cobs with the melted ghee and grill until blistered and charred. Cut the cooked kernels from the cob and set aside.

Melt the remaining ghee in a frying pan over high heat. Add the ajwain seeds and shallot and cook, stirring continuously, for 3 minutes or until starting to colour. Add the ginger and cook for a further 1 minute or until fragrant. Stir through the tomato puree and paste and return to a simmer. Add the ground spices and salt and cook for 2–3 minutes for flavours to combine. Stir through the corn, tomatoes and coriander to serve.

Sweet and Sour Bitter Melon DF, GF, V

A popular vegetable in Indian and south Asian cooking, but sadly overlooked in the West on account of its inherent bitterness, bitter melon is a vegetable I have learnt to embrace through my travels in India. When treated properly, this member of the gourd family offers essential balance to a meal, working as an ideal partner for richer, fattier dishes on the table. It's a good-for-gut food source, aids metabolism and is one of the staple vegetables in the Ayurvedic diet due to its therapeutic properties.

Serves 4

500 g small bitter melons, halved lengthwise
2 teaspoons sea salt flakes
1 teaspoon ground turmeric
½ teaspoon chilli powder
2 tablespoons lime juice
4 tablespoons chickpea (besan) flour
2 cups (500 ml) vegetable oil, for deep-frying
4 golden shallots, finely sliced
4 small green chillies, finely sliced
¼ teaspoon asafoetida
1 teaspoon ground cumin
1 teaspoon ground coriander
½ teaspoon freshly ground black pepper
2 tablespoons finely diced tomato
2 tablespoons shaved palm sugar (or brown sugar)
¼ teaspoon amchur (dried mango powder)
3 tablespoons coriander leaves
2 tablespoons fried shallot slices, see Glossary

Using a spoon, scrape out the seeds and insides of the melon and discard. Cut melon crosswise into 1 cm-thick slices to make half-moon rounds. Toss the slices with 1 teaspoon salt, the turmeric, chilli powder and 1 tablespoon of the lime juice and set aside in a colander over a flat plate for 30 minutes or until water is released from the melon. Press down on the melon to remove any excess water. Place in a zip-lock bag with the chickpea flour and toss to coat. Shake to remove any excess flour.

Heat the oil in a wok or kadhai to 180°C. Fry the melon slices for 2–3 minutes or until golden and crisp. Drain on paper towel. Reserve the oil.

Heat ⅓ cup (80 ml) of the reserved oil in a frying pan over medium heat. Add the shallot and cook for 4 minutes or until starting to colour. Add the green chilli and ground spices and cook for a further 1 minute or until fragrant. Stir through the diced tomato and palm sugar with 1 tablespoon water and remaining 1 teaspoon salt and cook, stirring constantly, for 2 minutes. Add the fried melon slices and stir to coat. Add the remaining lime juice and check seasoning, you may need to adjust with a little salt. Sprinkle with the amchur, remove from heat and garnish with coriander leaves and fried shallot slices to serve.

Tamarind Eggplant DF, GF, V

I collected this recipe years ago in Rajasthan and it's one of my all-time favourite eggplant dishes. I use it at any opportunity. I love its deeply satisfying sweet and sour notes. Serve it with other vegetable dishes on a shared table or as an accompaniment to grilled fish or barbecued meats.

Serves 6

600 ml vegetable oil, for deep-frying
4 x 300 g purple eggplants, quartered lengthwise
    and cut into 3 cm pieces
3 small red onions, peeled and finely diced
5 small green chillies, minced
8 garlic cloves, minced
1 tablespoon fresh curry leaves
150 g brown sugar
400 ml tamarind puree
1 teaspoon ground cumin
2 teaspoons sea salt flakes
4 tomatoes, seeded and diced
1 cup chopped coriander leaves
3 tablespoons fried shallot slices, see Glossary

Heat the oil in a wok or large pot to 180°C. Fry the eggplant, in batches, for 4–5 minutes or until golden. Remove from oil and drain on paper towel. Set aside. Reserve the oil.

To make the tamarind sauce, heat ⅓ cup (80 ml) of the reserved oil in a wok or frying pan over medium heat. Add the onion, chilli and garlic and cook, stirring continuously, for 1 minute or until beginning to colour. Add the curry leaves and cook for 1 minute or until wilted. Add the sugar, tamarind, cumin and salt and simmer gently for a further 5 minutes. Adjust seasoning, if necessary. There should be equal balance between the sweet, sour and salty flavours. Add the fried eggplant, stir to coat thoroughly and simmer for 3 minutes. Remove from heat, stir through the diced tomato and coriander leaves. Scatter with fried shallot slices to serve.

Bengali Sweet and Sour Eggplant DF, GF, V

Another variation on the sweet and sour theme, I collected this recipe in Kolkata from my friend, Bomti. It's a favourite on his lunch table.

Serves 4

2 cups (500 ml) vegetable oil, for deep-frying
3 purple eggplants, peeled and cut into
    2 cm-thick rounds
1 tablespoon mustard oil
1 teaspoon panch phoran, see Glossary
3 garlic cloves, crushed
1 teaspoon ground turmeric
1 teaspoon Kashmiri chilli powder
1 teaspoon ground coriander
3 tablespoons white vinegar
1 tablespoon caster sugar
1 teaspoon sea salt flakes
1 tablespoon chopped coriander

Heat the vegetable oil in a wok to 180°C. Fry the eggplant, in batches, for 8 minutes or until golden. Drain on paper towel. Set aside and keep warm.

Heat the mustard oil in a frying pan over medium heat. Once it starts to smoke, add the panch phoran and cook for 30 seconds or until fragrant. Add the garlic, turmeric, chilli powder and coriander and cook, stirring continuously, for 3–4 minutes. Add the fried eggplant, stirring to combine, and cook for a further 2 minutes. Add the vinegar, sugar and salt and simmer for 5 minutes. Remove from heat, top with chopped coriander and serve warm with roti or puri bread.

Stuffed Eggplant with Green Mango and Beetroot Salsa DF, GF, V

This recipe takes India's spicy flavours to a different level. I developed it for my restaurant menus, so it's one that requires some time and skill. The reward for your effort is contrasting layers of texture – it's a real flavour bomb. It's best to use eggplants with a fairly uniform width that aren't too fat, so when you cut them into their portions, they are even in size. Ideally, use eggplants that are no more than 11 cm in width. If they're too fat, they look inelegant on the plate and lose the desired effect.

Serves 6

3 x medium-size purple eggplants
300 ml vegetable oil
½ teaspoon chaat masala
2 tablespoons fried curry leaves

STUFFING

750 g potatoes, peeled and grated
3 purple eggplants
2 teaspoons sea salt flakes
1½ teaspoons freshly ground black pepper
3 tablespoons vegetable oil
1 brown onion, finely diced
2 tablespoons ginger garlic paste, see recipe
    page 436
3 small green chillies, sliced
2 teaspoons ground coriander
2 teaspoons ground cumin
1 teaspoon Kashmiri chilli powder
½ teaspoon amchur (dried mango powder)
½ teaspoon ground ginger
1 teaspoon ground turmeric
½ cup chopped coriander leaves

SALSA

½ green mango, peeled and finely julienned
1 small beetroot, peeled and finely julienned
2 red shallots, finely sliced
1 tablespoon shredded mint
1 tablespoon picked dill
⅓ cup (80 ml) curry dressing, see Salads
    page 90

To prepare the eggplant shells, slice the top and base off each eggplant. Cut each eggplant crosswise to make 2 x 9 cm-high rounds. Use a round cutter slightly smaller than the diameter of the eggplant and press down to remove the centre of the eggplant, leaving a thin, 6 mm exterior shell intact. Cut removed centres into 1 cm dice. Place the 6 prepared shells on a flat tray and set aside until ready to stuff.

Heat the oil in a large saucepan to 180°C. Fry the diced eggplant, in batches, for 5–6 minutes or until crisp and golden. Drain on paper towel (this will be added to the stuffing when it's made). Reserve the oil to cook the stuffed eggplants.

To prepare the stuffing, squeeze out excess water from the grated potato and spread onto a cloth to dry for 30 minutes. While the potato is drying, preheat hot coals, oven or barbecue to high heat. Smoke the whole eggplants for 20 minutes or until soft and skin has blistered. Place in a colander set over a bowl and set aside to cool and drain for 15 minutes.

When eggplant is cool enough to handle, remove charred skins and squeeze out any excess liquid. Place in a blender with 1 teaspoon salt, ½ teaspoon pepper and 2 tablespoons oil and blend until smooth. Set aside.

Heat the remaining 1 tablespoon oil in a frying pan over medium heat. Add the onion and cook for 4 minutes or until softened. Add the ginger garlic paste and chilli and cook for 3 minutes. Add the spices, remaining 1 teaspoon salt and 1 teaspoon pepper and cook until fragrant. Add the grated potato and cook, stirring frequently, for 5 minutes. Stir through the smoked eggplant puree and the fried eggplant and cook for a further 3 minutes. Remove from heat and allow to cool before folding through the coriander.

To stuff the eggplants, spoon the stuffing into the shells until full, pressing down to compact

and smoothing the surface. The eggplant can be prepared to this stage then covered and refrigerated until ready to cook. If you do place in the refrigerator at this stage, remember to stand the eggplants at room temperature for 30 minutes before cooking.

To cook the eggplants, preheat oven to 180°C. Heat ¼ cup (60 ml) of the reserved vegetable oil in a large, cast-iron or ovenproof frying pan over medium heat. Arrange the eggplants upright in the pan and cook for 3 minutes to seal the base. Carefully turn the eggplants and cook on the other side for a further 3 minutes or until stuffing is sealed into the shell and browned. Transfer pan to the oven and bake for 8 minutes or until heated through when tested with a skewer. Remove from oven and transfer to a flat tray lined with paper towel to soak up any residual oil.

While the eggplants are baking, make the salsa. Place the green mango, beetroot, shallot, mint and dill in a bowl with the curry dressing and toss to thoroughly coat. Divide stuffed eggplants between plates, arrange beetroot salsa on top, sprinkle with chaat masala and garnish with fried curry leaves.

Eggplant and Cherry Tomato Masala DF, GF, V

This spicy vegetable stew is traditionally served with fluffy *idli* (steamed rice cakes) and fresh coconut chutney. It pays homage to the vegetarian cooking of India's southern states, where each component is characteristically flavoured with tempered spices. To embellish it further, you could add chunks of salmon or ocean trout with the fried eggplant for the final cooking. You can also toss this through short pasta or noodles for a terrific home-style comfort dish.

Serves 6

40 ml vegetable oil
1 teaspoon mustard seeds
10 fresh curry leaves
2 teaspoons split urad dal (white lentils)
2 white onions, finely sliced
2 teaspoons sea salt flakes
1 tablespoon tomato paste
½ teaspoon chilli powder
½ teaspoon ground fennel
1 teaspoon ground coriander
1 teaspoon ground turmeric
1 cup (250 ml) tamarind puree
400 g eggplants, cut into 3 cm wedges and
    deep-fried
200 g cherry tomatoes, halved
coriander leaves, to serve

Heat the oil in a frying pan over medium heat. Add the mustard seeds and once they start to pop, add the curry leaves and the dal. Cook, stirring, for 1 minute or until the dal is golden. Add the onion and a little salt and cook, stirring frequently, for 5–6 minutes until the onion is brown. Remove half the onion and set side.

Add the tomato paste and ground spices to the remaining onion in the pan and mix well. Add the tamarind, bring to the boil and simmer for 10 minutes. Add the fried eggplant, cherry tomato and reserved onion and stir to combine. Return to the boil and simmer gently for 3 minutes or until the mixture has reduced slightly. Season with remaining salt, spoon into serving bowls and top with coriander leaves.

Vegetable Avial DF, GF, V

Avial is a traditional Keralan preparation that makes an excellent accompaniment to rice and gravy-based dishes. I have eaten countless variations of this across Kerala, where it's served for special occasions and during the harvest festival, typically on a banana leaf. Any seasonal vegetable can be used and this recipe calls for an assortment, such as asparagus, green beans, eggplant, carrot, snake gourd, potato, yam or plantain. This is a nourishing and healthy vegetable dish that can be whipped up in no time. I sometimes swirl a spoonful of coconut yoghurt through the vegetables after they've come off the heat for extra creaminess, but that's entirely optional.

Serves 4–6

150 g grated fresh coconut
½ teaspoon ground cumin
2 garlic cloves, minced
600 g mixed vegetables, cut into 6 cm batons
2 small white onions, finely sliced
5 small green chillies, halved lengthwise
2 teaspoons sea salt flakes
½ teaspoon ground turmeric
½ teaspoon chilli powder
3 tomatoes, diced
2 tablespoons coconut oil
2 tablespoons fried curry leaves

Place the grated coconut, cumin and garlic in a food processor with 2 tablespoons water and process to make a coarse paste. Set aside.

Place 3 cups (750 ml) water in a saucepan and bring to the boil. Add the vegetable batons, onion, green chilli, salt, turmeric and chilli powder and cook for 3 minutes or until al dente. Add the tomato and cook for a further 4 minutes or until softened. Add the coconut paste and cook, stirring, for a further 2 minutes. Add the coconut oil and curry leaves and stir to combine. Remove from heat and serve warm.

Stir-fried Kohlrabi DF, GF, V

Kohlrabi is an intriguing and often underrated vegetable. It looks similar to a turnip, but is actually a member of the cabbage family. With a delicate flavour and firm texture, this winter vegetable responds well to quick cooking and a splash of spice. Choose small ones for their tenderness and make sure to peel them before cooking. Called *subzi*, this is a dry-style vegetable preparation, much like a stir-fry, that I first tasted when travelling through the Punjab and Himalayan regions.

Serves 4

2 tablespoons mustard oil
1 teaspoon black mustard seeds
¼ teaspoon ajwain seeds, see Glossary
12 fresh curry leaves
1 tablespoon minced or grated ginger
2 small green chillies, finely sliced
½ teaspoon ground turmeric
1 teaspoon ground cumin
2 teaspoons ground coriander
1 teaspoon sea salt flakes
500 g kohlrabi, peeled and cut into 3 cm dice
3 tablespoons chopped coriander leaves
3 tablespoons red mustard cress, snipped
½ teaspoon garam masala

Heat the mustard oil in a wok or large, non-stick frying pan over medium heat. Add the mustard and ajwain seeds and curry leaves and cook for 20 seconds or until they start to pop. Add the ginger and chilli and cook, stirring, for 30 seconds or until fragrant. Add the ground spices and salt and cook for a further 30 seconds. Add the kohlrabi, tossing to ensure the kohlrabi is coated with the spices, and cook for 1 minute. Add 200 ml water, cover with a lid, and cook, stirring occasionally, for 5 minutes or until the kohlrabi is soft and the water is evaporated. Don't be alarmed if the oil separates during cooking, this is meant to happen and gives a nice gloss to the kohlrabi. Remove from heat, stir through the coriander and mustard cress and sprinkle over the garam masala to serve.

Potato and Fenugreek Leaves DF, GF, V

Aloo methi is a common potato dish enjoyed throughout India. It relies on a few staple ingredients that are immediately at hand. If you can't source fresh *methi* (fenugreek leaves), which are synonymous with Indian cooking, you can substitute them with tender mustard greens to achieve the same tangy, slightly bitter flavour and green colour. In Australia, you pretty much have to grow your own fenugreek if you want to use the leaves in your cooking. But it's possible to buy small punnets of fenugreek cress to snip as young leaves or to plant in your garden to grow larger, as I do. The plant can be sprouted from fenugreek seeds and grows like a small shrub in the garden.

Serves 4

¼ cup (60 ml) mustard oil
½ teaspoon cumin seeds
2 teaspoons minced garlic
3 teaspoons minced ginger
1 small red onion, finely diced
2 teaspoons ground turmeric
2 teaspoons sea salt flakes
3 medium-size potatoes, peeled and cut into 2 cm dice
200 g fresh fenugreek leaves (or mustard greens), washed and chopped
½ tomato, finely diced

Heat the oil in a wok over medium–high heat for 1 minute or until it starts to smoke. Once it's smoking, working quickly, stir in the cumin seeds and cook for 10 seconds. Add the garlic and ginger, stir to combine and immediately add the onion. Reduce heat to medium and cook, stirring, for 2 minutes, being careful not to burn. Stir through the turmeric, salt and potato and cook for 3–4 minutes.

Meanwhile, squeeze out any excess liquid from the fenugreek leaves in a cloth (this is to ensure the dish isn't watery) and add to the potatoes. Stir to combine, cover with a lid and cook for 4 minutes or until the leaves wilt and reduce in volume and the potatoes are cooked. Stir through the tomato to serve.

Spiced Potatoes GF, V

Translating to 'spiced potatoes', *aloo bhaji* is a simple dish to serve with *puri* (deep-fried bread) and is typically enjoyed for breakfast. I love the myriad vegetable dishes that Indians serve for breakfast and find myself utterly addicted to them when travelling there. But this can be served at any time of the day along with other dishes at a shared table. For an easy lunch snack, I spoon the cooked potato into the centre of a flatbread and roll it up to make a wrap, adding a dollop of spicy chutney. It brings a whole new meaning to the word 'sandwich'.

Serves 6

500 g potatoes (about 4 large), peeled
3 tablespoons ghee
½ teaspoon black mustard seeds
2 small green chillies, finely sliced
1 red onion, finely diced
2 teaspoons minced ginger
12 roasted cashews, roughly chopped
1 tomato, seeded and diced
½ teaspoon ground turmeric
½ teaspoon Kashmiri chilli powder
pinch of asafoetida
2 teaspoons sea salt flakes
3 tablespoons chopped coriander leaves

Place the potatoes in a saucepan of boiling water over medium heat and cook for 12–15 minutes or until al dente. Remove from pan and allow to cool slightly before breaking into large chunks for a more rustic look. Set aside.

Melt the ghee in a wok or frying pan over medium heat. Add the mustard seeds and, when they start to pop, add the green chilli and onion and cook for 3 minutes or until softened. Add the ginger and cook for a further 1–2 minutes. Add the cashew, tomato, turmeric, chilli powder and asafoetida and stir to combine. Add the potato and salt and cook for 2 minutes, stirring gently with a fork to break the potato up a little so the flavours can penetrate. Sprinkle with a little water to prevent the potato from drying out or sticking to the pan. Remove from heat and top with chopped coriander to serve.

Sesame Potatoes DF, GF, V

Across Rajasthan and the northern plains of India, you'll see farmers harvesting sesame crops and thrashing the branches to displace the tiny seeds during harvest. Sesame is called *til* in Hindi, so this potato dish is known as *aloo til*. I like to add roasted peanuts (another common crop) for texture and crunch and serve with roast chook or grilled lamb chops.

Serves 4

3 tablespoons white sesame seeds
12 chat (or new) potatoes, peeled and halved
2 tablespoons vegetable oil
1 teaspoon fenugreek seeds
2 teaspoons ginger garlic paste, see recipe
  page 436
2 teaspoons ground coriander
½ teaspoon ground turmeric
2 teaspoons sea salt flakes
2 small green chillies, finely sliced
2 teaspoons lemon juice
2 tablespoons roasted peanuts, chopped

Place the sesame seeds in a dry pan over low heat and cook, stirring frequently, for 1–2 minutes or until lightly toasted and golden. Remove from pan and set aside. Cook the potato in a saucepan of boiling water for 5 minutes or until parboiled. Drain and set aside.

Heat the oil in a frying pan over low heat. Add the fenugreek seeds and cook for 1 minute or until golden, being careful not to burn or they will become bitter. Add the potato with the ginger garlic paste and 3 tablespoons water, cover with a lid and cook for 5 minutes or until tender. Add the toasted sesame seeds, coriander, turmeric, salt, chilli and lemon juice, toss to coat the potatoes and cook for a further 1 minute. Toss through the chopped peanuts to serve.

Garam Masala Potatoes and Peas GF, V

An unbeatable combination of warming spices and contrasting textures makes this a real winner in my opinion. It's definitely a dish that can stand alone, but if you fancy making it more elaborate, as I've often done, you can toss through steamed mussels (removed from their shells) or serve with pan-seared chicken livers.

Serves 4

500 g small kipfler (or other waxy) potatoes, peeled and washed
100 g shelled fresh peas
75 g ghee
½ teaspoon brown mustard seeds
20 fresh curry leaves
2 teaspoons minced fresh ginger
1 green bird's eye chilli, minced
¼ teaspoon nigella seeds
1 teaspoon ground coriander
pinch of asafoetida
¼ teaspoon ground turmeric
2 teaspoons sea salt flakes
1 teaspoon garam masala, plus extra, to taste
⅓ cup (80 ml) curry dressing, see Salads page 90
50 g unsalted butter
200 g baby spinach leaves
½ cup fried curry leaves

Cook the potatoes in a saucepan of boiling water for 12 minutes or until just tender. Drain and set aside to cool for a few minutes before breaking roughly in half. The idea is for the potatoes to look more rustic, rather than a uniform dice. Blanch the peas in a saucepan of boiling water for 1 minute. Refresh under cold water, drain and set aside.

Melt the ghee in a wide-based pan over medium heat. Add the mustard seeds and cook for 30 seconds or until they start to pop. Add the curry leaves, ginger and chilli and stir to combine. Add the nigella seeds, ground coriander, asafoetida, turmeric and salt, stir to combine and cook for 30 seconds. Add the potato, toss to coat evenly with the spices and cook for 1 minute or until heated through. Add the peas with the garam masala and toss to combine. Remove from heat, add the curry dressing and stir to combine. Set aside and keep warm.

Melt the butter in a frying pan over medium heat. Add the spinach and cook, stirring, for 2 minutes or until wilted. Season with salt and pepper to taste and sprinkle with an extra pinch of garam masala to taste. Spoon the spinach onto plates and top with the potato and peas. Garnish with fried curry leaves and serve immediately.

Baked Sweet Potato, Ginger and Coriander DF, GF, V

Ideally, these potatoes taste best when cooked buried in hot coals to really accentuate their flavour. Here, I've baked them in the oven for modern convenience. This dish makes a wonderful accompaniment to a barbecue and, should you have any leftover, you can scoop out the potato with its seasoning and mash it for a sandwich filling or serve with steamed greens.

Serves 4

8 small sweet potatoes, scrubbed
1 teaspoon Kashmiri chilli powder
1 teaspoon ground cumin
1 teaspoon chaat masala
1 teaspoon black salt powder, see Glossary
2 small red chillies, thinly sliced
2 tablespoons lemon juice
2 tablespoons coriander leaves
1 tablespoon thinly sliced ginger

Preheat oven to 200°C. Wrap each sweet potato in foil and lay on a flat tray. Bake for 25 minutes or until soft in the centre when tested with a skewer. Allow to rest for 5 minutes before removing the foil.

While the sweet potato is resting, place the ground spices, black salt, chilli and lemon juice in a bowl and mix to combine. Cut each potato in half lengthwise and, while steaming hot, spoon over the spiced juice. Top with coriander and ginger and serve warm.

Gunpowder Potatoes GF, V

In this classic dish, cooked small potatoes are broken apart while still hot and lushed up with ghee and spices. This is a perennial favourite and everyone who tastes it becomes addicted. The gunpowder spice mix is the secret weapon that hails from Karnataka in the south, its inclusion bringing many a dish alive. I have found the best blend for the spice mix comes from Herbie's Spices, available at food stores or ordered online.

Serves 6

1 kg small chat (or new) potatoes, unpeeled and washed
½ teaspoon cumin seeds
½ teaspoon fennel seeds
1 teaspoon sea salt flakes
½ teaspoon freshly ground black pepper
2 teaspoons Herbie's Spices gunpowder spice mix, see Glossary
½ teaspoon ground kasoori methi (dried fenugreek leaves), see Glossary
4 tablespoons melted ghee
2 tablespoons shredded coriander leaves
3 small green chillies, finely sliced
4 green shallots, finely sliced

Cook the potatoes in a large saucepan of boiling water for 12 minutes or until al dente. Drain and set aside.

Heat a small frying pan over low heat. Add the cumin and fennel seeds and cook for 90 seconds or until lightly toasted. Set aside to cool.

Preheat oven to 220°C. Line an oven tray with baking paper. Cut the potatoes in half, place in a large bowl with the toasted spices, salt, pepper, gunpowder spice mix, kasoori methi and melted ghee and toss to coat. Arrange the potatoes on the prepared tray in a single layer and bake for 8 minutes or until crisp. Remove from oven, return to the bowl with the coriander, chilli and green shallot and toss to combine. Serve immediately.

Sweet and Sour Pumpkin GF, V

This is a lovely vegetable preparation I tasted at a family restaurant in Delhi, which specialises in food from Bihari state. The pumpkin is bathed in a spicy coating and, rather than cooking it in a saucepan, I prefer to roast it with the seasoning to yield sweet and tangy flavours and a better texture. I use the softer Japanese pumpkin varieties (such as Kent or similar) for this recipe, as the skin stays soft during cooking and doesn't need to be removed, which adds additional texture.

Serves 4

1 kg pumpkin, quartered and seeds removed
90 g ghee
1 teaspoon fenugreek
1 teaspoon fennel seeds
1 teaspoon cumin seeds
½ teaspoon asafoetida
2 small green chillies, finely sliced
3 teaspoons ginger garlic paste, see recipe page 436
½ teaspoon ground black salt
1 teaspoon ground turmeric
2 teaspoons garam masala
2 teaspoons ground coriander
1 teaspoon Kashmiri chilli powder
3 teaspoons amchur (dried mango powder)
1 teaspoon sea salt flakes
1 tablespoon caster sugar
1 tablespoon chopped coriander leaves
1 tablespoon almond flakes, lightly toasted
4 small dried chillies, fried in a little oil until crisp

Preheat oven to 200°C. Slice the pumpkin into 4 cm pieces, leaving the skin intact. Set aside.

Melt the ghee in a frying pan over medium heat. Add the whole spices and asafoetida and cook for 1 minute or until they start to pop. Add the chilli, ginger garlic paste and black salt and cook, stirring continuously, for 2 minutes or until starting to colour. Add the ground spices, sea salt and sugar, and cook, stirring to mix thoroughly, for a further 1 minute. Add the pumpkin and toss to thoroughly coat with the spice mix, making sure the pumpkin is glossy with the spiced ghee.

Transfer to an oven tray lined with baking paper and bake for 15 minutes. Turn the pumpkin and bake for a further 15 minutes or until tender. Serve topped with chopped coriander, toasted almond flakes, fried chillies and puris (fried bread).

Black Pepper Mushrooms GF, V

I've tried this dish in different parts of the south, from rural Karnataka to the Chettinad region of Tamil Nadu and the Andhra region of Hyderabad. I like to use a mix of small button mushrooms, shiitake and oyster mushrooms for contrasting textures. The savoury combination of the black pepper with the mushrooms gives a real umami hit. Don't be shy with your use of pepper, this dish is meant to be fiery.

Serves 4

400 g small mixed mushrooms, halved
3 tablespoons ghee
1 teaspoon cumin seeds
8 fresh curry leaves
2 spring onions (white bulb only), diced
1 tablespoons ginger garlic paste, see recipe
   page 436
2 small green chillies, finely sliced
¼ teaspoon ground turmeric
½ teaspoon chilli powder
2 teaspoons freshly ground black pepper, plus
   extra to taste
1 teaspoon sea salt flakes
1 tablespoon fried curry leaves

Rub the mushrooms with paper towel to remove any grit. Try not to wash them, as being a porous vegetable this diminishes their flavour. Melt 2 tablespoons of the ghee in a frying pan over medium heat. Add the cumin seeds and curry leaves and cook for 1 minute or until crackling. Add the onion and cook for 2 minutes or until softened. Add the ginger garlic paste and green chilli and cook, stirring, for 2 minutes or until fragrant, taking care not to burn. Add the mushroom, ground spices and salt, toss to coat and cook for 6–7 minutes or until mushrooms are tender. Transfer to serving bowl or plate and keep warm.

Melt the remaining 1 tablespoon ghee in a small frying pan and stir in a little extra freshly ground black pepper (just a twist or 2 of the grinder). Pour the peppered ghee over the mushrooms to give them a glossy coating. Sprinkle with fried curry leaves and serve with steamed rice or roti.

Bengali Mixed Vegetables DF, GF, V

Chorchori sounds far more romantic than mixed vegetables. But however you choose to say it, these vegetables seasoned with the trademark Bengali spice blend, panch phoran, and cooked until meltingly soft are delicious. Often served for a special feast, this recipe adds balance to the many dishes that make up the celebratory meal. It's just as good with steamed rice and dal for everyday cooking.

Serves 4

3 tablespoons mustard oil
1 teaspoon panch phoran, see Glossary
1 white onion, finely sliced
2 long green chillies, finely sliced
2 teaspoons minced ginger
2 teaspoons ground turmeric
1 teaspoon Kashmiri chilli powder
1 teaspoon caster sugar
2 potatoes, peeled and cut into 1 cm dice
1 cup cauliflower, florets and sliced stems
½ **cup** broccoli stems, diced
1 x 300 g purple eggplant, peeled and cut into 2 cm dice
1 cup diced pumpkin, peeled and cut into 1 cm dice
125 g peeled broad beans
4 Swiss chard leaves, shredded
2 teaspoons sea salt flakes
2 tablespoons chopped coriander leaves

Heat 2 tablespoons mustard oil in a large saucepan over medium heat. Once smoking, add the panch phoran and cook for 1 minute or until it begins to pop. Add the onion and cook for 4 minutes or until softened. Add the chilli, ginger, ground spices and sugar, and stir briefly before adding the vegetables, salt and 100 ml water. Reduce heat to low, cover and cook, stirring occasionally, for 15 minutes or until vegetables are softened and dry (the water should have evaporated). Drizzle with the remaining 1 tablespoon mustard oil and toss to combine. Top with coriander to serve.

Masala Baked Cauliflower DF, GF, V

On some of my more recent visits to Kolkata, I make time to have lunch with local art dealer Bomti Iyengar at his home in the centre of the city. His house cooks always prepare a feast, mostly of vegetable dishes, that is assiduously spiced and well-balanced. This dish fits with our current obsession of baking cauliflower whole and is given a flavour oomph by way of Indian spices. It also makes a great centrepiece for the shared table.

Serves 4

1 white onion, grated
2 tablespoons ginger garlic paste, see recipe page 436
1 teaspoon ground turmeric
1 teaspoon Kashmiri chilli powder
1 teaspoon ground cumin
1 teaspoon ground coriander
1 tablespoon tomato paste
3 tablespoons vegetable oil
1 teaspoon sea salt flakes
1 whole cauliflower, stem and leaves removed

Preheat oven to 200°C. Place all the ingredients except the cauliflower in a food processor or blender and blend to make a paste. Rub paste liberally over the cauliflower to evenly coat. Place on an oven tray lined with baking paper and bake for 1 hour or until tender. Serve hot.

Spice Roasted Root Vegetables
with Chilli Lime Butter GF, V

This is my go-to one-pot recipe when I am pushed for time. It's a home-style dish packed with the comforting flavours of winter and is super easy to throw together. Naturally, it's best made when root vegetables are at their peak, revealing their inherent sweetness. The butter acts as a sauce as it melts over the hot vegetables and can be made ahead of time and frozen to keep on hand when you need an instant flavour hit. It's delicious added to vegetables, noodles, pasta or even slathered over a roast chook for that extra dimension of magic.

Serves 4

⅓ cup (80 ml) grapeseed oil
2 teaspoons ginger garlic paste, see recipe
   page 436
½ teaspoon cumin seeds
1 tablespoon curry powder
1 teaspoon ground coriander
1 teaspoon ground turmeric
1 teaspoon sea salt flakes
½ teaspoon freshly ground black pepper
8 new (or chat) potatoes, halved
4 baby turnips
4 parsnips, peeled and halved lengthwise
1 sweet potato, peeled and cut into 3 cm pieces
4 baby beets, peeled and quartered
8 baby (or heirloom) carrots, peeled
4 tablespoons fresh curd (hung yoghurt), see
   Eggs and Dairy page 110
½ teaspoon nigella seeds

CHILLI LIME BUTTER
120 g unsalted butter
3 small green chillies, chopped
½ teaspoon dried chilli flakes
1 teaspoon curry powder
2 teaspoons sea salt flakes
1 tablespoon coriander leaves
zest of 1 lime, minced
1 tablespoon lime juice

To make the chilli lime butter, place all the ingredients in a food processor or blender and process until combined. Store in an airtight container in the fridge (or freezer) until ready to use.

Preheat oven to 200°C. To cook the vegetables, place the oil, ginger garlic paste, cumin seeds, curry powder, coriander, turmeric, salt and pepper in large bowl and mix to combine. Add the vegetables and toss to coat with the oil. Arrange the vegetables in single layer on an oven tray lined with baking paper and roast for 25–30 minutes or until tender.

Spread the drained curd over a large serving plate (or individual plates) and arrange baked vegetables on top. Sprinkle with the nigella seeds and dab knobs of the chilli lime butter generously over the top to serve.

Fried Mustard Greens DF, GF, V

Mustard greens have a slightly bitter taste and their tanginess is perfect for this dish. But you can also use gai lan, rainbow chard or silver beet leaves.

Serves 4

2 tablespoons mustard oil
3 small green chillies, finely sliced
2 tablespoons ginger garlic paste, see recipe page 436
1 red onion, finely diced
1 tomato, seeded and diced
600 g mustard greens, leaves torn and stalks cut into 2 cm lengths
1 teaspoon ground coriander
1 teaspoon sea salt flakes

Heat the mustard oil in a wok over medium heat until it starts to smoke. Add the green chilli and ginger garlic paste, immediately followed by the onion (to prevent burning) and cook, stirring constantly, for 4 minutes or until softened. Add the tomato, mustard leaves and stalks and continue to cook, stirring, for 2 minutes or until wilted and reduced in volume. Mix the ground coriander and salt together in a small bowl and stir through the greens to season.

Spinach in Buttermilk GF, V

Nourishing, healthy and easy for digestion, *palak kadhai* is a simple vegetable dish that's quick to prepare and can be served as a side dish with rice and dal or with a dry-style spicy curry.

Serves 4

2 tablespoons vegetable oil
½ teaspoon black mustard seeds
½ teaspoon cumin seeds
½ teaspoon split urad dal (white lentils)
12 fresh curry leaves
2 long green chillies, finely sliced
2 teaspoons minced ginger
pinch of asafoetida
500 g English spinach, washed, drained and chopped
1 cup (250 ml) buttermilk
1 cup thick plain yoghurt
2 teaspoons chickpea (besan) flour
1 teaspoon ground turmeric
1 teaspoon sea salt flakes

Heat the oil in a frying pan over medium heat. Add the mustard and cumin seeds and urad dal and cook until it starts to pop. Add the curry leaves, chilli, ginger and asafoetida and cook for 2 minutes. Add the chopped spinach, stirring to combine, then immediately pour in 1 cup (250 ml) water and bring to the boil. Reduce heat to low.

Meanwhile, whisk the buttermilk, yoghurt, chickpea flour, turmeric and salt together in a bowl, stirring to remove any lumps. Add a ladleful of the hot spinach water to the buttermilk to dilute and warm it, this ensures it doesn't curdle when added to the pan. Whisk the buttermilk mixture into the spinach and cook, stirring constantly, over low heat for 2 minutes. Once simmering, remove from heat and serve with steamed rice or roti.

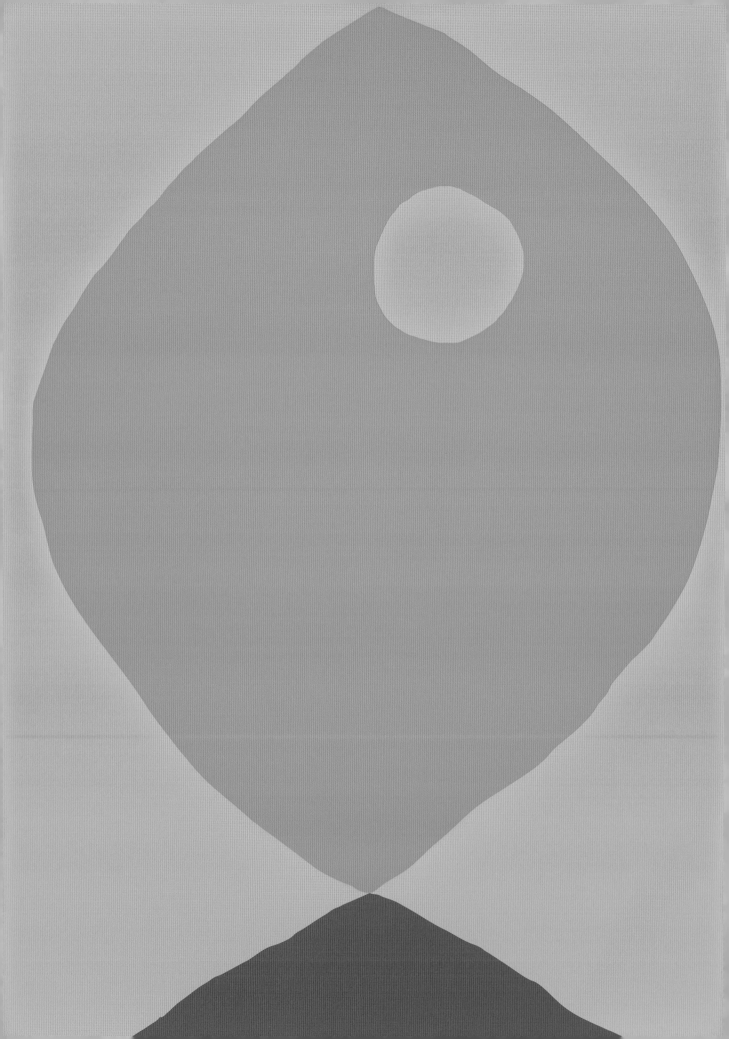

Seafood

The vast coastlines of India yield a huge volume and variety of fish and seafood. There's no doubt the consumption of both freshwater and saltwater fish, and shellfish, makes up a significant proportion of the country's culinary heritage. Kerala and Bengal are both predominantly fish-eating states and the prolific use of seafood in their cooking is testament to the abundance of the waters of the Coromandel and Malabar coastlines in the south.

There is also a bounty of fish from rivers, estuaries and lakes that are prized staples in Bengali, Himalayan and Assamese cooking. These cuisines refer to freshwater fish as 'sweet water fish', which they consider superior in taste to their saltwater cousins. A feature in regional cooking across India, the importance of fish and seafood can't be underestimated, with salted and dried fish also having played an important role throughout the country's history and export trade.

A visit to a fish market in India gives a frisson of high-octane energy and frenetic movement. Traditionally, the men fish and the women sell – they're the vendors and negotiators at every market. I've braved the crowded platform of Sassoon Docks in Mumbai just before dawn, a perilous pastime. I've watched the fishermen at sunrise unload their catch onto the sandy beach in Thalassery on the Malabar Coast before it is carted in buckets to the nearby fish market. I've enjoyed shopping with local friends at Park Circus Market in Kolkata, Mapusa Market in Goa or Russell Market in Bangalore, purchasing what we need to cook for lunch. The fishermen's harbour and Marine Drive in Chennai is home to the biggest fish market in India. Then there's the structural beauty of the cantilevered Chinese fishing nets in Kochi, at the backwaters of Kerala, the romantic symbol of many a travel brochure.

It's common practice in Indian kitchens to rub salt, ground turmeric and lime juice into fish before cooking. It's a time-honoured practice of seasoning and an antibacterial caution. What I love about cooking fish Indian-style is the astute use of spices and aromatics. Fish and seafood are immeasurably enhanced when cooked with coconut, turmeric, mustard seed, black pepper, chilli, coriander, tomato, ginger or tamarind. But seasonings shouldn't overpower the fish or seafood – it's a lesson in finding the ideal balance.

For each of these recipes, I have tried to offer substitutes for the fish varieties I use to give you more scope. When shopping for fish and seafood, it's of paramount importance to choose what's in season, in peak condition, sustainable and local – the suggestions in any recipe are a guide, not a blueprint. There is simply no excuse for using imported seafood in Australia when we have access to abundant resources from our own shores.

Tamarind Prawns DF, GF

The starting point for this recipe, *chemmeen varattiyathu*, was collected from a keen home cook in northern Kerala and is one that I have adapted and refined over the years. It's a firm favourite in my repertoire with a dazzling depth of flavour – I serve it as a starter accompanied with crisp pappadams. If you're time-poor, the sauce can be made a couple of days ahead and refrigerated.

Serves 6

1 teaspoon ground turmeric
1 teaspoon Kashmiri chilli powder
2 teaspoons roasted ground coriander
1 teaspoon sea salt flakes
⅓ cup (80 ml) vegetable oil
500 g raw king prawn meat, peeled (weight after shells removed), deveined and butterflied*
16 oven-roasted cherry tomatoes, halved
3 tablespoons freshly chopped coriander leaves
4 tablespoons fried curry leaves

TAMARIND SAUCE
3 tablespoons sunflower oil
1 teaspoon brown mustard seeds
1 teaspoon fenugreek seeds
6 red shallots, finely diced
2 small green chillies, minced
1 tablespoon ginger garlic paste, see recipe page 436
12 fresh curry leaves
2 ripe tomatoes, seeded and chopped
1 teaspoon Kashmiri chilli powder
½ teaspoon ground turmeric
1 teaspoon roasted ground coriander
1 teaspoon sea salt flakes
200 ml thick tamarind puree
1 tablespoons caster sugar

Place the turmeric, chilli powder, ground coriander, salt and vegetable oil in a bowl and mix to make a paste. Add the prawns and toss to coat well. Set aside.

To make the tamarind sauce, heat the oil in a frying pan over medium heat. Add the mustard seeds and fenugreek seeds and cook for 30 seconds or until they start to pop, taking care not to let them burn. Add the shallot and green chilli and cook for 2 minutes or until softened but not coloured. Stir in the ginger garlic paste and curry leaves and cook for 1 minute. Add the tomato and cook for 2 minutes or until softened. Add the ground spices, salt, tamarind and sugar and bring to a simmer. Cook for 5 minutes or until the sauce thickens. Remove from heat and set aside. If you've made the sauce ahead of time, you'll need to reheat it in a frying pan or large saucepan. Make sure it's hot when the prawns are being cooked, so you can do the final assembly.

To cook the prawns, heat a frying pan over high heat. Add the prawns and cook for 3 minutes or until half-cooked and starting to colour. Add the tamarind sauce to the prawns with the roasted cherry tomato and stir to combine. Cook for 1 minute only, just enough to warm through, remove from heat and stir through the chopped coriander. Top with fried curry leaves to serve.

*If you're buying whole prawns, rather than prawn meat, buy twice the quantity.

**Masterclass step-by-step
Tamarind Prawns ➜**

1

Heat the oil in a frying pan over medium heat. Add the mustard seeds and fenugreek seeds and cook for 30 seconds.

2

Add the shallot and green chilli and cook for 2 minutes.

3

Stir in the ginger garlic paste and curry leaves and cook for 1 minute.

4

Add the tomato and cook for 2 minutes or until softened.

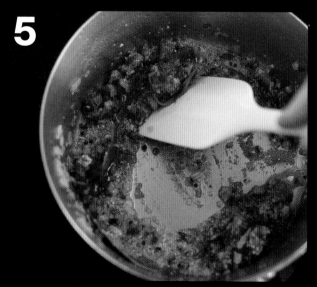

5

Add the ground spices and salt and stir to combine.

6

Add the tamarind and sugar and bring to a simmer.

7

Cook for 5 minutes or until the sauce thickens. Keep hot while cooking the prawns.

8

While the sauce is cooking, marinate the prawns in turmeric, chilli powder, ground coriander, salt and vegetable oil.

9

Cook the prawns in a frying pan over high heat for 3 minutes or until starting to colour.

10

Add the tamarind sauce.

11

Add the roasted tomato and stir to combine. Cook for 1 minute only.

12

Remove from heat and stir through the coriander. Top with fried curry leaves to serve.

Stir-fried Ginger and Coconut Prawns DF, GF

This dish is reminiscent of the flavours of southern India. I use extra-large (or jumbo) king or tiger prawns, as their fleshy texture is essential to the balance of the aromatics in the recipe.

Serves 4

3 tablespoons vegetable oil
2 teaspoons black mustard seeds
3 red shallots, finely sliced
3 tablespoons fresh curry leaves
1 tablespoon ginger garlic paste, see recipe
   page 436
3 small green chillies, sliced into thin rounds
1 teaspoon ground turmeric
½ teaspoon ground fennel
1 teaspoon freshly ground black pepper
1 teaspoon garam masala
100 ml young coconut water
400 g raw tiger prawn meat, peeled (weight after
   shells removed), deveined and butterflied*
2 tomatoes, diced
50 g shredded fresh coconut
2 tablespoons lime juice
2 tablespoons shredded mint leaves
2 tablespoons shredded coriander leaves
2 teaspoons sea salt flakes

Heat the oil in a heavy-based frying pan over medium heat. Add the mustard seeds and cook for 20 seconds or until they start to pop. Add the shallot and curry leaves and cook for 90 seconds or until the shallot is translucent. Stir through the ginger garlic paste and green chilli and cook, stirring continuously, for a further 90 seconds or until fragrant and softened. Add the turmeric, fennel, pepper and garam masala, mix well to combine and cook for 30 seconds. Add the coconut water, stir to combine (the mixture will become a paste) and increase heat to high. Add the prawn meat, tomato and coconut and cook, tossing to coat with the masala paste, for 3–4 minutes or until prawns change colour and are just cooked. If the paste becomes too dry, add an extra splash of coconut water to loosen. Remove from heat, add the lime juice, mint, coriander and salt and stir to combine. Serve hot with steamed rice or appams.

*If you're buying whole prawns, rather than prawn meat, buy twice the quantity.

Black Pepper Prawns DF, GF

Along the Konkan Coast from Mangalore (officially Mangaluru) to Mumbai, you can expect to find this dish not only in home kitchens, but also on the menu at seafood restaurants. In Australia, it's also an option to use Moreton Bay bug tails (sometimes referred to as bay or slipper lobster).

Serves 4

½ cup grated fresh coconut
1 tablespoon vegetable oil
1 teaspoon brown mustard seed
3 small garlic cloves, crushed
20 fresh curry leaves
1 brown onion, finely diced
2 small green chillies
1 tablespoon minced ginger
2 tomatoes, chopped
1 teaspoon freshly ground black pepper
¼ teaspoon ground turmeric
2 teaspoons ground coriander seed
1 teaspoon ground cumin
1 teaspoon sea salt flakes
12 x 120 g raw jumbo king prawns
1 teaspoon lime juice
1 tablespoon shredded coriander leaves

Preheat oven to 160°C. Scatter the coconut on a baking tray and roast for 5–6 minutes or until lightly coloured. Use a mortar and pestle to grind to a paste and set aside. Increase oven temperature to 200°C.

Heat the oil in a deep frying pan over medium heat. Add the mustard seeds, garlic and curry leaves and cook for 1 minute or until fragrant. Add the onion and cook for 2 minutes or until softened. Stir in the green chilli and ginger and cook for 1 minute. Add the tomato and cook for 5 minutes or until softened. Add the ground spices and salt and cook for a further 1 minute. Add 3 tablespoons water, stir to combine and cook for 3 minutes or until sauce is thickened. Stir through the roasted coconut paste and remove from heat. Set aside.

Without removing the shells, butterfly the prawns by making a split down the centre of the prawn's underside from head-to-tail, ensuring prawns stay in one piece. Spoon half the sauce onto a baking tray and top with the prawns, shell-side down, in single layer. Spoon over the remaining sauce and bake for 6–8 minutes or until cooked through. Drizzle with lime juice and sprinkle with shredded coriander to serve.

Mustard Prawns DF, GF

Shorshe chingri is a Bengali classic, defined by the pungent heat of mustard. It is typical that seafood from this region is first seasoned with ground turmeric and salt then fried before being added to a mustard gravy.

Serves 4

1 tablespoon black mustard seeds
1 tablespoon yellow mustard seeds
1 small green chilli, minced
2½ teaspoons sea salt flakes
1 teaspoon ground turmeric
16 large raw king prawns, peeled and deveined
¼ cup (60 ml) mustard oil
1 teaspoon nigella seeds
1 red onion, finely diced
1 tablespoon ginger garlic paste, see recipe page 436
2 teaspoons caster sugar
1 teaspoon Kashmiri chilli powder
4 tablespoons grated fresh coconut
1 small green chilli, extra, finely sliced
2 tablespoons chopped coriander leaves

Soak both mustard seeds in ⅓ cup (80 ml) cold water for 15 minutes to soften. Drain and place in a blender with the green chilli and ½ teaspoon salt to make a paste. Set aside.

Place the turmeric and 1 teaspoon salt in a bowl and mix to combine. Add the prawns and rub to coat. Heat the mustard oil in a frying pan over medium–high heat. When the oil begins to smoke, add the mustard paste and nigella seeds and cook, stirring, for 30 seconds or until mixture starts to pop. Add the onion and cook for 2 minutes or until softened. Add the ginger garlic paste, sugar and chilli powder, stir to combine and cook for 1 minute. Add the prawns and toss to coat with the mustard paste. Pour in 100 ml water and cook, stirring to loosen the mixture, for 2 minutes. Add the coconut, extra sliced green chilli and remaining 1 teaspoon salt and cook, stirring to combine, for a further 1 minute. Remove from heat and sprinkle with coriander to serve.

Fried Masala Prawns DF, GF

This recipe is typical to the *Koliwada* fishermen of the Konkan coast, particularly in the Mumbai communities where seafood reigns supreme and appears in myriad guises. Like many fried snacks, the prawns are served with either mint chutney or green chilli chutney.

Serves 4

1 tablespoon ginger garlic paste, see recipe page 436
½ teaspoon Kashmiri chilli powder
½ teaspoon ground turmeric
pinch of asafoetida
1 teaspoon sea salt flakes
2 tablespoons cornflour
600 g raw school or harbour prawns, heads removed and tail shells intact
1 litre vegetable oil, for deep-frying
mint chutney, to serve, see recipe page 361

Place the ginger garlic paste, ground spices, salt and cornflour in a bowl with just enough water to make a paste and mix to combine. Add the prawns and toss to coat well in the spice paste. Heat the oil in a wok or khadai to 180°C. Fry the prawns, in small batches, for 3 minutes or until crisp and cooked through. Remove with a slotted spoon and drain on paper towel. Serve hot with mint chutney.

Panch Phoran Spiced Prawns DF, GF

Panch phoran is the name given to Bengali five-spice, a blend of whole aromatic spices unique to the region that adds a vibrant boost of flavour. Prawns cooked in this aromatic spice blend take my tastebuds straight back to Kolkata, where I first tasted this dish.

Serves 4

500 g large raw king prawns, peeled and
    deveined with tails intact
1 tablespoon mustard oil
2 small green chillies, finely sliced
1 teaspoon panch phoran, see Glossary
1 brown onion, finely diced
2 tablespoons ginger garlic paste, see recipe
    page 436
1 teaspoon ground turmeric
1 teaspoon sea salt flakes
4 white cabbage leaves, finely shredded
1 handful baby spinach leaves
3 tablespoons chopped coriander leaves
1 tablespoon lime juice

Butterfly the prawns by making a split down the centre of the prawn's underside from head-to-tail, ensuring prawns stay in one piece. Set aside.

Heat the oil in a frying pan over medium heat. When it begins to smoke, add the green chilli and panch phoran and cook for 1 minute or until fragrant, taking care not to let it burn. Add the onion and cook for 4 minutes or until softened. Stir through the ginger garlic paste and cook for 30 seconds. Add the turmeric and salt, stir to combine and immediately add the prawns, stirring to coat with the spice mixture. Increase heat to high and cook, tossing the pan, for 4–5 minutes or until prawns have changed colour and are just cooked through. Add the cabbage, baby spinach and coriander and remove from heat. Stir through the lime juice and serve with steamed rice or a simple pulao.

Black Pepper and Garlic Butter Crab GF

A speciality of the Konkan Coast this recipe is a popular menu item at Mumbai's seafood restaurants, particularly at the world-renowned Trishna's, where it was made famous. I make sure I eat this dish each time I visit. Its buttery richness makes it so moreish and it's perfect served with parathas or pao (soft white buns).

Serves 4

160 g unsalted butter
5 garlic cloves, minced
2 small green chillies, minced
1 tablespoon freshly ground black pepper
500 g raw spanner (or blue swimmer) crabmeat,
    picked
1 teaspoon sea salt flakes
2 teaspoons lime juice
2 tablespoons finely chopped chives

Heat the butter in frying pan over medium heat. When it starts to melt, add the garlic and chilli and cook for 2–3 minutes or until starting to colour. Add the pepper and cook for a further 1 minute. Add the crabmeat, tossing to combine, and cook for 3 minutes or until crab is just cooked. Add the salt, lime juice and chives, remove from heat and serve hot with flaky parathas or *pao*.

Stir-fried Curry Mud Crab DF, GF

Crab is a favourite in the coastal dishes of India. With their thick, muddy-green shells that become red when cooked, the local crabs there are smaller but similar in appearance to the mud crabs we get from the Northern Territory and Queensland. This dish requires you to use your hands and all your senses, so it's great to serve at home where there are no inhibitions about getting into a mess – don a bib and dive in! In keeping with correct etiquette, place a large bowl on the table for discarded crab shells and a finger bowl for each person to clean their hands. Buy your crabs live and kill them humanely before you proceed with this recipe. Leftover cooked crabmeat can be tossed through eggs and seasoned with curry powder to make *kakuluwo* – a traditional curried omelette.

Serves 4

2 x 1 kg live mud crabs
4 garlic cloves
1 tablespoon chopped ginger
2 small red chillies
2 teaspoons sea salt flakes
¼ cup (60 ml) vegetable oil
4 tablespoons curry powder
1 tablespoon tamarind puree
2 teaspoons caster sugar
1 egg, beaten
½ cup (125 ml) coconut milk
2 green shallots, finely sliced diagonally
4 tablespoons coriander leaves

Kill crabs humanely by stunning (place in the freezer for 20 minutes before cooking), then lie each crab on its back and pierce it with a sharp, pointed object such as a knife. To clean the crabs, remove their carapaces (shells) and dead man's fingers (gills), reserving any mustard (roe) to stir into the mix after the egg, adding a deliciously rich flavour. Rinse the crabs well and cut each crab into quarters, keeping their large front pincers separate. Crack these slightly to split the shells to ensure even cooking and easy access when eating. Set aside.

Place the garlic, ginger, chilli and 1 teaspoon salt in mortar and pestle and pound to make a paste.

Heat a wok over high heat. Add the oil and the garlic chilli paste and cook for 1 minute or until it starts to colour. Add the curry powder and cook, stirring, for 2 minutes or until fragrant. Add the tamarind, sugar and remaining salt, stir in the egg and cook for 30 seconds or until the egg white just starts to change colour. Add any reserved crab mustard and cook for a further 30 seconds.

Add the crab pieces with the coconut milk, reduce heat to low and cook, stirring occasionally to make sure crab is evenly coated with the sauce, for 6 minutes or until the crab is cooked. The sauce should be quite dry, so it sticks to the crab shells and meat. Add the green shallots and toss to combine. Pile onto plates and sprinkle with coriander to serve.

Masala Freshwater Marron GF

In Kerala there are jumbo shrimps that look more like small lobsters. Fished from the Arabian Sea and the backwaters, they're similar in size to our native freshwater marron, which I prefer to use for this dish. Having said that, smaller lobsters or crayfish can also be used. Spiced coconut gravies, such as this one, are a favourite with seafood in the south, as they make good use of local star ingredients of coconut, pepper and cardamom, which accentuate the sweetness of the marron (or lobster).

Serves 4

8 x 300 g live marron
2 teaspoons lime juice
2 tablespoons coriander leaves
1 small green star fruit, finely sliced crossways
40 ml sunflower oil
1 tablespoon curry leaves
½ teaspoon black mustard seeds
1 large garlic clove, finely sliced

MASALA SAUCE
1 small brown onion, finely diced
3 garlic cloves, chopped
1 teaspoon chopped fresh turmeric
1 teaspoon chopped ginger
2 small green chillies, chopped
30 g ghee
1 teaspoon ground cumin
½ teaspoon nigella seeds
½ teaspoon ground turmeric
½ teaspoon ground cardamom
2 teaspoons sea salt flakes
1 teaspoon freshly ground black pepper
2 ripe tomatoes, seeded and diced
1 tablespoon kokum, soaked in hot water
   for 30 minutes, see Glossary
200 ml coconut cream

Kill marron humanely by stunning (place in the freezer for about 20 minutes before cooking), then piercing them between the eyes with a sharp knife. Fill a large saucepan with cold water, add the marron, cover with a lid and bring to a simmer. As soon as the water is simmering, remove the marron. Remove the tail meat from their shells and devein. Cut each tail crosswise into 3 thick medallions. Cut front claws from the head and remove claw meat. Discard shells and set aside.

To make the masala sauce, place the onion, garlic, fresh turmeric, ginger, chilli and 2 tablespoons water in a food processor and process to form a smooth paste. Heat the ghee in a frying pan over medium heat, add the paste and cook for 3 minutes or until fragrant. Stir in the ground spices, salt and pepper and cook for a further 2 minutes. Add the tomato and kokum and cook for 3 minutes. Add the coconut cream and bring to the boil. Once boiling, reduce heat to low and simmer gently for 10 minutes. Taste and adjust seasoning. Remove kokum from the sauce.

Add the marron medallions and the reserved claws to the simmering masala sauce and toss to coat. Cook for 3–4 minutes or until marron is just cooked. Remove from heat and stir through the lime juice, coriander and star fruit. Set aside.

In a separate small frying pan, heat the oil over medium heat. Add the curry leaves, mustard seeds and garlic and cook for 2 minutes or until crisp. Pour the tempered oil over the marron and serve with steamed rice or roti.

Green Masala Pipis DF, GF

Inspired by the seafood dishes and aromatic flavours of Goa, the coconut here lends a delicious sweetness to this dish. You can use clams or pipis in this recipe with equal success. Just make sure you soak and wash the clams in plenty of cold water before you start cooking to remove any sandy residue.

Serves 4

1 kg pipis
⅓ cup (80 ml) coconut oil
150 g red shallots, peeled and quartered
   lengthwise
¼ cup (60 ml) tamarind puree
50 ml coconut milk
1 teaspoon sea salt flakes
1 tablespoon coriander leaves

GREEN MASALA PASTE
50 g shredded fresh coconut
2 teaspoons ground coriander
3 teaspoons ground cumin
½ teaspoon freshly ground black pepper
½ teaspoon ground turmeric
8 small green chillies, chopped
1 tablespoon ginger garlic paste, see recipe
   page 436
2 tablespoons chopped coriander leaves

To make the green masala paste, place all the ingredients together in food processor and process to form a smooth paste. Set aside.

Soak the pipis in a large bowl of cold water for 1 hour. Rinse and drain. Heat 100 ml water in a large frying pan over high heat. Add the pipis, cover and cook for 2 minutes only, just until the shells start to open. Using a mesh spoon, remove pipis from pan and plunge immediately into a large bowl of iced water. Remove the top shells of each pipi and discard, leaving the meat attached to the bottom shells.

Heat the coconut oil in a deep-frying pan over high heat. Add the shallot and cook, stirring frequently to prevent burning, for 4 minutes or until golden. Reduce heat to medium, add the masala paste and cook, stirring, for 5 minutes or until fragrant. Add the tamarind, coconut milk and salt and stir to combine. Add the pipis, tossing the pan to coat in the masala paste, and cook for 2 minutes or until just warmed through. Top with coriander leaves and serve with steamed rice.

Fried Masala Fish DF, GF

Whole, red spot or eastern whiting, red mullet or other similar-sized fish work here, and pomfret sliced crosswise into cutlets are also great for this preparation. If cooking (or eating) whole fish scares you, you can easily use small fish fillets that cook just as quickly.

Serves 4

12 small whole fish, gutted and scaled
1 tablespoon lime juice
2 teaspoons sea salt flakes
1 tablespoon Kashmiri chilli powder
1 teaspoon freshly ground black pepper
2 teaspoons ground cumin
1 teaspoon ground turmeric
2 teaspoons ginger garlic paste, see recipe
   page 436
150 ml sunflower oil
2 dried chillies
2 tablespoons fried curry leaves

Place the fish, lime juice and 1 teaspoon salt in a tray and set aside to marinate for 30 minutes.

Place the ground spices, remaining salt and ginger garlic paste in a bowl and mix to combine. Rub liberally over the fish to coat.

Heat the oil in a frying pan over medium heat. Add the fish and cook for 2 minutes or until crisp. Gently turn fish over, being careful not to break the flesh, and cook on the other side for a further 2 minutes or until crisp. Drain fish on paper towel, reserving the oil.

Using the reserved oil, fry the dried chillies and drain on paper towel before breaking into small pieces. Arrange fish on a serving plate, garnish with the fried chilli and fried curry leaves to serve.

Mustard Fish GF

This is my modern take on the Bengali classic *bhekti sarson* – in this region, mustard and green chillies are the defining elements for flavouring seafood. When I visit the fish markets in Kolkata with friends, we look for whatever river fish is fresh and in season – they're spoilt for choice. Freshwater fish is prized and preferred in the Bengali diet, and many cooks will shun fish that comes from the sea as they consider the flavour inferior. I've used Murray cod here, but there's nothing to stop you from cooking this flavour-packed dish with other freshwater white fish, such silver perch (black bream), river trout or wild barramundi.

Serves 4

600 g Murray cod fillet, skin removed and
    trimmed
1 teaspoon ground turmeric
1 teaspoon ground cumin
½ teaspoon freshly ground black pepper
1 teaspoon black mustard seeds, coarsely ground
2 teaspoons sea salt flakes
2 teaspoons wholegrain Dijon mustard
2 teaspoons chopped ginger
2 garlic cloves
2 small green chillies, chopped
1 cup coriander leaves
1 tablespoons mustard oil
100 g thick plain yoghurt
2 tablespoons chopped coriander, extra

Cut the fish across the fillet into 4 even-size portions. Prepare 4 sheets of foil and 4 sheets of baking paper of the same size, ensuring the sheets are big enough to wrap the fillets. Place the ground spices, 1 teaspoon salt and wholegrain mustard in a bowl and mix to combine. Rub spice mixture liberally over the fish and set aside.

Place the ginger, garlic, chilli, coriander leaves, remaining 1 teaspoons salt and the mustard oil in a food processor and blend to make a paste. Place in a bowl with the yoghurt and stir to combine. Spread the yoghurt mixture over both sides of each fillet.

Preheat oven to 220°C. Place 1 sheet of baking paper on top of each sheet of foil and top with a fish fillet and its yoghurt coating. Wrap the fish in the paper to secure before enclosing with the foil. Don't wrap too tightly, the parcels can be slightly loose, just make sure they're sealed tightly at both ends. Place on an oven tray, side-by-side, and bake for 10 minutes or until fish is tender and just cooked. Remove from oven and set aside to rest for 5 minutes to allow the juices to settle. Unwrap the fish, discarding foil and paper. Garnish with chopped coriander and serve with steamed rice.

Tamarind-glazed Sea Mullet DF, GF

My preferred fish for this recipe, and one of my favourites to cook, is sea (or ocean) mullet. Its flavour and texture is a perfect match with the tamarind glaze. Other fish, such as mulloway, flathead or silver dory are also acceptable alternatives.

Serves 4

4 x 120 g sea mullet fillets, skin on
1 tablespoon vegetable oil
4 tablespoons fried curry leaves

TAMARIND GLAZE
1 tablespoon vegetable oil
½ teaspoon brown mustard seeds
2 teaspoons minced ginger
2 tablespoons tamarind puree
2 tablespoons brown sugar
1 tablespoon tomato puree
1 teaspoon sea salt flakes

To make the tamarind glaze, heat the oil in a frying pan over medium heat. Add the mustard seeds and cook for 30 seconds or until they start to pop. Stir in the ginger, before adding the tamarind, sugar, tomato puree, salt and ¼ cup (60 ml) water and simmer for 2–3 minutes or until glaze is slightly reduced and coats the back of a spoon. Set aside.

Heat a non-stick frying pan over medium–high heat. Brush the fish on both sides with the oil and season with salt and pepper. Place the fish, skin-side down, in the pan and use a fish weight, fish slide or right-angle spatula to press down on the fish for the first 40 seconds, this prevents the fillet from curling and keeps it in even contact with the pan. Cook fish, without turning, for 3 minutes or until crisp. Turn fish, skin-side up and add the tamarind glaze around the fish, shaking pan slightly to ensure the sauce gets under the fish. Reduce heat to medium and cook for a further 2–3 minutes, depending on thickness of fillet, or until just cooked through. Top with fried curry leaves and serve with steamed rice.

Fish in Coconut Milk DF, GF

Meen molee is perhaps the most well-known fish dish from Kerala. The fish is cooked in an aromatic coconut gravy infused with the gentle and delicate flavours of curry leaf, black pepper and green cardamom – all of which grow in abundance in Kerala and are the defining flavours of the region. You can use snapper, pearl perch, blue-eye trevalla, bass groper or any mild-flavoured, white-flesh fish.

Serves 4

½ teaspoon sea salt flakes
½ teaspoon freshly ground black pepper
½ teaspoon ground cardamom
400 g white-flesh fish fillet, skin removed,
    cut into 4 even portions
1 tablespoon sunflower oil
1 small red onion, finely sliced
2 small garlic cloves, sliced
1 tablespoon minced ginger
4 small green chillies, finely sliced
1 tablespoon fresh curry leaves
1 tomato, sliced into 4 rounds
1 cup (250 ml) coconut milk
½ cup (125 ml) coconut cream
10 roasted cashews, roughly chopped
10 golden raisins, fried
1 tablespoon fried curry leaves

Place the salt, pepper and cardamom in a bowl and mix to combine. Rub into the fish fillets and set aside.

Heat the oil in a frying pan over medium heat, add the onion, garlic, ginger and chilli and cook for 2 minutes. Add the curry leaves and cook until crisp. Push ingredients to one side of the pan away from the heat. Add the fish to the centre of the pan and cook for 1 minute. Carefully turn fish and spoon over the onion mixture to coat. Top each fillet with a slice of tomato and season with salt. Pour the coconut milk around the fish and bring to the boil. Reduce heat to low and simmer gently for 2–3 minutes. Pour in the coconut cream and cook until warmed through, being careful not to let the sauce boil. Remove from heat and garnish with cashews, raisins and fried curry leaves. Serve with steamed rice.

Fenugreek and Tomato Braised Mackerel DF, GF

When I was staying at Diphlu River Lodge in Kaziranga National Park, the chef there showed me how easy this traditional Assam fish preparation, known as *massur tenga*, is to make. There, it's typically cooked with a local river fish similar to a mild-tasting catfish, but at home I use blue mackerel.

Serves 6

2 tablespoons mustard oil
2 teaspoons fenugreek seeds
2 tomatoes, roughly chopped
100 g spinach leaves, shredded
1 teaspoon ground turmeric
1 teaspoon sea salt flakes
600 g blue mackerel fillets, skin removed and cut into 1 cm slices
2 teaspoons lime juice

Heat the oil in a braising pan over medium heat. Add the fenugreek seeds and cook for 90 seconds or until aromatic, taking care not to burn. Add the tomato, spinach leaves and turmeric and cook for 2 minutes or until softened. Add 150 ml water and the salt and bring to a simmer. Add the fish and cook for 5–7 minutes or until tender and just cooked. Remove from heat and add the lime juice. Check seasoning and adjust, if necessary. Serve with steamed rice.

Masala Baked Kingfish GF

Kingfish is given a gentle kick of spice in this simple preparation. If you can't find kingfish, Spanish mackerel or cobia make for suitable substitutes as the texture of these fish responds well to their masala bath. As an alternative, you can thread fish chunks onto metal skewers and cook over hot coals before finishing in the oven for a few minutes.

Serves 4

50 g thick plain yoghurt
500 g kingfish fillet, skin removed and trimmed
tamarind chutney, to serve, see Pickles and Chutneys page 362

MASALA PASTE
2 teaspoons brown mustard seeds
2 teaspoons fenugreek
2 teaspoons cayenne
1 teaspoon garam masala
1 teaspoon sea salt flakes
3 teaspoons sriracha chilli sauce
1 teaspoon tamarind puree

To make the masala paste, heat a non-stick frying pan over medium heat. Add the mustard seeds and fenugreek and cook for 30 seconds or until fragrant. Place in a bowl with the remaining ingredients and mix to make a paste. Add the yoghurt and mix until well combined. Cut the fish into 4 even-size portions and toss gently to coat in the yoghurt and masala mixture. Set aside in the fridge for 1 hour to marinate.

Preheat oven to 200°C. Place the fish and the marinade on a baking tray lined with baking paper and bake for 15 minutes or until fish is just cooked through. Serve with tamarind chutney and roti or paratha.

Fish Steamed in Banana Leaf DF, GF

Patra ni machi is a popular way to enjoy fish in Kerala and Gujarat, where the spice paste varies slightly between regions. This version is from the Parsi repertoire and is defined by its green colour and pungency. You can easily substitute the mackerel with kingfish or bonito.

Serves 4

4 x 120 g portions Spanish mackerel, cut from the centre of the fillet for even thickness
4 banana leaves, see Glossary
4 lime wedges, to serve

MASALA PASTE
2 tablespoons ginger garlic paste, see recipe page 436
4 small green chillies
60 g shredded fresh coconut
1 tablespoon fresh curry leaves
2 tablespoon coriander leaves
2 tablespoon mint leaves
¼ cup (60 ml) lime juice
½ teaspoon ground turmeric
1 teaspoon sea salt flakes
½ teaspoon freshly ground black pepper
½ teaspoon garam masala

To make the masala paste, place all ingredients in a food processor and blend to make a smooth paste. Rub the paste over both sides of the fish to thoroughly coat. Set aside to marinate for 10 minutes.

Remove the central ribs from the banana leaves and cut into 20 cm squares. Place the squares on a bench, arrange a piece of fish and the masala marinade in the centre of each leaf and carefully fold over the edges, one at a time, to make a parcel. Secure parcels with a toothpick.

Place the fish parcels in a steamer tray and steam over gently boiling water for 10–12 minutes or until fish is cooked through when tested with a skewer. Remove from heat and set aside to rest for 3 minutes. Unwrap fish, discarding the banana leaves, and transfer to serving plates. Serve with lime wedges.

Swordfish Tikka GF

Ask your fishmonger to cut you a thick slice of fish for this recipe, as you need to be able to cut the fish into 3 cm cubes. If the fillet or slice is too thin, the fish won't cook evenly and will break apart. With a similar texture to swordfish, silver trevally, albacore tuna or bass groper will also work in this dish.

Serves 6

500 g swordfish fillet, skin removed and cut into 3 cm cubes
6 lime wedges, to serve

TIKKA MARINADE
250 g fresh curd (hung yoghurt), see Dairy page 110
1 tablespoon mustard oil
1 tablespoon lime juice
2 teaspoons ginger garlic paste, see recipe page 436
1 teaspoon garam masala
1 teaspoon ajwain seeds, see Glossary
1 teaspoon Kashmiri chilli powder
1 teaspoon turmeric
2 teaspoons sea salt flakes
1 tablespoons chickpea (besan) flour

To make the tikka marinade, place all ingredients together in a bowl and mix until well combined. Add the fish and gently toss to coat, taking care not to break the fish pieces. Set aside to marinate for 10 minutes before threading fish onto metal skewers, leaving a slight gap between each piece.

Preheat a grill plate over hot coals (I like to use a benchtop hibachi grill) or a barbecue plate to high heat and cook the skewers for 3 minutes. Turn skewers and cook for a further 2 minutes or until just cooked through. Serve with lime wedges.

Turmeric and Ginger Grilled Tuna GF

Buying sashimi-grade tuna will make all the difference to the outcome of this recipe, yielding a superior texture and flavour. This is a very straightforward dish and can also be cooked on a hotplate or barbecue. Serve it with cabbage thoran and ginger chutney.

Serves 4

600 g sashimi-grade tuna loin fillet, trimmed
1 tablespoon ginger garlic paste, see recipe page 436
½ teaspoon ground ginger
½ teaspoon ground turmeric
½ teaspoon garam masala
½ teaspoon ground cumin
½ teaspoon Kashmiri chilli powder
1 teaspoon sea salt flakes
½ teaspoon freshly ground black pepper
2 tablespoons lime juice
2 tablespoons ghee
cabbage and coconut thoran, to serve, see Salads page 87
ginger chutney, to serve, see Pickles and Chutneys page 364

Slice the tuna across the fillet into 4 x 3 cm-thick even-size steaks. Place the ginger garlic paste, ground spices, salt, pepper, lime juice and 1 tablespoon of water in a bowl and mix to make a paste. Rub the spice paste over both sides of the tuna steaks.

Melt the ghee in a frying pan over medium–high heat. Add the tuna and cook, without touching (this ensures it develops a crust), for 2 minutes. Turn the tuna and cook on the other side for a further 2 minutes. It's important to note, the cooking time depends on the thickness of the tuna. Make sure there's a visible pink band in the centre of the fish, otherwise it will be overcooked and alter the soft texture. Remove tuna from the pan and rest for 2 minutes. Serve topped with cabbage thoran and with ginger chutney.

Yoghurt Baked Fish, Walnut Crumble and Tomato Kasundi Pickle

This is a wonderful heart-warming dish enhanced by textural contrasts, from soft and yielding to crunchy, and balanced with deeply flavoured pickle. I like to use snapper, coral trout, blue-eye trevalla or other deep-sea, white-flesh fish for this recipe. If you have the tomato kasundi pickle already made, this is a very quick dish to prepare. Serve it with buttered spinach or wilted mustard greens.

Serves 6

6 x 120 g snapper fillets, skin removed
½ cup (125 g) thick plain yoghurt
½ cup tomato kasundi pickle, to serve,
   see Pickles and Chutneys page 350

YOGHURT MARINADE
250 g thick plain yoghurt
1 teaspoon cornflour
1 egg
2 green shallots, finely sliced
1 tablespoon finely chopped chives
1 tablespoon extra virgin olive oil
2 teaspoons lime juice
1 teaspoon sea salt flakes
1 teaspoon freshly ground black pepper

WALNUT CRUMBLE
50 g sourdough breadcrumbs
50 g walnuts, chopped
30 g unsalted butter
1 tablespoon shredded parsley
1 teaspoon chopped mint
1 teaspoon chopped dill

To make the walnut crumble, preheat oven to 180°C. Mix the breadcrumbs, walnut and butter in a bowl, using your fingers to rub the butter through until the crumbs are moist. Spread the crumble onto a baking tray and bake for 6–8 minutes or until lightly toasted. Stir the herbs through the crumble when ready to serve.

To make the yoghurt marinade, place all the ingredients in a bowl and mix to combine. Add the fish and coat well in the marinade. Set aside for 5 minutes.

Increase oven temperature to 200°C. Transfer fish to a baking dish that comfortably fits the fish, cover with foil and bake for 12 minutes or until just cooked through. To serve, spread 1 tablespoon of yoghurt across centre of each plate and top with a dollop of tomato kasundi pickle. Coat the top of each fish with walnut crumble to make a crust and place on the pickle to serve.

Salmon and Vegetable Masala GF

Inspired by Tamil flavours of the south and straightforward to prepare, I think of this vegetable masala as an Indian take on a ratatouille, using similar vegetables with extra embellishment. I have used salmon in this instance, but the options are quite broad, depending on what's in season and available, which should always be the rule of thumb when buying seafood. If I'm after a fish with a more delicate texture, I sometimes use the fillets from smaller fish, such as flathead, whiting, garfish, leatherjacket or John Dory.

Serves 4

2 tablespoons ghee
1 small green chilli, minced
2 teaspoons curry powder
½ teaspoon sea salt flakes
½ teaspoon freshly ground black pepper
4 x 120 g king salmon fillets, skin on
2 teaspoons chopped coriander
1 teaspoon chopped mint

VEGETABLE MASALA
120 g pumpkin, cut into 1 cm dice
5 tablespoons sunflower oil
12 cherry tomatoes, halved
600 ml vegetable oil, for deep-frying, plus an
    extra 3 tablespoons
200 g eggplant, cut into 1 cm dice
1 small red onion, finely diced
2 teaspoon ginger garlic paste, see recipe
    page 436
1 teaspoon curry powder
1 zucchini, quartered lengthwise and cut into
    1 cm dice
1 red capsicum, roasted, peeled and cut into
    1 cm dice
1 tablespoon lemon juice, strained
2 tablespoons chopped coriander
2 tablespoons ginger chutney, see Pickles
    and Chutneys page 364

To prepare the vegetable masala, preheat oven to 175°C. Toss the diced pumpkin in 4 tablespoons of the sunflower oil to coat and place on baking tray. Season lightly with salt and pepper and roast for 15 minutes or until soft. Remove from oven and set aside. At the same time, place the cherry tomato on a separate baking tray, drizzle lightly with remaining 1 tablespoon sunflower oil, season with salt and pepper and roast for 10 minutes or until soft and starting to caramelise. Remove from oven and set aside.

Heat the vegetable oil in deep fryer or large saucepan to 180°C. Fry the diced eggplant, in small batches, until golden. Drain on paper towel. Set aside.

Heat the extra 3 tablespoons vegetable oil in a frying pan over medium heat. Add the onion and cook for 4 minutes or until softened. Add the garlic ginger paste and cook for 2 minutes or until starting to colour. Add the curry powder and stir to combine. Add the zucchini, reduce heat to low and cook for 5 minutes or until zucchini is soft.

In a large bowl, mix together the onion and zucchini, eggplant, roasted pumpkin, tomato, roasted capsicum, lemon juice, chopped coriander and ginger chutney and stir to combine. Set aside.

To cook the fish, melt the ghee in a frying pan over medium heat. Add the chilli and when it starts to sizzle, add the curry powder, salt and pepper, stirring to combine. Add the fish, skin-side down, and cook for 3 minutes or until skin is crisp. Turn and cook on the other side for a further 2 minutes, ensuring fish is still rosy-pink in the centre. Add the chopped herbs and swirl through the pan to coat the fish. Spoon the masala vegetables onto plates, top with the fish and drizzle over pan juices to serve.

Baked Fish with Mustard Cashew Masala GF

Here is another popular fish preparation with gentle, fragrant flavours. I like to serve this in a small pot accompanied with a crisp kachumber salad for textural contrast. Any deep-sea, firm-flesh fish is suitable for this recipe, such as kingfish, trevally, trumpeter or groper.

Serves 6

3 tomatoes, grated
1 tablespoon tomato kasundi pickle, see Pickles
  and Chutneys page 350
3 teaspoons sea salt flakes
1 tablespoon caster sugar
100 ml vegetable oil
2 teaspoons coriander seeds, roasted and ground
2 teaspoons cumin seeds, roasted and ground
1 cup (250 ml) fish stock or water
1 tablespoon chickpea (besan) flour
½ cup thick plain yoghurt
50 ml cream
6 x 150 g mulloway cutlets, cut from centre
  of fillet for even thickness
1 tablespoon mustard oil
25 ml lime juice
2 tablespoons chopped coriander leaves
½ long green chilli, finely sliced
kachumber salad, to serve, see Salads page 82

MUSTARD CASHEW MASALA
2 teaspoons brown mustard seeds
1 teaspoon ground turmeric
1 teaspoon chilli powder
60 g grated fresh coconut
1 tablespoon minced ginger
4 garlic cloves, chopped
3 small green chillies, chopped
1 brown onion, chopped
2 tablespoons raw cashews, chopped
1 tablespoon mustard oil

To make the mustard cashew masala, place all the ingredients together in food processor and blend to form a paste. Set aside.

Place the grated tomato and tomato kasundi pickle in a frying pan over medium heat and cook for 8–10 minutes or until reduced by half. Add 2 teaspoons of the salt and the sugar, stir to combine and set aside.

Heat the vegetable oil in a wide-based pan over low heat. Add the ground coriander and cumin and cook for 30 seconds or until fragrant. Immediately stir in the mustard cashew masala, increase heat to medium, and continue stirring for 5 minutes or until aromatic and starting to colour. Add the reduced tomato and the stock and cook for 10 minutes. Reduce heat to low.

Meanwhile, combine the chickpea flour and yoghurt in a bowl, this prevents the yoghurt from splitting during cooking, and stir into the masala sauce. Add the cream and cook for 5 minutes. Remove from heat while you cook the fish.

To cook the fish, preheat oven to 200°C. Brush the fish skin with mustard oil and sprinkle with a little sea salt. Heat a heavy-based, ovenproof frying pan over medium heat. Add the fish, skin-side down, and cook for 3 minutes or until golden and crisp. Turn fish over, pour the mustard cashew sauce around the fish, transfer to the oven and bake for 4–5 minutes, depending on thickness of fish, or until cooked through. Rest for 2 minutes to allow juices to settle.

Carefully lift the fish from the pan and place on serving plates. Add the lime juice, remaining 1 teaspoon salt, coriander and chilli to the sauce in the pan and stir to combine. Spoon sauce over the fish and serve with kachumber salad and steamed basmati rice.

Fried Turmeric Fish with Coconut Beetroot Salad GF

A visual treat that reminds me of an impressionist Fauve painting, this recipe is a clash of vibrant colours and enticing flavours. You can use any deep-sea, white-flesh fish such as mahi mahi, bass groper or snapper to yield the required thickness for the cutlets.

Serves 4

½ teaspoon chilli powder
1 teaspoon ground turmeric
1 teaspoon freshly ground black pepper
1 tablespoon minced ginger
3 garlic cloves, minced
2 teaspoons minced fresh turmeric
2 teaspoons sea salt flakes
1 tablespoon coconut vinegar
4 x 150 g wild barramundi portions, cut from centre of the fillet for even thickness
¼ cup (60 ml) vegetable oil
4 tablespoons coconut beetroot salad, to serve, see Salads page 81
1 punnet Swiss chard cress, snipped
1 punnet mustard cress, snipped
2 tablespoons fried curry leaves

Place the ground spices, ginger, garlic, turmeric, salt and coconut vinegar in a large bowl and mix to combine. Add the fish and toss gently to coat. Cover and set aside to marinate for 20 minutes.

Heat a frying pan over medium heat. Add the oil and fry the fish, skin-side down, for 4 minutes or until skin is crisp. Add a splash of water, making sure the paste doesn't burn, reduce the heat slightly, if necessary. Turn the fish and cook on the other side for a further 3–4 minutes, depending on the thickness of the fish, or until cooked through.

Divide fish between plates and spoon over the coconut beetroot salad. Scatter with the Swiss chard and mustard cress and fried curry leaves to serve.

Meat

Religious diversity in India underscores both the cooking and inclusion of various meats in diets across the country, as the major religions come with certain dietary restrictions. For example, Hindus and Sikhs don't eat beef, while the Muslim and Parsi communities forbid pork. So it stands to reason that lamb, mutton, goat and chicken are the most commonly consumed meats for those who do allow meat in their diet. For those unversed in the religious traditions of the land, it can be confusing, as some Hindu families forbid the cooking of meat at home, yet they'll happily go out to a restaurant or *dhaba* (roadside eatery) to eat kebabs, tandoori, biryani or other meat dishes. Meanwhile, the Buddhist and tribal communities from the mountains and the north-east, the Catholics in Goa, and the Syrian Christians in Kerala do include beef and pork in their diet. India is fascinating in that you can witness first-hand how different religions and customs produce utterly different ways of cooking, even in the same city or town.

In the past, long before the population explosion of the 20th century, when India was covered in extensive forests, game meats were commonly cooked. These were the spoils of hunting in a time when wildlife was abundant. The cooking of animals such as wild boar, sambar deer (venison), hare, hedgehog, rabbit, partridge and other game birds are mentioned in historical, religious and royal texts. But, over time, the consumption and preference of animal protein in diets shifted to what we now consider everyday meats.

Naturally, different cultures have left their stamp on how meat is enjoyed throughout India. The Mughals were responsible for introducing fragrant meat biryanis, kebabs and yoghurt-rich meat dishes into the broader Indian repertoire and, in many regions, Muslim communities have built on cooking styles that stem from the imperial kitchens. Indeed, it's the Muslims who are the butchers and vendors in any market in India, handling the preparation of goat, mutton, lamb or beef for consumption. Of course, the British undoubtedly influenced food habits and practices during their colonial rule and current regional cuisines have adapted inherited legacies to suit local ingredients and tastes. This distinctive food culture, born from a hybrid of British culinary traditions and indigenous ingredients and cooking practices, has come to be known as the 'taste of empire'.

Whatever the origins, you'll find meat preparation in India often relies on yoghurt and buttermilk, both of which add moisture during cooking as well as imparting a glorious tanginess and yielding tenderness. More often than not, meats are marinated in yoghurt and spices before being cooked.

If you've been reticent to cook with mutton (lamb that has been allowed to mature to sheep) or goat, then there are myriad recipes to get you started. While aged meat takes longer to cook, it responds beautifully to slow, gentle cooking. Try these meats and the varying Indian cooking methods from this chapter and you'll be rewarded with dishes rich in complexity and flavour.

Chicken Pepper Fry DF, GF

This punchy recipe is a classic from the Chettinad region of Tamil Nadu. It has a decent kick of pepper and spice that lingers on the palate.

Serves 4

2 tablespoons vegetable oil
1 cinnamon stick
2 green cardamom pods, cracked
2 white onions, finely diced
2 tablespoons ginger garlic paste, see recipe
   page 436
1 tablespoon curry leaves
2 tomatoes, seeded and diced
2 teaspoons sea salt flakes
1 kg chicken wings, wing tips removed
2 teaspoons lime juice
2 tablespoons fried curry leaves

BLACK PEPPER MASALA
1½ teaspoons fennel seeds
1½ teaspoons cumin seeds
1½ teaspoons coriander seeds
2 teaspoons black peppercorns
2 small dried chillies

To make the black pepper masala, place all the ingredients in a frying pan over low heat and dry roast for 1 minute or until fragrant. Allow to cool before grinding to fine powder in a spice grinder.

Heat the oil in a heavy-based frying pan over medium heat. Add the cinnamon and cardamom and cook for 20 seconds or until fragrant. Add the onion and cook for 4 minutes or until softened and starting to colour. Stir in the black pepper masala and cook for 1 minute or until fragrant. Add the ginger garlic paste, curry leaves, tomato and salt and cook, stirring, for 2 minutes. Add the chicken and cook for 2 minutes, stirring to thoroughly coat with the masala base. Add 100 ml water (the water is to stop the masala base from burning, not to make a sauce), cover pan with a lid, reduce heat to low and cook for 6 minutes. Turn the chicken and cook for a further 6 minutes or until tender. The chicken should be nicely coated with the cooked masala paste. Stir through the lime juice and discard the cinnamon stick. Top with fried curry leaves and serve with appams or steamed rice.

**Masterclass step-by-step
Chicken Pepper Fry →**

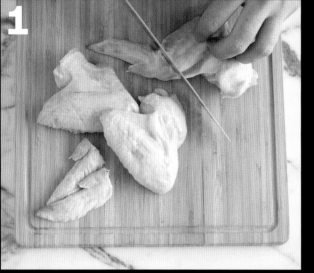

1 Remove wing tips from the chicken wings.

2 To make the black pepper masala, dry roast ingredients over low heat. Once cooled, grind in a spice grinder.

3 Heat the oil in a heavy-based frying pan over medium heat. Add the cinnamon and cardamon and cook for 20 seconds.

4 Add the onion and cook for 4 minutes or until softened.

5 Add the black pepper masala and cook for 1 minute.

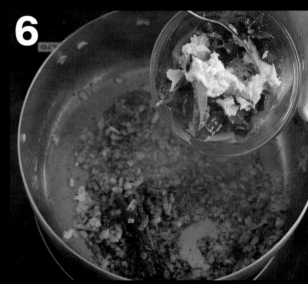

6 Add the ginger garlic paste, curry leaves and tomato and salt and cook, stirring, for 2 minutes.

7 Add the chicken.

8 Cook for 2 minutes, stirring to coat with the black pepper masala.

9 Add 100 ml water, cover pan with a lid, reduce heat to low and cook for 6 minutes.

10 Turn the chicken and cook for a further 6 minutes or until tender.

11 Stir through the lime juice and discard cinnamon stick.

12 Top with fried curry leaves to serve.

Chettinad Chilli Chicken GF

The Chettinad region in Tamil Nadu has some of the spiciest food in India and their rich culinary traditions owe much to their links with nearby Malaysia and Indonesia, with whom they were long-term spice traders. As such, this layering of spice complexity has become the signature of the region. The red masala paste here can be made in advance and kept in an airtight jar in the fridge for up to two weeks.

Serves 4

75 g ghee
2 brown onions, diced
2 tablespoons ginger garlic paste, see recipe
 page 436
3 small red chillies, minced
20 fresh curry leaves
2 teaspoons chilli powder
4 chicken marylands, cut into thigh and leg joints
3 tomatoes, seeded and chopped
100 ml chicken stock (or water)
2 teaspoons sea salt flakes
1 tablespoon lime juice
½ cup coriander leaves

CHETTINAD MASALA PASTE
1 teaspoon white poppy seeds
2 large dried chillies
100 g grated fresh coconut
½ teaspoon fennel seeds
½ teaspoon ground cinnamon
¼ teaspoon ground cardamom
½ teaspoon ground cloves
½ teaspoon ground turmeric
½ teaspoon garam masala
2 tablespoons vegetable oil
1 tablespoon finely diced brown onion
2 teaspoons ginger garlic paste, see recipe
 page 436

To make the Chettinad masala paste, place the poppy seeds in a frying pan and cook over low heat for 20 seconds or until lightly toasted. Remove from pan and soak in 1 tablespoon of water for 20 minutes. Add the chillies to the pan and cook for 2 minutes or until fragrant. Allow to cool before grinding to a fine powder in a spice grinder. Place the poppy seed mixture, coconut, ground chilli and other spices in a food processor or blender and process to a fine paste.

Heat the oil in a frying pan over medium heat. Add the onion and cook for 4 minutes or until golden. Add the ginger garlic paste and cook for 2 minutes. Stir in the spiced coconut paste and cook, stirring to combine, for 4–5 minutes. If the mixture becomes too dry, add a splash of water to prevent it from burning. Set aside to cool.

To cook the chicken, melt the ghee in a wide-based pan over medium–high heat. Add the onion and cook for 4 minutes or until softened. Add the ginger garlic paste and minced chilli and cook, stirring to combine, for 30 seconds. Add the curry leaves and cook, stirring, for 30 seconds or until crisp. Add the ground chilli and 3 tablespoons of the Chettinad masala paste and cook, stirring to combine, for 2–3 minutes. Add the chicken and cook, turning once to ensure the pieces are evenly coated in the paste, for 5 minutes. Add the tomato and cook for a further 4 minutes. Add the stock, reduce heat to low, cover and simmer for 10 minutes or until the chicken is tender. Season with salt and lime juice. Scatter with the coriander and serve with steamed rice.

Parsi-style Sweet and Sour Chicken with Potato Straws DF, GF

This dish is found on menus at the popular Irani cafes in Mumbai and Hyderabad. *Salli murgh* translates as 'chicken with crisp potato straws', and is one of the defining dishes in the Parsi repertoire. The Parsis came to India centuries ago from Persia fleeing religious persecution and have woven their way into the everyday vernacular. The heritage of their cooking may be Persian, but it has also been heavily influenced by both the British and Indian food cultures.

Serves 4

⅓ cup (80 ml) vegetable oil
2 white onions, finely diced
1 tablespoon ginger garlic paste, see recipe
 page 436
400 g ripe tomatoes, pureed
1 tablespoon brown sugar
1 teaspoon sea salt flakes
½ teaspoon freshly ground black pepper
½ teaspoon ground cinnamon
2 teaspoons garam masala
1 teaspoon ground turmeric
½ teaspoon Kashmiri chilli powder
1 teaspoon ground cumin
8 x 1.6 kg chicken thighs, bone in
2 cups (500 ml) vegetable oil, extra,
 for deep-frying
2 medium potatoes, peeled and sliced into
 fine matchsticks
½ cup coriander leaves
saffron rice, to serve, see Rice page 306

Heat the oil in a large frying pan over medium heat. Add the onion and cook for 4 minutes or until softened. Increase heat to high and cook, stirring often, for a further 4 minutes or until golden brown. Add the ginger garlic paste and cook gently for 1 minute or until fragrant. Add the tomato puree, sugar, salt, pepper and the ground spices and bring to the boil. Reduce heat to medium and cook for 15 minutes or until thickened and the masala has released some oil. This is essential to the character of the gravy. Taste and adjust seasoning, if necessary. Add the chicken and 100 ml water to the masala, stir to combine and bring to the boil. Cover with a lid, reduce heat to low and cook, stirring occasionally, for 20 minutes or until the chicken is tender. Make sure the gravy doesn't dry out too much, add an extra splash of water, if necessary.

While the chicken is cooking, prepare the potato straws. Heat the extra vegetable oil in a deep saucepan to 180°C. Fry the potato straws, in small batches, until golden and crisp. Remove from the oil with a slotted spoon and drain on paper towel. Set aside and keep warm.

Check the consistency of the masala sauce – it should coat the back of a spoon. If it's too watery, simply remove the chicken and cook until reduced. Stir the coriander through the chicken, top with the potato straws and serve with saffron rice.

Butter Chicken GF

Murgh makhani is one of the most popular and widely known dishes of India. Invented in a Delhi restaurant owned by three Sikhs, the accidental flavour combination was born out of necessity to feed a busload of hungry Punjabi Hindu refugees during Partition. Traditionally made with marinated chicken cooked in a tandoor oven (chicken tikka) and served in a creamy tomato gravy, it's authentically Indian. The silken and creamy sauce is mildly spiced and enriched with butter and cream, which yields the chicken meltingly tender. The ratio of gravy to chicken is about double, you're looking for a very soupy gravy that's perfect for mopping up with roti, paratha, or steamed rice. This recipe was kindly given to me by Indian star chef Alfred Prasad from his extensive restaurant repertoire. He comments that it's best to use tinned whole tomatoes, as they give a more consistent flavour and colour to the sauce. This recipe is a simplified home-style version that doesn't require a tandoor oven.

Serves 6

CHICKEN TIKKA
1 tablespoon canola (or vegetable) oil
¼ cup (35 g) chickpea (besan) flour
1 tablespoon ginger garlic paste, see recipe
    page 436
75 g thick plain yoghurt
1 teaspoons Kashmiri chilli powder
¼ teaspoon ground turmeric
½ teaspoon garam masala
1 teaspoon sea salt flakes
500 g chicken thigh fillets, cut into 3 cm pieces
2 teaspoons vegetable oil
15 g unsalted butter
¼ teaspoon ground kasoori methi (dried
    fenugreek leaves), see Glossary
¼ teaspoon ground cardamom
2 tablespoons single cream
1 tablespoon double cream

SAUCE
1 tablespoon canola oil
1 tablespoon minced ginger
1 long green chilli
600 g tinned tomatoes, pureed
2 teaspoons honey
10 cashews, soaked and ground to
    a smooth paste
¾ teaspoons Kashmiri chilli powder
¼ teaspoon ground cardamom
¼ teaspoon ground kasoori methi (dried
    fenugreek leaves), see Glossary

¼ teaspoon garam masala
½ teaspoon sea salt flakes
20 g unsalted butter

HERB BUTTER
1 teaspoon chopped dill leaves
1 teaspoon chopped coriander leaves
¼ teaspoon ground kasoori methi (dried
    fenugreek leaves), see Glossary
½ teaspoon sea salt flakes
10 g unsalted butter, softened

To make the chicken tikka, place the oil and chickpea flour in a small saucepan over low heat and cook for 5 minutes or until smooth to make a roux. Transfer to a plate to cool. Place the ginger garlic paste, yoghurt, ground spices and salt in a large bowl and mix well to combine. Add the chicken, chickpea flour roux and vegetable oil and mix well. Transfer to a non-reactive container and marinate in the fridge for at least 4 hours. You'll need to bring the marinated chicken back to room temperature roughly 30 minutes before grilling.

Preheat oven to 200ºC. Place the chicken on a wire rack in a baking tray and bake for 10–15 minutes. Change oven to the grill setting, turn the chicken, and grill on the top shelf for 2–3 minutes or until brown and cooked through. Remove from the grill and set aside to cool.

To make the sauce, heat the oil in a large saucepan over medium heat. Add the minced ginger and green chilli and cook for 2 minutes. Add the tomato, honey, cashew paste, chilli powder, cardamom, kasoori methi and garam masala, cover with a lid and cook for 20 minutes or until thickened to gravy consistency. Transfer to a bowl and use a stick blender to blend the sauce until smooth. Return sauce to the saucepan over medium heat, add the salt and butter and mix well. Cook until just reheated. Remove from heat to prevent sauce from splitting and set aside.

To make the herb butter, place the chopped herbs, kasoori methi and salt in a bowl with the softened butter and mix to combine. Transfer to a sheet of doubled-layered plastic wrap, roll tightly into a cylinder and freeze for 15–20 minutes.

Heat a large saucepan over medium heat, add the remaining butter and cook until a nut-brown colour. Add the chicken and cook for 2 minutes. Sprinkle with kasoori methi and cardamom, add the sauce, single cream and double cream and stir to combine. Once the sauce reaches boiling point, remove from heat, transfer to a serving plate and top with slices of herb butter. The butter will melt into the sauce.

Barbecued Chicken Legs GF

Ideally these would be cooked in a tandoor oven, but given that Western kitchens aren't equipped with this traditional wood-burning oven, I cook them over a charcoal (or wood-fired) barbecue grill plate, to similar effect. Serve them with lime wedges and mint chutney for added vibrancy.

Serves 4

2 tablespoons ginger garlic paste, see recipe
   page 436
2 tablespoons lime juice
1 teaspoon sea salt flakes
½ teaspoon freshly ground black pepper
8 x chicken legs, skin on
150 g thick plain yoghurt
2 tablespoons mustard oil
1 teaspoon Kashmiri chilli powder
½ teaspoon ground turmeric
1 teaspoon garam masala
½ teaspoon kasoori methi (dried fenugreek
   leaves), see Glossary
lime wedges
mint chutney, to serve, see Pickles and Chutneys
   page 361

Place the ginger garlic paste, lime juice, salt and pepper in tray and mix to combine. Add the chicken and rub with the paste to coat. Set aside for 10 minutes.

Place the yoghurt, mustard oil, spices and kasoori methi in a bowl and mix to combine. Add the chicken and massage the yoghurt into the meat until thoroughly coated. Cover and refrigerate for 2 hours to marinate.

Heat a wood-fired grill plate to hot. Add the chicken and cook for 12 minutes, turning every few minutes, or until slightly charred and cooked through. Serve hot with lime wedges and mint chutney.

Fried Chicken and Carrot Raita GF

Every food culture has their own version of fried chicken, and this Indian rendition doesn't disappoint with its punchy, spicy flavours. Typical of menus in Bangalore and Hyderabad and referred to locally as 'Chicken 65', it's a regional favourite with enormous popularity. Taste it yourself and you'll understand why.

Serves 4

2 tablespoons ginger garlic paste, see recipe
   page 436
2 small green chillies, minced
2 teaspoons Kashmiri chilli powder
1 teaspoon freshly ground black pepper
40 ml lime juice
3 eggs, lightly beaten
600 g chicken tenderloin fillets, halved lengthwise
2 tablespoons rice flour
2 tablespoons cornflour
1 teaspoon sea salt flakes
½ teaspoon chilli powder
1 litre vegetable oil, for deep-frying
2 tablespoons fried curry leaves

CARROT RAITA
2 large carrots, peeled and grated
1 teaspoon cumin seeds
½ teaspoon chilli powder
1 small green chilli, minced
1 teaspoon minced ginger
1 teaspoon sea salt flakes
400 g thick plain yoghurt
1 tablespoon boondi (puffed lentils), see Glossary

To make the carrot raita, blanch the carrot in boiling water for 30 seconds, drain and rinse under cold water. Drain again and squeeze out any excess moisture. This is to ensure the softened carrot is as dry as possible. I use a clean, unused Chux or a piece of muslin cloth to wring out the carrot.

Place the cumin seeds in a frying pan over low heat and cook for 1 minute or until fragrant. Allow to cool before grinding to a fine powder in a spice grinder. Place the carrot and cumin in a bowl with all remaining ingredients and stir gently to just combine. Set aside.

To prepare the chicken, place the ginger garlic paste, green chilli, Kashmiri chilli, ½ teaspoon of the pepper, lime juice and egg in a bowl and stir to combine. Add the chicken strips, cover and refrigerate for 1 hour to marinate. Remove chicken from the marinade, shaking off excess liquid (I use a large sieve for this) and discard marinade.

Place the rice flour, cornflour, remaining pepper, salt, and chilli powder in a bowl and stir to combine. Add the chicken and toss to finely coat in the flour. Heat the oil in a deep fryer or deep saucepan to 180°C. Fry the chicken, in small batches, for 4 minutes or until golden and tender. Drain on paper towel. Arrange fried chicken on a plate, top with the fried curry leaves and serve with the carrot raita and pappadams or chapati.

Masala Chicken Livers and Peas GF

The Irani cafes in Mumbai are some of my favourite haunts when I visit the city and these spiced livers are something you'll find on the menu at any of them. Parsi heritage permeates Mumbai's food traditions and this humble but satisfying dish is incredibly delicious. You can make a wrap to enclose the livers using hot, flaky parathas or roti, or serve them on toast as the English would. Otherwise, in the true Parsi tradition, serve them with a warm, soft milk bun.

Serves 4

75 ml buttermilk
1 tablespoon ginger garlic paste, see recipe
  page 436
½ teaspoon ground cumin
½ teaspoon ground turmeric
1 teaspoon hot chilli powder
1 teaspoon garam masala
1 teaspoon sea salt flakes
400 g chicken livers
2 tablespoons ghee
2 garlic cloves, finely sliced
4 tablespoons cooked green peas
2 teaspoons lime juice
1 teaspoon roasted rice, ground
2 tablespoons shredded coriander leaves
1 tablespoon fried curry leaves

Place the buttermilk, ginger garlic paste, ground spices and salt in a bowl and stir to combine.

Trim the livers, removing the connective tissue. Cut each liver into 2 lobes and add to the buttermilk mixture. Cover and refrigerate for 30 minutes to marinate.

Remove livers from the fridge and return to room temperature for 10 minutes before cooking. Melt the ghee in a frying pan over medium heat, add the garlic and cook for 20 seconds or until softened and starting to colour. Add the livers with the marinade, toss the pan over the heat, and cook, stirring occasionally, for 3–4 minutes or until livers are just cooked with a slight rosy-pink centre. They taste so much better when not overcooked and their texture is more yielding. Remove from heat and stir through the cooked peas, lime juice, ground rice, coriander and fried curry leaves. Serve with hot roti, paratha or soft white buns (*pau*).

Saffron Yoghurt Baked Quails GF

A Mughal-inspired dish rich in spices and perfumed with heady saffron, the quails here are given a delicious tanginess thanks to a yoghurt bath ahead of baking. The Persian influence on India's food culture is manifest in the Mughal legacy of the royal courts and has contributed enormously to the culinary customs of India today.

Serves 6

6 x jumbo (large) quails
⅓ cup (80 ml) cream
2 teaspoons saffron threads
¼ cup (60 ml) ghee
3 red shallots, finely diced
3 garlic cloves, minced or crushed
1 teaspoon Kashmiri chilli powder
½ teaspoon ground turmeric
½ teaspoon freshly ground black pepper
½ teaspoon ground cardamom
¼ teaspoon ground cloves
2 teaspoons sea salt flakes
300 g thick plain yoghurt
1 tablespoon lemon juice
3 tablespoons fried shallot slices, see Glossary
lemon rice, to serve, see Rice page 306

Split the quails along the backbone to butterfly and place in a single layer in a snug-fitting baking dish. Set aside.

Heat the cream in a small saucepan over low heat to simmering point. Stir in the saffron, remove from heat and set aside to infuse for 15 minutes.

Melt the ghee in a frying pan over medium heat. Once it starts to melt, stir in the shallot and garlic and cook, stirring occasionally, for 8 minutes or until starting to become golden. Add the ground spices and salt, stir to combine and continue to cook for a further 2 minutes or until fragrant. Add the saffron cream and stir to combine. Remove from heat and allow to cool to room temperature. Once cool, add the yoghurt and pour over the quails. Cover and refrigerate for 1 hour to marinate. Allow to return to room temperature for 30 minutes before cooking.

Preheat oven to 200°C. Remove the quails and marinade from their baking dish. Wash the dish and line with baking paper. Return quails to the dish, side-by-side in a single layer, and pour over the marinade. Drizzle with the lemon juice and roast for 14 minutes or until slightly pink and juicy in the centre. Remove from oven and set aside to rest for 5 minutes. Cut each quail in half along the breastbone. Arrange on plates, top with fried shallots and serve with lemon rice.

Yoghurt Baked Duck GF

A heritage favourite from a Rajasthani friend of mine, this has been a treasured recipe across generations. If you can't find or prefer not to cook duck, this recipe is made just as easily with chicken.

Serves 4

4 x 180 g duck marylands
170 ml mustard oil
2 teaspoons freshly minced garlic
1 red onion, finely diced
1 tablespoon white vinegar
2 tablespoons freshly chopped coriander leaves
1 teaspoon freshly minced green chilli

YOGHURT MARINADE
2 tablespoons mustard oil
1 tablespoon Kashmiri chilli powder
1 tablespoon ground coriander
2 teaspoons ground turmeric
2 teaspoons sea salt flakes
2 tablespoons ginger garlic paste, see recipe
   page 436
225 g thick plain yoghurt
75 ml buttermilk

To make the yoghurt marinade, place all the ingredients together in a bowl and mix to combine. Massage the marinade into the duck until thoroughly coated. Set aside for 30 minutes.

Heat the mustard oil in a large, deep saucepan over medium heat. Add the garlic and onion and cook, stirring, for 3 minutes or until softened and starting to colour. Add the duck with the marinade and 100 ml water and stir to combine. Cover with a lid, reduce heat to low and simmer for 25 minutes. Turn the duck pieces over in the gravy and cook for a further 25 minutes or until cooked. You may need to add a little extra water if the gravy dries out too much. Remove lid, add the vinegar and cook for 2–3 minutes. Remove from heat and stir through the coriander and chilli. Serve with chapati or roti.

Rajasthani-style Roast Chicken GF

This is nothing short of good, old-fashioned Indian-style comfort food that's easy to prepare and full of flavour. I collected this family recipe many years ago when travelling through the Rajasthani outback. Roast chicken never looked or tasted so good!

Serves 4

1.5 kg whole chicken, butterflied
1 tablespoon mustard oil
1 red onion, sliced
1 tablespoon white vinegar
2 tablespoons shredded coriander leaves
2 small green chillies, finely sliced
cardamom and onion pulao, to serve,
    see Rice page 305

MARINADE
2 tablespoons mustard oil
2 tablespoons ginger garlic paste, see recipe
    page 436
250 g thick plain yoghurt
2 teaspoons Kashmiri chilli powder
2 teaspoons ground coriander
1 teaspoon ground turmeric

Preheat oven to 200°C. Place all the marinade ingredients together in a bowl and mix to combine. Massage the marinade into both sides of the chicken. Set aside for 30 minutes.

Heat the oil in a cast-iron baking dish that comfortably fits the chicken over medium heat. Add the onion and cook for 5 minutes or until softened. Add the vinegar and stir to combine. Arrange the chicken with its marinade, skin side-up, on top of the onion and roast for 35–40 minutes or until cooked through and golden. Remove from oven and set aside to rest for 10 minutes to allow the juices to settle. Joint the chicken, slice the breast fillets in half and arrange on a serving plate. Top with coriander leaves and green chilli and serve with cardamom and onion pulao or a salad of bitter greens (such as rocket, dandelion, radicchio, chicory).

Goan Roast Suckling Pork DF, GF

Goans love their pork. It's an everyday meat thanks to their Portuguese heritage and its enduring influence on the food customs of their tiny coastal state.

Serves 6

1.2 kg suckling pork belly
2 teaspoons sea salt flakes
2 teaspoons fennel seeds, roasted and ground
1 teaspoon freshly ground black pepper
1 tablespoon honey

MARINADE
1 teaspoon chilli powder
1 teaspoon ground cumin
½ teaspoon ground turmeric
2 tablespoons ginger garlic paste, see recipe
  page 436
1 teaspoon sea salt flakes
2 tablespoons lemon juice
1 tablespoon coconut (or rice) vinegar

Score the skin of the pork belly with a sharp knife at 1 cm intervals, being careful to not cut right through to the fat layer. Place the pork in a deep baking dish, skin side-up, and pour over 3 cups (750 ml) boiling water. This will help to make the crackling crisp during the cooking process. Lift the pork out, discard the water and return pork to the dish skin side-down. Prick the flesh (not the skin) with a fork to allow the marinade to penetrate the meat more thoroughly. Set aside.

To make the marinade, place all the ingredients and 1 tablespoon water in bowl and use a stick blender to make a paste. Rub the marinade liberally all over the pork flesh, but not the skin. Place the pork, skin side-up, in a baking dish that fits the pork comfortably and refrigerate, uncovered, overnight. This helps the skin to dry out, making for crisp crackling.

Preheat oven to 150°C. Remove the pork from the refrigerator and bring to room temperature for 1 hour before you start cooking.

Place the salt, ground fennel and pepper in a bowl and mix to combine. Rub liberally over the pork skin. Pour 1 cup (250 ml) boiling water into the baking dish, being careful not to splash the skin.

Transfer dish to the centre shelf in oven and roast for 2 hours. Increase oven temperature to 220°C, check if a little more water is needed to prevent the meat from drying out and roast for a further 25–30 minutes or until pork is cooked and the crackling is crisp and golden.

Remove pork from oven and allow to rest in a warm place for 15 minutes. You can cover with foil at this stage. Lift pork from the tray and transfer to a chopping board. Remove any excess fat from the pan juices and pour the juices into a saucepan. Place the saucepan over high heat, add the honey and bring to the boil. Cook for 2–3 minutes or until reduced and thickened. Cut the pork into thick slices and drizzle with the sauce to serve.

Hot and Spicy Lamb Ribs DF, GF

The glaze on these ribs has the consistency of a reduced sauce, making it stick to the meat for an unctuous and finger-licking meal. This dish is great served simply with tomato rice. You can substitute the lamb for suckling pork spareribs, they work equally well with the glaze, but you may need to adjust the cooking time slightly. Ask your butcher to cut the lamb ribs into single pieces for you.

Serves 6

1 tablespoon ground coriander
½ teaspoon garam masala
2 teaspoons ground ginger
2 teaspoons freshly ground black pepper
1 teaspoon ground fennel
1 teaspoon hot chilli powder
2 garlic cloves, crushed
1 teaspoon sea salt flakes
1 tablespoon lime juice
1 kg lamb spareribs
½ cup (75 g) chickpea (besan) flour
2 tablespoons cornflour
600 ml vegetable oil, for deep-frying
1 long red chilli, finely sliced
1 tablespoon shredded coriander leaves
tomato rice, to serve, see Rice page 308

TAMARIND GLAZE
¼ cup (60 ml) vegetable oil
3 teaspoons black mustard seeds
2 tablespoons minced fresh ginger
6 small red chillies, minced
200 ml tamarind puree
180 g brown sugar

To make the tamarind glaze, heat the oil in a frying pan over medium heat. Add the mustard seeds and cook for 20 seconds. When they start to pop, add the ginger and chilli and toss to combine. Add the tamarind and sugar with ½ cup (125 ml) water and bring to the boil. Reduce heat to low and cook for 5 minutes or until reduced slightly and mixture coats the back of a spoon. Season with salt and set aside.

To prepare the ribs, place the ground spices, garlic, salt and lime juice in a bowl and mix to combine. Rub the spice mixture liberally over the ribs to coat and set aside for 15 minutes.

Mix the chickpea flour and cornflour in bowl and dust the ribs to lightly coat, shaking off any excess. Heat the oil in a wok or large saucepan to 160°C. Fry the ribs, in batches, for 6 minutes or until crisp, golden and cooked through. Set aside and keep warm.

Heat the tamarind glaze in a wide-based frying pan over medium heat. When the glaze starts to bubble, add the fried ribs in single layer, making sure each rib is coated with the glaze, and cook for 5 minutes or until sticky. Top with chilli and coriander and serve with tomato rice.

Spiced Lamb and Mushrooms in Yoghurt Gravy GF

Yakhni, meaning 'cooked in yoghurt', is a typical Hindu preparation that I learnt from one of my Kashmiri Pandit acquaintances in Srinagar. Here the meat is fragrant with aromatic spices and simmered in a yoghurt gravy, which gives a gentle tang and intoxicating depth of flavour to the lamb. Morel mushrooms grow wild in the hills of Kashmir and add a wonderful earthy richness to the gravy. I love this recipe because it's both simple and satisfying.

Serves 6

100 ml mustard oil
1 cinnamon stick
2 bay leaves
2 black cardamom pods, cracked
3 green cardamom pods, cracked
3 cloves
1 kg lamb shoulder, off the bone and cut into
    4 cm dice
1 tablespoon ground fennel
2 teaspoons ground ginger
2 teaspoons sea salt flakes
1 litre meat stock (or water)
10 g dried morel mushrooms, soaked in ½ cup
    (125 ml) cold water for 30 minutes to soften
650 g thick plain yoghurt, whisked
3 teaspoons cornflour
½ teaspoon ground cardamom
1 teaspoon black cumin (shah jeera) seeds
saffron rice, to serve, see Rice page 306

Heat the oil in a large, heavy based pan over medium–high heat. Add the cinnamon, bay leaves, black and green cardamom pods and cloves and cook for 30 seconds or until fragrant. Add the lamb, stir to combine and cook, stirring frequently, for 6 minutes. Add the ground fennel, ginger and salt and stir to combine. Add the stock (or water) and bring to the boil. Reduce heat to low and cook for 40 minutes or until lamb is tender, adding a little extra water if necessary to prevent it from drying out. Remove lamb from the pan and set aside. Discard the whole spices.

Increase heat to medium and return the sauce to the boil. Add the softened morel mushrooms with their soaking water and cook for 5 minutes. Stir the whisked yoghurt into the gravy and return to the boil again, stirring continuously. In a small bowl mix the cornflour with 1 tablespoon cold water and whisk into the yoghurt gravy (this will thicken the gravy). Cook for 15 minutes or until thickened. Return the cooked lamb to the pan with the ground cardamom, stir thoroughly to combine and cook for a further 5 minutes. Sprinkle over the black cumin seeds and serve with saffron rice.

Slow-braised Kid in Cashew Coconut Gravy DF, GF

White kid gosht is one of the most revered dishes in Parsi cuisine. The preparation of the baby goat (or kid) slow-cooked in a masala-rich cashew and coconut gravy elevates this dish to top ranking at a Parsi wedding, as I've experienced first-hand. It is totally acceptable to use lamb instead of goat meat, if you prefer, and to be honest, it's a lot easier to procure on an everyday basis. Serve with steamed rice or roti.

Serves 6

3 tablespoons ginger garlic paste, see recipe
   page 436
2 teaspoons cumin seeds, roasted and ground
1 kg kid goat (or lamb) meat, cut into 4 cm pieces
¼ cup (60 ml) vegetable oil
3 white onions, finely diced
5 black cardamom pods, cracked
6 cloves
1 cinnamon stick
4 dried chillies, broken into pieces
2 teaspoons sea salt flakes
150 g potato, peeled and cut into 3 cm pieces
90 g raw cashews, soaked in cold water for
   30 minutes, drained
1 cup (250 ml) coconut milk

Mix to combine the ginger garlic paste and cumin together in a small bowl and rub into the meat. Set aside to marinate for 1 hour.

Heat the oil in a large frying pan over medium–high heat. Add the onion, cardamom, cloves, cinnamon and chilli and cook for 6–7 minutes or until onion is softened and just starting to colour. Reduce heat to low, add the marinated meat and cook for 20 minutes or until any water has evaporated. Add 1 cup (250 ml) water with the salt and cook for a further 25 minutes. Add the potato and another ½ cup (125 ml) water and continue to cook for 15 minutes or until potato is slightly firm in the centre but still holding its shape.

Meanwhile, blend the softened cashews and coconut milk in a food processor to make a paste. When the potato is almost tender, add the cashew paste to the sauce and continue to cook for 10 minutes or until the meat and potato are both tender. Check seasoning, adding a little extra salt, if necessary. Serve with white basmati rice, roti or bread.

Masala Lamb Cutlets and Kachumber Salsa GF

These cutlets, lathered in a gently spiced yoghurt marinade, give an added dimension to the cooked chop. Add this fresh and zesty salsa and you have a dish that delivers a large reward for very little effort.

Serves 4

1 teaspoon ground mace
1 teaspoon ground cardamom
1 teaspoon ground fennel seeds
1 tablespoon minced ginger
3 garlic cloves, chopped
½ bunch coriander, leaves and stalks chopped
3 tablespoons lime juice
1 teaspoon Kashmiri chilli powder
½ teaspoon ground turmeric
1 teaspoon sea salt flakes
12 French-trimmed lamb cutlets
¼ teaspoon saffron threads
3 tablespoons thick plain yoghurt
1 tablespoon grapeseed oil

KACHUMBER SALSA
2 ripe tomatoes, seeded and diced
3 tablespoons finely diced cucumber
1 small red onion, finely diced
1 small green chilli, finely sliced
2 tablespoons shredded coriander leaves
½ teaspoon black salt, see Glossary
2 tablespoons lime juice

Place the mace, cardamom and fennel in a bowl and mix together to make a garam masala. Place the ginger, garlic and coriander in a food processor with 1 tablespoon water and blend to make a paste. Add the garam masala, lime juice, chilli powder, turmeric and salt and blend to combine. Rub spice mixture over the lamb cutlets to coat. Cover and refrigerate for 1 hour to marinate.

Place the saffron in a small cup with 1 tablespoon boiling water and set aside to cool and infuse for 15 minutes. Stir the cooled saffron water into the yoghurt. Add the yoghurt to the lamb and mix to thoroughly coat, rubbing liberally over the meat. Set lamb aside at room temperature for 30 minutes.

Preheat oven to 180°C. Line a baking tray with baking paper. To make the kachumber salsa, place all the ingredients in a bowl and mix well to combine. Set aside.

Heat a frying pan over high heat. Add the oil and lamb and cook, in batches, taking care not to overload the pan, for 1 minute on each side to seal. Transfer cutlets to the prepared baking tray and arrange in a single layer. Roast for 3 minutes or until still pink in the centre. Allow to rest for 5 minutes for the juices to settle. Scatter the kachumber salsa over the cutlets to serve.

Savoury Mince and Potatoes GF

This recipe has been cooked for me numerous times by Parsi friends. It's a nod to the food legacy left by the British, where savoury mince, called *kheema*, is the epitome of comfort food and a staple for the thrifty cook. I have used lamb, but this recipe can just as easily be made with minced beef or chicken. In strict adherence to tradition, the meat is chopped by hand, as it's believed this yields a superior texture and flavour.

Serves 6

2 tablespoons ghee
2 red onions, finely diced
2 tablespoons ginger garlic paste, see recipe
    page 436
3 small green chillies, minced
1½ teaspoons ground turmeric
2 teaspoons ground cumin
1 teaspoon freshly ground black pepper
2 teaspoons sea salt flakes
800 g coarse lamb mince
200 g potatoes, peeled and cut into 1 cm dice
½ cup shelled green peas
2 tomatoes, seeded and diced
2 teaspoons caster sugar
2 tablespoons lime juice

Melt the ghee in large frying pan over medium heat. Add the onion and cook for 5 minutes or until starting to brown. Add the ginger garlic paste, chilli, ground spices and salt and cook, stirring, for 1 minute. Add the lamb and continue to cook, stirring to break up any lumps, for 5 minutes or until brown. Add 400 ml water and simmer for a further 5 minutes. Add the potato and cook for 8–10 minutes or until al dente. Add the peas and tomato, stir to combine and cook for a further 4–5 minutes. If the mixture becomes too dry, add a splash of water. Remove from heat and stir through the sugar and lime juice. Serve with soft white buns (*pau*) or on toast.

Sesame and Chilli Beef Kebabs GF

This is a hearty snack typical of the Muslim and Buddhist communities of the mountains. You'll often find these kebabs served from a roadside vendor at truck stops along the highways of the north.

Serves 6

800 g beef strip loin, trimmed
⅓ cup (80 ml) mustard oil
2 tablespoons ginger garlic paste, see recipe
    page 436
1 teaspoon sea salt flakes
1 teaspoon dried chilli flakes
2 tablespoons white sesame seeds
1 tablespoon white poppy seeds
1 teaspoon cumin seeds
1 teaspoon coriander seeds
2 tablespoons desiccated coconut
125 g thick plain yoghurt
½ teaspoon freshly ground black pepper
1 teaspoon garam masala
mint yoghurt chutney, to serve, see Pickles and
    Chutneys page 362

Cut the beef into 6 cm-thick slices then cut each slice into 1 cm-thick strips to make long, thin strips.

Place the oil, ginger garlic paste, salt and chilli flakes in a shallow dish with the beef strips and toss to coat. Place the sesame and poppy seeds, cumin seeds, coriander seeds and coconut in a spice grinder and grind to make a fine powder. Place in a bowl with the yoghurt, pepper and garam masala and mix to combine. Pour the spiced yoghurt over the beef and stir to coat the beef. Cover and refrigerate for 2 hours.

Thread the meat onto metal skewers. Using 2 beef slices per skewer, bunch the meat up so it's compacted. The meat should sit just at the pointed end of the skewer, so it's easy to remove once cooked.

Preheat a grill plate over hot coals or barbecue plate to high heat and cook the skewers for 3 minutes. Turn and cook for a further 3 minutes. Serve hot with chapati or parathas and mint yoghurt chutney.

Dry Fried Beef and Coconut DF, GF

This recipe's Malayalam name, *ulathiya irachi*, translates to the rather dull-sounding 'beef fry', but this dish is anything but boring. In the Kerala community, beef is widely used and this popular Syrian-Christian dish imparts an extra layer of flavour thanks to coconut oil. You'll find its satisfying taste develops even more after a couple of days and it reheats quite easily. Instead of using a pressure cooker, as is the usual practice, I steam the beef first with the spices to keep it succulent. As an alternative to rice or *idli* (steamed rice cakes), I've tossed the beef through soft rice noodles with green beans.

Serves 4

1 teaspoon ground fennel
¼ teaspoon ground cloves
2 teaspoons ground chilli
1 teaspoon ground turmeric
1 tablespoon ground coriander
1 teaspoon ground cinnamon
3 tablespoons ginger garlic paste, see recipe
    page 436
4 golden shallots, finely diced
3 small green chillies, minced
3 teaspoons sea salt flakes
50 ml coconut cream
500 g beef sirloin, cut into 2 cm strips
50 ml coconut oil
2 spring onion bulbs, finely sliced lengthwise
2 tablespoons fresh curry leaves
1 cup shredded fresh coconut
100 g green beans, finely sliced and blanched
160 g fresh rice noodles, softened in boiling water
    and drained

Place the ground spices together in a wide bowl and mix to combine. Add the ginger garlic paste, shallot, chilli, salt and coconut cream to the spice mix and stir well to combine. Add the beef and mix to thoroughly coat. Cover and set aside to marinate for 20 minutes.

Place the bowl in a bamboo steamer, cover, and steam for 30 minutes. Remove from heat, transfer beef to a wire rack over a tray and allow to cool and dry out for 1 hour at room temperature.

Heat the oil in a wok or a large frying pan over medium–high heat. Add the spring onion and cook for 1 minute or until beginning to colour. Add the curry leaves and when they start to pop, add the beef and cook for 2–3 minutes, tossing the wok to prevent the beef from sticking or burning. Add the shredded coconut, beans and noodles and toss gently to combine. Remove from heat and divide between bowls to serve.

Minute Steak and Curry Butter GF

This is not a recipe you're likely to find anywhere in India. I've taken the liberty of cooking steak and chips through an Indian lens, using the essential spicy characteristics of the cuisine but with a Western twist. The slab of curry butter melts and seasons the cooked meat just as café de Paris butter does in the French tradition – it's the exact same principle. Serving the steak with gunpowder potatoes (see page 154) gives the dish an enviable depth of flavour, making good use of the aromatic spice blend common to the cooking of Andhra Pradesh.

Serves 4

600 g scotch fillet
3 tablespoons vegetable oil
½ teaspoon sea salt flakes
1 teaspoon ground coriander
½ teaspoon freshly ground black pepper
gunpowder potatoes, to serve, see Vegetables
    page 154

CURRY BUTTER
120 g unsalted butter, softened
2 teaspoons lemon juice
2 garlic cloves, minced
2 teaspoons mild curry powder
2 teaspoons sea salt flakes
1 teaspoon freshly ground black pepper

To make the curry butter, place all the ingredients in a food processor and blend until thoroughly combined. Spoon the butter onto a long sheet of plastic wrap, spreading across the centre. Roll into a cylinder and tie both ends to seal. Refrigerate for 3 hours or until firm.

To prepare the steak, cut the fillet into 4 equal-size portions across the grain and pound each piece with a meat mallet on both sides until 6 mm-thick. Brush the meat with oil and season generously with salt, coriander and pepper.

When you're ready to cook, heat a cast-iron skillet over high heat. When the skillet is very hot, cook the steaks, 2 at a time, making sure they don't overlap in the pan, on both sides for 1 minute before transferring to a warm tray. If your pan is small, cook 1 at a time. Allow to rest for 2–3 minutes while you cook the remaining steaks. Divide between plates and top with a slice of curry butter. The butter will slowly melt into the hot meat, creating a sauce. Serve with warm gunpowder potatoes.

Spiced Lamb Kebabs GF

Kebabs (chunks or slices of meat) and kofta (minced meat), marinated with spices and threaded onto skewers then cooked over glowing charcoal embers or in the tandoor oven, are synonymous with Indian cooking. They have a distinct identity and the many variations hold particular allure to so many people. Some of the best kebab shops or roadside vendors I've visited were in the cities of Lucknow, Delhi, Amritsar, Mumbai, Kolkata and Srinagar or along the main arterial highways frequented by long-haul truck drivers. Originating in Persian cuisine, kebabs were elevated to an art form in India by the Mughals many centuries ago and have played a central role to Muslim culinary lore ever since. Serve with flatbread, red onion slices and chutney for a simple feast. I have used lamb meat here, but there's nothing stopping you from using venison, chicken or beef with this spiced yoghurt marinade. If using wooden skewers, soak them in water overnight so they don't burn on the fire.

Serves 4

1 teaspoon garam masala
1 teaspoon ground fennel
1 teaspoon ground turmeric
1 teaspoon Kashmiri chilli powder
1 teaspoon nigella seeds
½ teaspoon saffron threads
1 teaspoon sea salt flakes
2 teaspoons white sesame seeds
1 tablespoon ginger garlic paste, see recipe
    page 436
2 tablespoons chopped coriander leaves
2 teaspoons lime juice
¼ cup (60 ml) vegetable oil, plus extra,
    for brushing
⅓ cup (80 ml) thick plain yoghurt
1 kg lamb leg meat (off the bone), cut into
    3 cm cubes

Start your fire a couple of hours before you'd like to cook, this way you can create the desired heat and a bed of hot coals. Too much flame will scorch the meat and give uneven cooking, so the flames need to die down. Hot coals are sufficient to maintain the heat during cooking.

Place all ingredients, except the lamb, in a bowl and mix to combine. Add the lamb and mix to coat in the marinade. Cover and marinate in the fridge for 1 hour.

Allow lamb to return to room temperature. Thread 2–3 cubes of lamb onto each skewer, depending on the length of the skewers. You need to leave enough room at each end as a handle for turning the kebabs as they cook.

Brush a cast-iron grill plate with vegetable oil and place over the coals, making sure it is elevated above the coals to allow enough air flow and oxygen between the coals and the grill. Arrange the skewers side-by-side on the grill plate and cook for 4–5 minutes or until browned. Carefully turn the skewers and cook on the other side for a further 3–4 minutes or until meat is tender but still rosy in the centre. Set aside to rest for a few minutes to allow juices to settle. Remove the skewers when serving.

Curries

The aroma of roasted spices and heady sauces or gravies as they simmer in the kitchen is enough to whet anyone's appetite. The strong tradition of curry in the culinary repertoire of India is well known and has evolved over the centuries across the world, wherever Indians found their adopted homes. During British colonial rule, curry became the Anglicised name for sauce-based dishes, derived from *kari*, the Tamil word for sauce. The word is still used across many different countries and has simply come to define a dish that has a spicy sauce.

It's vital to remember that curry is not a single dish or flavour. As a genre, it is anything but homogenous. There are no rigid recipes, traditions have been passed down through generations orally without strict written instructions, and each recipe is open to interpretation. But what curry does conjure in the mind, no matter how diverse the interpretation, is flavour.

A curry gravy or sauce can be based on coconut milk, tamarind, pureed nuts, onion or roasted chillies, tomato, buttermilk, yoghurt, cream, stock or water, in addition to the spices and aromatics used to flavour the dish. All these variations are regionally specific, so there exists an almost infinite number of preparations that would fall under the category of curry.

Curries should complement the other dishes served alongside, so when cooking, it's important to consider spiciness, colour, flavour and texture as part of a whole meal. While not all curries are the same, there is a general method to follow when building a curry sauce.

Whole spices and, sometimes, fresh curry leaves, are first fried in hot oil. This process is called tempering and is designed to flavour the oil and cook the seeds. Diced or pureed onion and other aromatics are added next, this lowers the temperature of the oil and prevents the whole spices from burning. The aromatic base is then cooked until softened and starting to colour. Ground spices are added next, as they won't burn at this stage, they're cooked into the base until fragrant. This helps to build the flavours before the liquid is added. Finally, the sauce or gravy is seasoned with salt, a vital inclusion, as it brings out the flavours and creates the desired balance.

Be guided by the different regional curries, whether it's a mild, creamy *korma* or a tangy seafood curry from the Konkan coast; a hot and sour *vindaloo* from Goa; a delicate fish *molee* from Kerala; a fiery *laal maas* meat curry from the Rajasthani desert; a tomato and yoghurt *kadhai*-style curry popular when cooking vegetables; a vibrant rogan josh from Kashmir; or *dhansak*, the intensely aromatic curry of the Parsi community.

Find your own favourite from the broad choice I've offered in this chapter and open your world up to the endless possibilities of curry.

Chicken Kofta Korma

This is a typical, gently spiced curry of Kashmir and Punjab in the north, where the addition of cream is common practice. Meatballs or *koftas* are made in every region of India and usually cooked over hot coals, but these lightly spiced ones are simmered in their gravy for a more delicate, softer texture. The korma is very adaptable, so if you don't have time to make koftas, you can easily make this curry with diced chicken or potatoes.

Serves 6

70 g ghee
1 teaspoon black mustard seeds
2 white onions, finely sliced
½ teaspoon dried chilli flakes
2 tablespoons ginger garlic paste, see recipe
    page 436
1 teaspoon ground turmeric
1 teaspoon ground coriander
60 g thick plain yoghurt
½ cup (125 ml) pouring cream
2 teaspoons sea salt flakes
2 tablespoons almond meal
1 tablespoon flaked almonds, toasted

CHICKEN KOFTAS
600 g chicken thigh fillets, minced
1 white onion, grated, excess juice squeezed out
2 tablespoons ginger garlic paste, see recipe
    page 436
125 g fresh white breadcrumbs
2 eggs, lightly beaten
2 teaspoons sea salt flakes
1 teaspoon freshly ground black pepper
1 teaspoon ground coriander
½ teaspoon ground cardamom
½ teaspoon ground nutmeg
1 tablespoon chopped coriander leaves
1 tablespoon chopped mint

To make the koftas, mix all the ingredients together in a large bowl. Using your fingers, work the mixture well until thoroughly combined. Using wet hands (have a small bowl of cool water beside you), roll the mixture into small, 3 cm-diameter balls. Place balls in a single layer on baking paper, cover and refrigerate until ready to cook.

To make the curry, melt the ghee in a large, heavy-based pan over medium heat. Add the mustard seeds and cook until they start to pop. Add the onion and cook for 4 minutes or until softened. Add the chilli flakes and continue to cook, stirring frequently, for 5 minutes or until onion is starting to brown. Add the ginger garlic paste and cook for a further 2 minutes or until fragrant. Add the ground spices and yoghurt and cook for 3 minutes. Stir through the cream and salt with 1 cup (250 ml) water and bring to the boil. Reduce heat to low and simmer, uncovered, for 10 minutes. Stir in the almond meal and cook for a further 3 minutes or until thickened. Add the koftas to the gravy and stir to coat. Cover with a lid and simmer, turning halfway through, for 15 minutes or until koftas are cooked. Garnish with flaked almonds and serve hot with parathas.

Masterclass step-by-step Chicken Kofta Korma ➔

1

Melt the ghee in a large pan over medium heat. Add the mustard seeds and cook until they start to pop.

2

Add the onion and cook for 4 minutes. Add the chilli flakes and cook for 5 minutes.

3

Add the ginger garlic paste and cook for 2 minutes or until fragrant.

4

Add the ground spices and stir to combine.

5

Add the yoghurt.

6

Add the cream and salt and cook for 3 minutes.

7

Add 1 cup (250 ml) water and bring to the boil.

8

Reduce heat to low and simmer for 10 minutes. Add the almond meal.

9

Cook for 3 minutes or until thickened.

10

Meanwhile, mix all ingredients in a bowl to make koftas.

11

Using wet hands, roll the mixture into 3 cm balls and place in a single layer on baking paper.

12

Add the koftas to the gravy and stir to coat.

13

Cover with a lid and simmer, turning halfway through, for 15 minutes or until cooked.

14

Garnish with flaked almonds and serve with hot parathas.

Curried Potatoes GF, V

Of Bengali origins, *alur dum* is a simple, dry-style curry using everyday ingredients that would be found in any humble kitchen pantry. Small, new season potatoes are ideal for this dish.

Serves 4

4 tablespoons ghee
2 bay leaves
2 cm cinnamon stick, broken into small pieces
4 green cardamom pods, crushed
4 cloves
3 tomatoes, seeded and diced
1 kg small chat potatoes, boiled and peeled
½ teaspoon sea salt flakes

SPICE MIX
1 tablespoon ground coriander
3 tablespoons ground cumin
1 tablespoon freshly ground black pepper
¼ teaspoon ground turmeric
2 teaspoons sea salt flakes
2 teaspoons white sugar

To make the spice mix, combine all ingredients in a small bowl and mix thoroughly. Store in an airtight container for up to 1 week and use as required. Mix 4 tablespoons of the prepared spice mix in a bowl with enough water to make a paste. Set aside.

Heat the ghee in a frying pan over medium heat. Add the bay leaves and whole spices and cook for 1 minute. Add the prepared spice paste and cook for a further 2 minutes or until fragrant, but not burning. Add the tomato and cook until softened and broken down. Add 1 cup (250 ml) water and bring to the boil. Add the boiled potatoes and continue to boil for 4 minutes. Reduce heat to low, cover with a lid and simmer until most of the water has been absorbed. Season with salt and serve with *puri* (deep-fried flatbreads) or rice.

Potato and Cauliflower Curry GF, V

This curry originates from the holy city of Varanasi. It follows the principals of the Ayurvedic Satvik Khana diet, which promotes calmness, purity and balance by omitting the use of onion and garlic and using spices sparingly.

Serves 4

⅓ cup (80 ml) mustard oil
250 g cauliflower florets
2 cloves
3 green cardamom pods, cracked
2 teaspoons minced ginger
12 fresh curry leaves
300 g potato, peeled, diced and parboiled
1 teaspoon ground turmeric
½ teaspoon ground cinnamon
½ teaspoon chilli powder
2 teaspoons sea salt flakes
1 teaspoon caster sugar
3 tomatoes, seeded and diced
150 g thick plain yoghurt
½ teaspoon garam masala
1 tablespoon roughly chopped mint leaves
1 tablespoon roughly chopped coriander leaves

Heat half the oil in large frying pan over high heat. Add the cauliflower and cook, tossing the pan frequently for even cooking, for 2 minutes or until just starting to colour. Remove cauliflower from the pan with a slotted spoon.

In same pan, add the remaining oil, cloves, cardamom, ginger and curry leaves and cook for 30 seconds or until fragrant. Add the potato, toss to combine, and return the cauliflower to the pan. Add the ground spices, salt and sugar and toss to coat the vegetables with the spices. Add 2 cups (500 ml) water and bring to the boil. Once boiling, reduce heat to medium–low, add the tomato and simmer for 6–8 minutes or until potato is soft and liquid has reduced. If the gravy becomes too dry, add a little extra water. Stir through the yoghurt and simmer for 2 minutes. Remove from heat and season with garam masala. Sprinkle with the chopped herbs to serve.

➜

Pumpkin Curry GF, V

The natural sweetness of pumpkin balanced with warming, aromatic spices makes this dish wonderfully nourishing and comforting.

Serves 6

2 small dried chillies, broken into pieces
1 teaspoon coriander seeds
1 teaspoon cumin seeds
2 tablespoons ghee
3 tablespoons toor dal (yellow split lentils), washed
2 teaspoons brown mustard seeds
20 fresh curry leaves
½ teaspoon fenugreek seeds
3 garlic cloves, minced
1 small green chilli, minced
2 teaspoons minced ginger
1 teaspoon ground turmeric
600 g pumpkin, peeled, seeds removed and cut into 3 cm pieces
2 cups (500 ml) coconut milk
2 teaspoons sea salt flakes
2 tablespoons lemon juice
½ cup coriander leaves

Place the dried chilli, coriander and cumin seeds in a pan over low heat and cook for 2 minutes or until fragrant. Allow to cool before grinding to a fine powder in spice grinder. Set aside.

Heat the ghee in a wide, heavy-based saucepan over medium heat. Add the dal and mustard seeds and cook for 45 seconds or until they start to pop. Add the curry leaves, fenugreek seeds, garlic, green chilli, ginger and turmeric and cook for 2 minutes or until fragrant. Add the pumpkin, coconut milk, roasted spice powder and salt, and gently bring to the boil.

Reduce heat to low, cover with a lid and simmer for 15 minutes or until the pumpkin is soft but still holding its shape. Add the lemon juice and coriander, taste and adjust seasoning if necessary. Serve with steamed rice or parathas.

Coconut Beetroot Curry DF, GF, V

This truly luscious curry from Kerala on the Malabar Coast is rich with coconut milk and fragrant with curry leaves.

Serves 4

6 medium beetroots, unpeeled
2 tablespoons organic extra-virgin coconut oil
2 tablespoons fresh curry leaves
4 small green chillies, finely sliced
1 teaspoon minced ginger
3 red shallots, finely sliced
1 teaspoon ground cumin
¼ cup (60 ml) coconut (or rice) vinegar
2 teaspoons sea salt flakes
2 teaspoons caster sugar
600 ml coconut milk
2 tablespoons fried curry leaves

Cook the beetroot whole in large pot of lightly salted boiling water until al dente. Allow to cool for 10 minutes before peeling the beetroot while still warm. The skins will come away more easily than when cold. I wear disposable gloves when doing this to prevent my hands from discolouring. Cut each beetroot in half lengthwise and cut each half lengthwise again into 6 even-size wedges. Set aside.

Heat the oil in a braising pan over medium heat. Add the curry leaves, chilli, ginger and shallot and cook for 2 minutes or until softened, making sure it doesn't burn. Stir in the cumin and cook for 20 seconds before adding the beetroot. Stir to combine and add the vinegar, salt and sugar. Simmer, stirring continuously, for 1 minute. Add the coconut milk, reduce heat to low and cover with lid. Cook for 10 minutes or until beetroot is tender. Add a little water if sauce reduces too much. Remove from heat, taste and adjust seasoning – it may need extra salt. Scatter with the fried curry leaves and serve with rice.

➜

Mushroom Curry DF, GF, V

Shakti chef, Tika, cooked this curry for me when I was travelling through Sikkim and the eastern Himalayas. In the lush Sikkimese hills, mushrooms are abundant and black cardamom grows prolifically. Both lend this curry – and many dishes of the region – an earthy and slightly smoky flavour.

Serves 4

4 dried morel mushrooms
2 tablespoons vegetable oil
2 black cardamom pods, cracked
2 white onion, finely diced
1 tablespoon ginger garlic paste, see recipe
    page 436
2 teaspoons ground coriander
1 teaspoon ground cumin
2 teaspoons ground turmeric
2 teaspoons Kashmiri chilli powder
2 teaspoons sea salt flakes
2 ripe tomatoes, seeded and diced
400 g mixed mushrooms (oyster, whole shimeji,
    and small, sliced Swiss brown)
1 teaspoon garam masala
3 tablespoons chopped coriander leaves

Soak the morels in ½ cup (125 ml) water for 20 minutes. Remove from water, halve lengthwise and set aside. Reserve the mushroom water for cooking.

Heat the oil in a frying pan over medium heat. Add the black cardamom and onion and cook until softened. Stir in the ginger garlic paste and cook for a further 1–2 minutes or until starting to colour.

Add the ground spices and salt and cook for a further 1 minute. Add the tomato and reserved mushroom water and cook for 2–3 minutes. Add the mixed mushrooms and morels, reduce heat to low and simmer gently for 3–4 minutes or until mushrooms are tender. Remove the black cardamom pods and sprinkle with garam masala and coriander to serve.

Vegetable Buttermilk Curry GF, V

This typical vegetable curry from Tamil Nadu and the south is given a slightly sour flavour from the fenugreek and buttermilk – good for gut health. A generous dollop of gently spiced tamarind chutney adds a little sweetness to balance the flavours and also works to enhance the Ayurvedic properties of the dish.

Serves 4

3 tablespoons coconut oil
2 tablespoons split urad dal (white lentils)
2 teaspoons fenugreek seeds
2 teaspoons coriander seeds
4 dried chillies, broken into pieces
3 tablespoons shredded fresh coconut
1 tablespoon minced ginger
50 ml young coconut water
2 cups (500 ml) buttermilk
1 teaspoon ground turmeric
2 teaspoons sea salt flakes
1 teaspoon black mustard seeds
1 teaspoon cumin seeds
½ teaspoon dried chilli flakes
12 fresh curry leaves
3 small carrots, peeled and sliced diagonally
2 small zucchini, sliced diagonally
100 g fresh green peas
4 teaspoons tamarind chutney, to serve,
    see Pickles and Chutneys page 362

Heat half the coconut oil in a frying pan over medium heat. Add the dal, fenugreek and coriander seeds and dried chilli and cook for 1–2 minutes or until fragrant, ensuring it doesn't burn. Allow to cool then pound in mortar and pestle (or a blender) with the fresh coconut, ginger and coconut water to make a paste. Add to a bowl with the buttermilk, turmeric and salt and stir to combine. Set aside.

Heat the remaining coconut oil in heavy-based pan over medium heat. Add the mustard and cumin seeds and cook for 30 seconds or until they start to pop. Add the chilli flakes and curry leaves and cook a further 20 seconds or until fragrant.

Add the carrot and zucchini, stirring to combine, and cook for 2 minutes. Pour in the buttermilk mixture and simmer until the vegetables are al dente. Add the peas and cook for a further 2 minutes. Check seasoning and add extra salt, if necessary. Divide curry between bowls and serve with tamarind chutney.

Stuffed Potatoes in Tomato Yoghurt Curry v

This recipe is inspired by the rich legacy of the Mughal Empire, which, in turn, influenced the heritage of northern Indian food. Royal cooks of the era devised ingenious and often labour-intensive ways of preparing food, but like this recipe, the rewards were well worth the effort. As with many dishes of that pedigree, this curry is cooked *dum*-style, where a rope of dough is used to tightly seal a pot, enabling the delicious contents to steam gently inside.

Serves 6

12 even-size chat or new potatoes (about the size of an egg), peeled
1 litre vegetable oil, for deep-frying, plus extra 100 ml
1 teaspoon fennel seeds
1 teaspoon nigella seeds
2 small red onions, finely diced
½ teaspoon ground cardamom
75 g raisins
75 g raw cashews
sea salt flakes
1½ cups (225 g) plain flour
2 tablespoons coriander leaves

TOMATO YOGHURT GRAVY
1 tablespoon vegetable oil
1 red onion, finely diced
1 tablespoon ginger garlic paste, see recipe page 436
350 ml thick plain yoghurt
½ cup (125 ml) tomato puree
2 tablespoons blanched almonds, ground to a paste with a little water
1 teaspoon fennel seeds
½ teaspoon ground mace
½ teaspoon ground cardamom
1 tablespoon ground coriander
2 teaspoons ground cumin
¼ teaspoon ground cloves
½ teaspoon nigella seeds
sea salt flakes

To prepare the potatoes, slice one end off each potato, about a quarter of the way down. Using a melon baller, scoop out the centre of each potato, ensuring the potato walls are not punctured or broken.

Heat the oil in large wok or deep-fryer to 180°C. Fry the potato shells, in batches, until golden. Drain on paper towel. Cook the scooped out centres and potato tops in boiling water for 4 minutes or until softened. Drain and cool slightly before mashing with a fork. Set aside.

Heat the extra 100 ml oil in a wok or kadhai over medium heat. Add the fennel and nigella seeds and cook until fragrant. Add the onion and cook for 3–4 minutes or until transparent. Add the mashed potato, cardamom, raisins and cashews and cook for 2 minutes. Season to taste with salt. Carefully spoon the stuffing into fried potato shells. Set aside.

To make the tomato yoghurt gravy, heat the oil in a deep saucepan over medium heat. Add the onion and cook until softened and just beginning to colour. Add the ginger garlic paste, yoghurt, tomato puree, almond paste and spices and cook, stirring to combine, for 10 minutes or until fragrant. Season with salt. Reduce heat to very low and arrange the stuffed potatoes in single layer in the base of the pan. Spoon over the sauce to coat the potatoes.

Preheat oven to 150°C. To make the dough for sealing the saucepan, mix the flour and 180 ml (¾ cup) water together in bowl until a workable dough forms. If the dough is too wet, add a little extra flour. If too dry, then add a little extra water. Roll the dough out on lightly floured surface into a sausage shape long enough to wrap around the top edge of the saucepan. Cover the saucepan with a lid and wrap the dough around the edge, pressing firmly to seal completely.

Bake the potatoes for 20 minutes. Remove from oven and set aside to rest for 10 minutes. Break the dough seal and discard. Divide the potatoes between plates, strain the gravy through a sieve and spoon over the potatoes. Sprinkle with coriander leaves and serve hot.

Turmeric, Potato and Chickpea Curry GF, V

This is one of my go-to curries for when I'm short on time. It's absolutely fine to use canned chickpeas in this dish – I always keep them in my pantry for when I need to cook something delicious in a hurry. If you prefer to make this recipe dairy-free, simply omit the yoghurt when serving.

Serves 6

2 tablespoons vegetable oil
1 onion, diced
3 garlic cloves, minced
1 tablespoon grated ginger
1 tablespoon grated fresh turmeric
2 cinnamon sticks
1 tablespoon ground cumin
1 tablespoon ground coriander
½ teaspoon Kashmiri chilli powder
1 teaspoon ground turmeric
400 g peeled tomatoes, chopped
400 g cooked chickpeas
600 g potatoes, cooked and diced
3 teaspoons sea salt flakes
100 g baby spinach leaves
2 teaspoons lemon juice
3 tablespoons thick plain yoghurt

Heat the oil in a frying pan over medium–high heat. Add the onion, garlic, ginger and turmeric and cook for 4 minutes or until softened. Add the spices, stir to combine and cook for 2 minutes. Add the tomato and 2 cups (500 ml) water and bring to a simmer. Reduce heat to medium–low, add the chickpeas, potato and salt and simmer for 10 minutes. Fold through the spinach leaves until just-wilted and remove pan from heat. Stir through the lemon juice and check the seasoning. Drizzle with yoghurt to serve.

Tomato Paneer Curry GF, V

I learnt to cook this curry at Shreyas Retreat, an Ayurvedic and yoga retreat in Karnataka. *Mattar paneer* is a staple dish in the kitchens of southern India and also a popular dish in Mumbai's Irani cafes. The tomato masala in this recipe is the foundation for many dishes and can be a lifesaver for last-minute cooking, so I like to make it ahead of time to keep in the fridge. A side dish of kachumber salad makes a great accompaniment to this curry.

Serves 4

200 g paneer, cut into 2 cm cubes
½ teaspoon ground turmeric
½ teaspoon freshly ground black pepper
½ teaspoon sea salt flakes
¼ cup (60 ml) vegetable oil
1 red capsicum, cut into 2 cm diamonds
1 red onion, cut into 2 cm diamonds
120 g fresh green peas
2 tablespoons chopped coriander leaves

TOMATO MASALA
2 tablespoons vegetable oil
½ teaspoon cumin seeds
3 small red onions, finely diced
10 raw cashews
½ teaspoon ground turmeric
2 tablespoons ginger garlic paste, see recipe
  page 436
2 teaspoons sea salt flakes
3 tomatoes, seeded and diced
2 teaspoons ground coriander
1 teaspoon ground cumin
½ teaspoon garam masala
1 teaspoon chilli powder
⅛ teaspoon ground cardamom
⅛ teaspoon ground cinnamon

To make the tomato masala, heat the oil in small frying pan over low heat. Add the cumin seeds and cook for 1 minute or until fragrant. Increase heat to medium, add the onion and cook, stirring, for 10 minutes or until softened and starting to caramelise. Add the cashews, turmeric, ginger garlic paste and 1 teaspoon salt, stir to combine and cook for 2 minutes. Add the tomato and 3 tablespoons water and simmer for 10 minutes or until sauce has thickened slightly. Stir through the coriander, cumin, garam masala, chilli powder and remaining salt and cook for a further 2 minutes. Remove from heat and allow to cool slightly before blending with ½ cup (125 ml) water in a food processor until smooth. Check seasoning, it may need a little extra salt. Set aside.

Season the paneer cubes with turmeric, pepper and salt. Heat half the oil in a frying pan over medium–high heat and fry the paneer, tossing, for 2 minutes or until coloured. Remove from pan and set aside.

Heat the remaining oil in the same pan. Add the capsicum and onion and cook for 4–5 minutes or until softened and starting to colour. Return the paneer to the pan with the green peas and toss to combine.

Meanwhile, in a separate saucepan, reheat the tomato masala. Add the ground cardamom and cinnamon and simmer for 2 minutes. Pour the tomato masala over the paneer mixture and stir gently to thoroughly coat. Remove from heat, sprinkle with coriander and serve with roti or chapati.

Curried Mussels DF, GF

This is a delicious recipe I collected from Thalassery in northern Kerala. Mussels are abundant in this coastal town and appear in many dishes, often with coconut milk as the preferred base for the fragrant sauce.

Serves 4

4 tablespoons organic extra-virgin coconut oil
8 garlic cloves, finely sliced
20 fresh curry leaves
½ teaspoon dried chilli flakes
2 tablespoons finely sliced fresh ginger
2 teaspoons ground turmeric
1 teaspoon freshly ground black pepper
3 teaspoons garam masala
1 cup (250 ml) coconut milk
1 teaspoon sea salt flakes
1 kg live mussels (in their shells), cleaned and
    beards removed
1 teaspoon lime juice
½ cup roughly chopped coriander leaves

Heat the oil in a large saucepan over low heat. Add the garlic, curry leaves and dried chilli and cook for 30 seconds or until fragrant and the garlic is just starting to colour. Add the ginger and cook for a further 30 seconds before stirring through the ground spices. Increase heat to medium, add the coconut milk and salt and bring to the boil. Once boiling, throw in the mussels, cover with a lid and simmer for 3–4 minutes or until mussels have opened. Remove pan from heat, stir through the lime juice and coriander leaves and serve hot with roti or paratha.

Konkan Fish and Eggplant Curry DF, GF

Along the Konkan Coast between Mumbai and Goa, seafood is fresh and plentiful. Every village has a fish market where the women take command and their seafood curries are prized throughout the region for their elegant richness. I like to use ling fillets for this curry as the fish retains its texture and moisture during cooking, but you could just as easily use snapper, hapuka, gurnard or flathead.

Serves 8

1 dried kokum, see Glossary
½ cup (90 g) rice flour
sea salt flakes
freshly ground black pepper
1 kg white fish fillets, trimmed, skin removed and cut into 5 cm pieces
1 litre vegetable oil, for deep-frying
2 x 250 g purple eggplants, cut into 4 cm pieces

CURRY GRAVY

2 tablespoons coconut oil
3 tablespoons brown mustard seeds
3 tablespoons fennel seeds
20 fresh curry leaves
¼ teaspoon dried chilli flakes
1 brown onion, finely sliced lengthwise
1½ tablespoons ginger garlic paste, see recipe page 436
3 small red chillies, minced
1 teaspoon ground turmeric
1 teaspoon Kashmiri chilli powder
1 teaspoon freshly ground black pepper
1 tablespoon sea salt flakes
100 ml tamarind puree
½ cup (125 ml) fresh tomato puree (blend 2 ripe tomatoes)
1½ cups (375 ml) coconut cream
1 long red chilli, halved, deseeded and sliced diagonally
1 long green chilli, halved, deseeded and sliced diagonally
½ cup coriander leaves
¼ cup fried shallot slices, see Glossary
¼ cup fried curry leaves

Soak the kokum in 100 ml water for 30 minutes. Discard kokum and reserve water.

Season the rice flour with a little salt and pepper and dust the fish in the flour to lightly coat, shaking off any excess. Heat the oil in a deep-fryer or large saucepan to 180°C. Fry the fish, in batches, for 2 minutes, taking care not to cook through. Drain on paper towel and set aside. In the same oil, fry the eggplant for 3–4 minutes or until golden. Drain and set aside.

To make the curry gravy, heat the coconut oil in a wide-based pan over low heat. Add the mustard and fennel seeds and cook for 30 seconds or until they start to pop. Add the curry leaves and chilli flakes and cook for 30 seconds. Add the onion and cook for 5 minutes or until softened. Stir through the ginger garlic paste and red chilli and cook, stirring frequently, for 2 minutes or until softened.

Mix together the ground spices and salt in a small bowl. Add to the onion, stir to combine and cook for a further 1 minute or until fragrant. Add the reserved kokum water, tamarind, tomato puree and coconut cream and bring to a simmer. Reduce heat to low and simmer for 5 minutes. Add the red and green chilli, fried fish and eggplant and stir to combine. Cook for a further 5 minutes before removing from heat. Stir through the coriander and garnish with fried shallots and curry leaves. Serve with steamed rice and pappadams.

Kerala Fish Curry DF, GF

This beautifully spiced curry benefits from firm, white fish fillets, such as Spanish mackerel, kingfish, snapper, mahi mahi, bar cod or hapuka, as the texture and moisture works perfectly with the flavours of the sauce.

Serves 4

4 garlic cloves, crushed
1 teaspoon minced fresh turmeric
2 teaspoons minced ginger
4 small green chillies, minced
3 tablespoons coconut oil
1 brown onion, finely sliced
12 fresh curry leaves
2 teaspoons ground turmeric
2 teaspoons ground coriander
1 teaspoon ground cumin
1 teaspoon freshly ground black pepper
¼ teaspoon ground cloves
½ teaspoon ground cardamom
400 ml coconut milk
1 teaspoon sea salt flakes
600 g white fish fillets, skin removed and cut into large pieces
30 ml lime juice, strained
3 tablespoons chopped coriander leaves
3 tablespoons fried curry leaves

Place the garlic, turmeric, ginger and chilli in a blender or food processor with 1 tablespoon of the oil and blend to make a paste. Set aside.

Heat a wok or frying pan over medium heat. Add the remaining oil and onion and cook for 3 minutes or until onion is softened. Add the garlic paste and curry leaves and cook for 2 minutes. Add the ground spices, stir to combine, and cook for a further 2 minutes or until fragrant. Add the coconut milk and salt and gently bring to the boil. Reduce heat to low and simmer for 5 minutes to allow the flavours to infuse. Add the fish and simmer for 4–5 minutes or until just cooked. Season with salt and lime juice. Stir through the coriander leaves and scatter over the fried curry leaves to serve.

Kerala Prawn Curry DF, GF

Nimmy Paul from Fort Kochi in Kerala is one of the city's most treasured home cooks. Cooking dishes from both her Syrian-Christian heritage and her home state, she opens her house to visitors eager to learn the culinary secrets of Kerala. Her recipe for this typical curry is gently flavoured, making an ideal accompaniment to steamed rice and a vegetable thoran. If you're unable to find green mango, simply substitute tomato, instead.

Serves 4

1 kg raw king prawns, peeled and deveined
    (yields 400 g prawn meat)
2 teaspoons ginger paste
1 teaspoon chilli powder
1 teaspoon ground coriander
½ teaspoon ground turmeric
1 teaspoon sea salt flakes
2 tablespoons coconut oil
1 teaspoon black mustard seeds
20 fresh curry leaves
4 red shallots, finely sliced
2 small green chillies, finely sliced
2 teaspoons minced ginger
2 garlic cloves, minced
1 small green mango, peeled and cut into
    2 cm dice
½ cup (125 ml) coconut milk

Mix to combine the prawn meat with the ginger paste and set aside to marinate for 15 minutes. Mix the ground spices and salt in a bowl with just enough water to make a paste. Set aside.

Heat the oil in a frying pan over medium heat. Add the mustard seeds and cook for 20 seconds or until they start to pop. Add the curry leaves and cook for a further 20 seconds. Add the shallot, chilli, minced ginger and garlic and cook for 4 minutes or until softened. Add the spice paste and stir to combine. Reduce heat to low and cook until the oil separates. Stir through ½ cup (125 ml) water to loosen the gravy. Add the mango and cook for 5–6 minutes or until softened. Stir in the prawn meat and cook for a further 4 minutes or until prawn is just cooked. Remove from the heat and stir through the coconut milk to serve.

Goan Prawn Curry DF, GF

It seems every Goan cook has their own version of *ambot tik*, a traditional prawn curry with a soupy gravy. I've had versions from keen home cooks and restaurant chefs alike, but despite their differences, they all have a higher ratio of sauce to prawns. The richness of the coconut milk is cut with the sourness of tamarind and green mango, making it all the more delicious when served with black pepper and cumin brown rice (page 286).

Serves 4

2 tablespoons organic extra-virgin coconut oil
1 white onion, finely diced
1 tablespoon minced ginger
2 ripe tomatoes, finely chopped
2 teaspoons tomato paste
16 large raw tiger prawn tails, peeled and deveined
2 teaspoons sea salt flakes
2 tablespoons tamarind puree
1 small green mango, peeled and julienned
3 small green chillies, finely sliced
2 tablespoons fried curry leaves
black pepper and cumin brown rice, to serve, see Rice page 286

COCONUT MASALA
3 dried Kashmiri chillies, broken into pieces
5 garlic cloves
1 tablespoon ground coriander
1 teaspoon ground cumin
1 teaspoon ground turmeric
1 teaspoon freshly ground black pepper
2/3 cup grated fresh coconut
2 cups (500 ml) coconut milk

To make the coconut masala, blend all the ingredients together in food processor until smooth. Set aside.

Heat the coconut oil in wide-based frying pan or kadhai over medium heat. Add the onion and cook for 5 minutes or until starting to colour. Add the ginger and cook for 1 minute. Add the tomato, tomato paste and ½ cup (125 ml) water and cook for 2–3 minutes or until the tomato begins to break down. Reduce heat to low, stir through the coconut masala and simmer, stirring occasionally, for 10 minutes. Add the prawns and salt and continue to cook for a further 2 minutes. Add the tamarind, green mango and chilli and cook for 2–3 minutes or until prawns are just cooked. Top with fried curry leaves and serve with black pepper and cumin brown rice.

Fish, Coconut Clam Curry and Crab Salsa DF, GF

Despite its deep traditions, Indian cooking can easily lend itself to new interpretations. For this recipe, I've used classic curry flavours with a Western twist, offering another perspective of modern Indian cooking. I like kingfish for this curry, but you can just as easily use bass grouper, snapper or Spanish mackerel. The important thing is to choose a fish with a similar texture that's fresh from the ocean that day.

Serves 6

1 x 800 g kingfish fillet, skin on
2 tablespoons vegetable oil
½ teaspoon sea salt flakes
½ teaspoon freshly ground black pepper
2 tablespoons fried curry leaves

VEGETABLES
2 small Japanese eggplants, cut into 1 cm-thick rounds and deep-fried in hot oil until golden
9 small new potatoes, cooked and halved
1 young coconut, flesh cut into thin lengths (reserve 200 ml coconut water for the curry)
12 oven-roasted cherry tomatoes, halved
3 tablespoons coriander leaves

CRAB AND GREEN MANGO SALSA
90 g cooked blue swimmer (or spanner) crabmeat
¼ small green mango, peeled and sliced into fine matchsticks
1 red shallot, finely sliced
1 tablespoon shredded mint
1 tablespoon shredded coriander
2 tablespoons lemon juice
⅓ cup (80 ml) lemon-infused extra-virgin olive oil
½ teaspoon sea salt flakes
¼ teaspoon freshly ground black pepper
½ teaspoon chaat masala

COCONUT CLAM CURRY
¼ cup (60 ml) vegetable oil
20 g brown onion, diced
20 fresh curry leaves
2 tablespoons minced ginger
6 garlic cloves, minced
2 small red chillies, minced
10 black peppercorns
6 cloves
2 teaspoons fennel seeds
1 teaspoon Kashmiri chilli powder
1 teaspoon coriander seeds
1 teaspoon ground turmeric
400 ml coconut cream
1 tablespoon sea salt flakes

200 ml chicken stock
200 g diced tomato
1 kg clams (or pipis), steamed and removed from shells

To make the crab and green mango salsa, place all the ingredients together in a bowl and toss to combine. Set aside.

To make the coconut clam curry, heat the oil in a large frying pan over medium heat. Add the onion, curry leaves, ginger, garlic and chilli and cook for 4 minutes or until golden. Add the spices and cook until fragrant. Add the coconut cream, salt, stock, tomato, and the 200 ml reserved coconut water from the vegetables and simmer for 25 minutes. When ready to serve, add the clams to the sauce to heat through.

Preheat oven to 200°C. Trim the fish fillet, remove the central blood line and cut the fish into 6 even-size portions (each portion should weigh approximately 75 g). Brush with oil and season with salt and pepper. Heat a heavy-based frying pan over medium–high heat. Add the fish, skin-side down in single layer, and use a fish slice to press down on the fish to prevent it from curling up. The flesh will tighten upon impact with the heat, so a gentle weight on top for the first 30 seconds keeps the fish in even contact with the pan. Cook for 2–3 minutes or until skin is crisp and golden. Turn the fish, transfer pan to the oven and roast for 2–3 minutes or until just cooked through. The cooking time depends on the thickness of fish fillet. Remove from oven and set aside to rest for 2 minutes.

Place the vegetable components together in a bowl and mix to combine. Divide vegetables between plates and ladle the curry over the vegetables, distributing the clams evenly between the plates. Top with the fish, skin-side up. Arrange the crab salsa over the fish and top with fried curry leaves.

Lobster Curry DF, GF

Assuming you have the red masala paste on-hand, this dish demands minimum effort for maximum flavour. Make the sauce in advance and keep it in the fridge, that way, you need only quickly cook the shellfish. It's one of my staples when I don't have much time for elaborate preparation, because the flavours are so immediate and rewarding. You can just as easily substitute the lobster for freshwater marron, crayfish, slipper or bug tails.

Serves 6

150 ml coconut milk
40 ml tomato puree
2 teaspoons sea salt flakes
900 g raw lobster tail meat, deveined
1 tablespoon fried shallot slices, see Glossary
2 tablespoons fried curry leaves

RED MASALA PASTE
2 teaspoons white poppy seeds
200 g grated fresh coconut
1 teaspoon ground fennel seeds
½ ground cinnamon
¼ teaspoon ground cardamom
¼ teaspoon ground cloves
1 teaspoon ground turmeric
1 teaspoon garam masala
1 teaspoon chilli powder
½ cup (125 ml) vegetable oil
1 brown onion, finely diced
1 tablespoon ginger garlic paste, see recipe
  page 436

To make the red masala paste, place the poppy seeds in a frying pan over low heat and cook for 30 seconds. Soak the toasted seeds in water for 20 minutes. Place in a food processor with 50 ml water, the coconut and ground spices and blend to make a paste. Set aside.

Heat the oil in a frying pan over medium–high heat. Add the onion and cook for 5–6 minutes or until softened. Add the ginger garlic paste and cook for a further 2–3 minutes. Stir through the spiced coconut paste, reduce heat to medium–low and cook, stirring occasionally, for 10 minutes or until fragrant. Set aside to cool. Store in an airtight container in the refrigerator for up to 2 weeks or until required.

Preheat oven to 180°C. Place 3 tablespoons of the red masala paste, the coconut milk, tomato puree and salt in a saucepan over medium–high heat. Stir to combine and simmer for 10 minutes. Cut the lobster tail meat evenly into 12 x 75 g crosswise medallions. Lay the lobster in a small baking dish (it should fit the lobster snugly), pour over the masala sauce and cover with foil. Bake for 4–5 minutes or until just cooked. Divide lobster between plates, spoon over the sauce and top with fried shallot and curry leaves. Serve with steamed rice.

Coconut Duck Curry DF, GF

Farmed on the backwaters of Lake Vembanad, ducks are readily available in Kerala, where this unctuous curry originates, going by its local name *naadan thaaravu*. The region's other prized ingredients of coconut, chillies, black pepper and turmeric blend beautifully with the rich duck meat to make for a deeply flavoured dish.

Serves 4

4 tablespoons coconut oil
4 duck marylands, cut into thigh and leg joints
1 tablespoon finely chopped ginger
12 garlic cloves, crushed
1 tablespoon shredded fresh turmeric
20 small red shallots, peeled and chopped
4 small green chillies, sliced
1 tablespoon ground coriander
2 teaspoons ground black pepper
1 tablespoon ground turmeric
1 x 400 g can peeled tomatoes, roughly chopped and juice reserved
400 ml coconut milk
60 g raw cashews
2 teaspoons ground cumin
1 tablespoon sea salt flakes
100 ml coconut cream
½ cup coriander leaves

Heat the coconut oil in a frying pan over medium heat. Add the duck pieces and cook for 4 minutes or until browned. Remove from pan and set aside.

Add the ginger, garlic and fresh turmeric to the pan and cook for 1 minute or until just beginning to colour. Add the shallot and cook for a further 2 minutes or until softened. Add the chilli and toss to combine. Stir in the ground spices and cook for a further 1 minute or until aromatic. Add the tomato with the juice and the coconut milk, increase heat to high and bring to the boil. Return the duck to the pan, cover with a lid, reduce heat to low and braise for 25 minutes or until duck is tender and cooked through.

Soak the cashews in water for 20 minutes or until softened. Blend with a little of the soaking water to make a paste. Add the cashew paste and ground cumin to the duck and cook for 5 minutes. Season with salt. To serve, stir through the coconut cream and coriander leaves and remove from heat – don't allow it to boil. Serve with steamed rice or appam.

Tomato Duck Curry DF, GF

I've enjoyed variations of this curry in both Bengal and Assam, where duck farming is popular. The herds there are generally tended by nomadic tribes and small-scale farmers, meaning the meat is wonderfully full-flavoured. I prefer to use marylands rather than breast meat for this recipe, as the thigh and leg joints give more tenderness and tend not to dry out.

Serves 4

100 ml vegetable oil
½ teaspoon cumin seeds
1 teaspoon black mustard seeds
1 cinnamon stick
2 cloves
4 green cardamom pods
3 white onions, finely sliced
4 small green chillies, minced
1 tablespoon ginger garlic paste, see recipe
    page 436
1 teaspoon chilli powder
1 teaspoon ground turmeric
2 teaspoons ground cumin
4 duck marylands, cut into thigh and leg joints
2 ripe tomatoes, chopped
1 tablespoon tomato paste
1 teaspoon sea salt flakes
1 cup (250 ml) freshly squeezed orange or
    mandarin juice
½ teaspoon garam masala
2 tablespoons chopped coriander leaves

Heat 2 teaspoons of oil in a wide-based frying pan over medium–low heat. Add the whole spices and cook until they start to colour. Add the remaining oil and onion and cook, stirring occasionally to prevent burning, for 10 minutes or until just starting to brown. Add the chilli and ginger garlic paste and cook for 2 minutes or until fragrant. Stir through the chilli powder, turmeric and cumin and cook for a further 1 minute. Add the duck pieces and mix thoroughly with the onion, using tongs to roll the pieces in the pan to coat. Cook for 2–3 minutes before adding the tomato, tomato paste, salt, orange juice and ½ cup (125 ml) water. Bring to the boil and cover with a lid. Reduce heat to low and simmer, turning the duck halfway through cooking, for 45 minutes or until duck is tender. Add a little extra water if the sauce dries out too much. The sauce should cling to the duck when finished, not be too wet. Remove from the heat and discard cinnamon stick. Season with salt and sprinkle with the garam masala. Top with the coriander leaves and serve with chapati.

Black Pepper Chicken and Onion Curry DF, GF

This dish is an enduring favourite from Hyderabad, where black pepper is a prominent seasoning and heavily used in the robust, Andhra-style cooking. Subtlety is not key here, there should be a very obvious pepper kick to this curry, so add a little more if your palate prefers. For extra zing, I like to add a few extra grinds from the pepper mill just as I serve.

Serves 4

1 tablespoon ginger garlic paste, see recipe
    page 436
1 teaspoon sea salt flakes
2 tablespoons lemon juice
2 teaspoons ground turmeric
2 teaspoons ground coriander
1 teaspoon chilli powder
1 tablespoon freshly ground black pepper
4 x 180 g chicken marylands, cut into thigh
    and leg joints
100 ml vegetable oil
2 brown onions, sliced lengthwise
½ cup onion puree (blend 1 white onion
    with 2 tablespoons vegetable oil)
2 tablespoons finely shredded ginger
4 tablespoons coriander leaves, roughly chopped
2 tablespoons fried shallot slices, see Glossary

Place the ginger garlic paste, salt, lemon juice, turmeric, coriander, chilli and half the pepper in a bowl and mix to combine. Rub into the chicken. Place in the fridge to marinate for 2 hours.

Heat the oil in a large frying pan over medium heat. Add the remaining black pepper and the onion and cook, stirring, for 5 minutes or until softened and starting to colour. Reduce heat slightly, stir in the onion puree and cook for a further 10 minutes or until onion is browned. Increase heat to medium–high, add the chicken with its marinade and cook for 5 minutes to remove any excess liquid. Add 1 cup (250 ml) water and simmer, turning the chicken halfway through, for 15 minutes or until chicken is just cooked through. Check seasoning and add a little extra salt, if necessary. Transfer to a serving dish and garnish with shredded ginger, coriander leaves and fried shallots.

Chicken Cashew Curry GF

Made using white meat, cashew paste and yoghurt, this curry has an endearingly mild aroma and pale colour, but still packs a punch with its layered flavours. It was inspired by a southern-style korma curry typical of Tamil Nadu and Karnataka. Don't be stingy with the fried curry leaves, it's a case of the more the better. They bring all the flavours together, so scatter them liberally over the curry before serving.

Serves 8

4 tablespoons raw cashews
1 teaspoon dried chilli flakes
3 tablespoons shredded fresh curry leaves
1 teaspoon chilli powder
1 large dried chilli, broken into small pieces
1 teaspoon freshly ground black pepper
1 teaspoon ground turmeric
1 teaspoon garam masala
1 tablespoon ginger garlic paste, see recipe
   page 436
3 tomatoes, seeded and diced
150 g thick plain yoghurt
1 teaspoon sea salt flakes
1.2 kg chicken thigh fillets, cut into 4 cm pieces
2 tablespoons fried curry leaves

Soak the cashews in 150ml cold water (enough to cover) and set aside to soften for 2 hours. Strain off half the water and place cashews and remaining water in a high-speed blender and process to form a paste. Add the chilli flakes and shredded curry leaves and blend to combine. Set aside.

Place the spices, ginger garlic paste, tomato, yoghurt and salt in a bowl and stir to combine. Add the chicken and mix thoroughly to coat. Set aside to marinate for 30 minutes.

Place the chicken and marinade in a wide-based frying pan over medium heat. Simmer gently for 15 minutes or until marinade has reduced and coated the chicken, it shouldn't be too wet at this stage. Add the cashew paste and cook, stirring, for a further 2–3 minutes or until combined. Remove from heat and sprinkle over the fried curry leaves to serve.

Mysore Chicken Curry GF

I first tasted this southern-style curry, *koli saaru*, in the home kitchens of Mysore (officially, Mysuru), where it's a popular dish. Cooking the chicken on the bone in the gravy makes for a succulent and fragrant result. You'll want to serve this dish with steamed rice or fresh roti to mop up the beautifully aromatic sauce.

Serves 6

6 dried small chillies
1 tablespoon coriander seeds
1 teaspoon cumin seeds
1 teaspoon black peppercorns
100 ml coconut oil
6 whole red shallots, peeled
6 garlic cloves
1 cup shredded fresh coconut
1 teaspoon ground turmeric
¼ cup (60 ml) buttermilk
½ teaspoon fenugreek seeds
2 white onions, finely diced
1 tablespoon fresh curry leaves
6 x 180 g chicken thighs, on bone with skin

Place the dried chillies, coriander seeds, cumin seeds and peppercorns in a cast-iron pan and cook for 3 minutes or until fragrant. Set aside and wipe the pan clean.

Heat 2 tablespoons coconut oil in a separate pan and cook the whole shallots and garlic cloves until softened. Heat the cleaned cast-iron pan over low heat, add the grated coconut and turmeric and cook, without browning, until fragrant. Place all these ingredients together in a food processor and blend to make a paste. Add the buttermilk and mix to combine. Set aside.

Heat another 2 tablespoons of the coconut oil in a frying pan over medium heat. Add the fenugreek seeds and, once they start to change colour, add the onion and cook until just starting to colour. Add the curry leaves and once they start to pop, remove the pan from the heat. Place mixture in a bowl and set aside.

In the same pan, heat the remaining coconut oil over medium heat and cook the chicken, skin-side down, for 3 minutes or until starting to brown. Turn the chicken and return the onion mixture to the pan with the buttermilk paste. Cook, stirring to coat the chicken, for 20 minutes or until chicken is tender. Season with salt and serve with steamed rice.

Pork Vindaloo DF, GF

In the Western world, vindaloo is perhaps one of the most defining dishes of India. Its origins are in Portuguese Goa on the west coast, where the combination of garlic and vinegar give a unique character to the food of the region. The history of this dish is evident in its name, with *vinho* meaning wine and *alho* translating as garlic in Portuguese, both make the basis of this fiery curry sauce. But while the recipe has come to use vinegar instead of wine, it's still made with a heady amount of garlic. With a liberal use of fiery, small chillies, vindaloo is spicy and hot by nature and typically made with pork, an everyday meat in Goa. As it is so rich, it's a good idea to serve small quantities alongside complementary dishes, such as steamed greens and tangy pickles.

Serves 6

1.2 kg pork neck
2 teaspoons ground chilli
1 teaspoon ground cumin
½ teaspoon ground cloves
2 teaspoons freshly ground black pepper
1 teaspoon ground cinnamon
1 teaspoon ground turmeric
½ teaspoon ground cardamom
6 garlic cloves, minced
2 small red chillies, minced
2 teaspoons minced ginger
75 ml coconut vinegar, plus extra 2 tablespoons
75 ml malt vinegar
¼ cup (60 ml) vegetable oil
6 golden shallots, finely sliced
100 ml tamarind liquid
1 litre white chicken stock
3 ripe tomatoes, roughly chopped
1 tablespoon jaggery, shaved
2 teaspoons sea salt flakes
2 tablespoons fried garlic slices

Cut the pork neck in half lengthwise then cut each piece into 4 cm-thick slices.

Place the ground spices, garlic, chilli, ginger and both vinegars in a bowl and stir to combine. Add the pork and set aside to marinate for 30 minutes.

Preheat oven to 160°C. Heat the oil in a baking dish over medium heat on the stovetop. Add the shallot and cook for 3 minutes or until softened and starting to colour. Add the pork with the marinade and cook for 4–5 minutes on both sides. Add the tamarind liquid, stock, tomato and jaggery, cover with a lid and transfer dish to oven. Roast for 90 minutes or until pork is tender.

Remove dish from oven and remove pork from the sauce. Set the pork aside in a warm place. Pour the sauce into a saucepan over high heat and bring to the boil. Cook until reduced by half or until slightly thickened. Season the sauce with the extra coconut vinegar and salt, taste and adjust seasoning, if necessary.

Slice the meat into 2 cm-thick slices, arrange on plates and spoon over the sauce. Sprinkle with fried garlic and serve with steamed basmati rice.

Pork Curry <small>DF, GF</small>

I discovered this aromatic pork curry while travelling through Sikkim in the Himalayas, where the local cooking is simple and rustic, drawing on neighbouring Nepali and Tibetan influences. Pork is a popular meat among the Christian and Buddhist communities of the Himalayas, Goa, Kolkata, Assam, Kerala, and the Coorg (officially Kodagu) region of Karnataka.

Serves 4

2 tablespoons ginger garlic paste, see recipe page 436
2 tablespoons tomato puree
¼ cup (60 ml) vegetable oil
2 teaspoons black mustard seeds
20 fresh curry leaves
2 brown onions, diced
3 small green chillies, halved lengthwise
1 teaspoon ground cumin
1 teaspoon ground turmeric
1 teaspoon Kashmiri chilli powder
800 g pork shoulder, cut into 3 cm pieces
1 tablespoon white vinegar
3 tablespoons chopped coriander leaves

GARAM MASALA
2 teaspoons cumin seeds
2 teaspoons coriander seeds
3 cloves
1 teaspoon fennel seeds
12 black peppercorns
½ teaspoon black mustard seeds
½ teaspoon ground cinnamon

To make the garam masala, place all the spices in a non-stick frying pan over medium heat and toast for 40–50 seconds or until golden and aromatic. Allow to cool before using a spice grinder to grind to a fine powder. Set aside.

Place the ginger garlic paste, tomato puree and 2 teaspoons water in a food processor and blend until a smooth paste forms. Set aside.

Heat the oil in a large braising pan over low heat. Add the mustard seeds and cook for 30 seconds or until they start to pop. Add the curry leaves, onion and chilli and cook, stirring frequently, for 5 minutes or until browned. Add the tomato mixture and ground spices and cook, scraping the bottom of the pan with a wooden spoon to prevent burning, for 10–12 minutes or until reduced and liquid has begun to release its oils.

Increase heat to high, add the pork and cook, stirring occasionally, for 2 minutes or until pork is coated and slightly browned. Add the vinegar, ½ cup (125 ml) water and 3 teaspoons of the garam masala and bring to the boil. Cover, reduce heat to low and simmer, stirring frequently to ensure sauce doesn't dry out, for 2 hours or until pork is tender. If the sauce reduces too much, add a little boiling water. Season with an extra 2 teaspoons garam masala, stir through the coriander and serve with steamed rice.

Rajasthani Goat Curry GF

Laal maas is the definitive curry of the desert region of Rajasthan and a particular favourite of the royal palaces. The goat meat is cooked in thickened yoghurt curd seasoned liberally with red chillies and aromatic spices and is traditionally eaten with chapatis made from wheat or millet, depending on the season. If goat is difficult to come by, you can easily make this curry using lamb or mutton.

Serves 6

150 ml vegetable oil
1 teaspoon cumin seeds
5 cloves
1 black cardamom pod, cracked
5 green cardamom pods, cracked
¼ teaspoon mace blades
15 small red chillies
250 g red onions, finely sliced
50 g ginger garlic paste, see recipe page 436
600 g young goat leg meat, cut into 3 cm dice
1 teaspoon ground turmeric
2 teaspoons chilli powder
2 teaspoons sea salt flakes
225 g fresh curd (hung yoghurt), see Eggs and Dairy page 110
2 tablespoons freshly chopped coriander leaves

Heat the oil in a heavy-based saucepan over medium heat. Add the cumin seeds and let them crackle for 30 seconds before adding the cloves, black and green cardamom pods, mace and chillies. Cook for 30–40 seconds or until fragrant. Add the onion and cook, stirring frequently, for 10 minutes or until it starts to brown. Add the ginger garlic paste and cook for 3 minutes. Reduce heat to low, add the goat and cook for 10 minutes or until seared and coated with the spiced onion. Add the turmeric, chilli powder and salt, stir to combine and cook for a further 8–10 minutes. Add the fresh curd and stir to combine. Increase heat to medium and cook for a further 10 minutes. Reduce heat to low and simmer for at least 30 minutes or until the meat is tender. Remove from heat and allow to stand for 5 minutes. Sprinkle with the fresh coriander and serve with chapati, roti or steamed rice.

Almond Lamb Curry GF

Rajput cuisine is rich in meat preparations and this curry is another Rajasthani delicacy. *Safed maas* translates to 'white lamb', referring to the pale colour of the sauce, but its grand taste is anything but lacklustre. Indeed, the secret to the delicious gravy lies in the perfect union of its mostly colourless ingredients, including pureed onion, ginger garlic paste, salt, pepper, cashew paste and cardamom.

Serves 4

50 g raw cashews, soaked in cold water for 1 hour to soften
100 g shredded fresh coconut
50 g blanched almonds
150 g Indian melon seeds (char magaz)
600 g boneless lamb shoulder, cut into 3 cm pieces
100 g ghee
½ teaspoon nigella seeds
3 green cardamom pods, cracked
½ teaspoon whole black peppercorns
9 cloves
1 bay leaf
1 brown onion, finely diced
1 tablespoon ginger garlic paste, see recipe page 436
100 g thick plain yoghurt
1 tablespoon chickpea (besan) flour
3 cups (750 ml) white chicken stock
1 teaspoon freshly ground white pepper
3 teaspoons sea salt flakes
100 ml thick cream
2 tablespoons vegetable oil
3 dried Kashmiri chillies
1 teaspoon garam masala
3 tablespoons coriander leaves

Place the softened cashews, coconut, blanched almonds and melon seeds in a food processor and blend with just enough water to make a smooth paste. Set aside.

Blanch the lamb in a large pot of simmering water for 2 minutes. Drain and set aside.

Melt the ghee in large, heavy-based pan over medium heat. Add the whole spices, using just 3 cloves (reserve the remaining 6 for tempering at the end), and bay leaf and cook for 90 seconds or until sizzling. Add the onion and cook for 5 minutes or until softened. Add the ginger garlic paste and cook for a further 2 minutes or until fragrant. Add the blanched lamb and cook for 3 minutes, stirring to coat the lamb with the paste.

Meanwhile, mix together the yoghurt and chickpea flour. Add to the lamb and stir to combine. Pour over the stock, add the pepper and salt and bring to a simmer. Reduce heat to low, cover, and gently cook for 45 minutes or until half the liquid has been absorbed and the meat is tender. Add the coconut cashew paste and cook, stirring, for 2–3 minutes. Add the cream and cook for a further 5 minutes.

In a separate pan, heat the vegetable oil over low heat. Add the dried chillies, garam masala and remaining 6 cloves and cook briefly until crisp. Drain from oil and add to the lamb. Remove lamb from heat, taste and adjust seasoning, if necessary. Sprinkle with coriander and serve with a rice pulao.

Lamb Rogan Josh GF

This is one of the most well-known Indian curries to the Western world. The dish originated in the Kashmiri region in Muslim and Hindi households, where every keen cook has their own version. Its vibrant red colour comes from the dried Kashmiri chilli powder, which gives a lovely depth of colour without the associated heat. When in India, the dried petals of the cockscomb flower add to the lustrous red colour.

Serves 4

¼ cup (60 ml) mustard oil
6 green cardamom pods, cracked
1 black cardamom pod, cracked
½ teaspoon black peppercorns, cracked
2 large brown onions, finely sliced
2 tablespoons ginger garlic paste, see recipe
    page 436
2 teaspoons ground turmeric
3 teaspoons Kashmiri chilli powder
1 teaspoon ground fennel seeds
2 teaspoons ground coriander
¼ teaspoon ground cloves
2 cinnamon sticks
2 teaspoons sea salt flakes
300 g thick plain yoghurt, lightly whisked
8 x 120 g lamb chump chops
2 tablespoons tomato puree

Heat the oil in heavy-based pot over medium heat. Add the green and black cardamom pods and black pepper and cook for 30 seconds or until fragrant. Add the onion and cook, stirring occasionally, for 5 minutes or until softened. Add the ginger garlic paste and cook for a further 2–3 minutes. Add the ground spices, cinnamon sticks, salt and yoghurt and stir to combine. Add the lamb chops with 100 ml water and stir to combine. Reduce heat to low, cover pot and simmer gently for 1 hour, adding a little extra water, if necessary. It needs just enough liquid to keep the lamb from drying out. Stir through the tomato puree and cook, covered, for a further 15 minutes or until the meat is tender and falling off the bone. Serve with a saffron pulao.

Lamb and Chickpea Curry GF

This typical Hindu curry from Bengal is serious comfort cooking with heart-warming and nourishing flavours that soothe the soul. It's traditionally made with goat meat, procured from the butcher early in the morning to ensure freshness, but I've adapted this recipe using more accessible lamb. It's better to plan ahead and soak the chickpeas overnight. Although slightly more time-consuming, they do give a better texture than using the canned variety.

Serves 4

125 g dried chickpeas
2 tablespoons ginger garlic paste, see recipe
    page 436
2 cinnamon sticks
250 g thick plain yoghurt
1 kg lamb shoulder, off the bone, cut into 3 cm
    dice (ask your butcher to do this for you)
2 tablespoons mustard oil
2 red onions, finely sliced
1 tablespoon ground coriander
2 teaspoons ground cumin
2 teaspoons garam masala
3 teaspoons Kashmiri chilli powder
1 teaspoon ground turmeric
½ teaspoon ground cardamom
½ teaspoon freshly ground black pepper
2 tablespoons fresh curry leaves
2 teaspoons sea salt flakes
2 cups (500 ml) buttermilk
3 ripe tomatoes, seeded and chopped
1 bunch English spinach leaves, washed, stems
    removed and torn
½ cup roughly chopped coriander leaves
4 tablespoons fried curry leaves

Soak the dried chickpeas in a large pot of cold water overnight. Drain, rinse and set aside.

Place the ginger garlic paste and cinnamon sticks in a bowl with the yoghurt and mix to combine. Add the lamb and stir until the meat is thoroughly coated. Cover and set aside to marinate in the fridge for 2 hours.

Heat the oil in a heavy-based pot over medium heat. Add the onion and cook, stirring occasionally, for 5 minutes or until translucent. Stir in the ground spices, curry leaves and salt and cook for 3 minutes or until fragrant. Add the lamb with the yoghurt marinade and stir to combine. Add the buttermilk, tomato and 1 cup (250 ml) water and bring to a simmer. Reduce heat to low, cover with a lid and simmer very gently, stirring occasionally, for 1 hour.

Add the chickpeas to the lamb, stir to combine and cook for a further 20 minutes or until chickpeas are soft and lamb is meltingly tender. Discard the cinnamon sticks.

Add the spinach and stir to combine. Once the leaves have wilted, remove curry from the heat and stir through the coriander. Transfer curry to a large bowl and scatter with fried curry leaves to serve.

Mutton Korma GF

This recipe is based on the mild, Muslim-style korma curries of the Mughals in Lucknow. It's more aromatic than spicy-hot, making it a great introduction to the infinite world of curries for timid palates. While I've tasted many different regional meat curries during my travels through India, most using goat meat (often curiously referred to as lamb or mutton), here I've used mutton. The aged meat imparts a greater depth of flavour, but you can just as easily use lamb, hogget or young goat meat. It's best to use shanks, though, as meat on the bone gives a more succulent, richly flavoured result.

Serves 6

120 g ghee
2 brown onions, finely diced
50 g blanched almonds
½ teaspoon ground mace
½ teaspoon ground cloves
2 teaspoons freshly ground black pepper
¼ teaspoon ground green cardamom
4 small green chillies, finely sliced
4 garlic cloves, minced
1 tablespoon minced ginger
2 fresh bay leaves
2 teaspoons ground coriander
2 teaspoons garam masala
3 teaspoons sea salt flakes
2 teaspoons Kashmiri chilli powder
6 mutton shanks
150 g thick plain yoghurt
1 tablespoon chickpea (besan) flour
1 litre beef stock (or water)
25 ml lemon juice, strained
2 tablespoons fried shallot slices, see Glossary
2 tablespoons toasted almond flakes
saffron rice, to serve, see Rice page 306

Melt half the ghee in a frying pan over medium heat. And the onion and cook for 10 minutes or until translucent. Remove onion from pan and set aside. Add the almonds to the pan and cook for 5 minutes or until golden. Remove from pan and drain on paper towel. Allow to cool before blending the onion and almonds in a food processor with the mace, cloves, pepper, and cardamom to make a smooth puree. Set aside.

Melt the remaining ghee in a wide-based, ovenproof pan over medium heat. Add the green chilli, garlic, ginger and bay leaves and cook for 2 minutes or until softened but not coloured.

Preheat oven to 160°C. Mix together the ground coriander, garam masala, salt and chilli powder and rub into the shanks. Add the shanks to the pan and cook for 3 minutes, turn and cook on the other side for a further 3 minutes. Remove from pan and set aside, reserving pan juices.

Mix the yoghurt with the chickpea flour to combine. Add to the pan and cook, stirring, for 30 seconds or until mixture is absorbed by the pan juices. Add the spiced onion puree and cook, stirring, for a further 2 minutes. Return shanks to the pan with the stock, cover with a lid, transfer to the oven and cook for 2 hours or until meat is tender. Leave a little longer if need be.

Remove meat from the gravy and set aside in a warm place. Place the pan with the gravy over high heat and cook for 5 minutes or until the gravy is reduced and thickened slightly. Return the meat to the pan with the lemon juice and adjust seasoning with a little extra salt, if necessary. Scatter with the fried shallot slices and toasted almonds and serve with saffron rice.

Rice

Historically, India was one of the earliest countries to grow rice and its importance in the everyday diet cannot be underestimated. It's difficult to imagine an Indian meal without the ubiquitous ingredient, whether it's steamed, fried or made into a pulao or biryani. India is blessed with different varieties of rice, from the prized long grain basmati of the north, grown in the foothills of the Himalayas, to the short grains of the south that are softer, less fragrant and require less cooking time, and also the more rustic red rice of the coastal and desert regions that are common in everyday village cooking. Rice plays an important role in daily domestic rituals, it's a symbol of good fortune and fertility, and the calendar is punctuated with festivals throughout the year associated with the rice harvest. As a food source, it embodies the very spirit of India.

The Persians brought their biryanis and pulaos with them when they invaded northern India and these preparations underwent a dramatic change in the royal Mughal kitchens, where they were made more elaborate with the addition of fragrant aromatics and spices. The grand biryani is a celebration dish. Made with mutton, lamb, chicken, fish, eggs or vegetables, it's hearty, spice-laden and exotic. The rice is layered with spiced protein and a yoghurt marinade and is cooked *dum*-style, where the pot is covered and sealed with a rope of dough or foil, effectively steaming the dish to ensure the flavour penetrates the rice. The grade of basmati is of paramount importance when making biryani, my preferred brand in Australia is Daawat; it's classified 'premium deluxe' with the longest grains.

Pulao, adapted from the Persian pilaf, is a fragrant, subtly spiced rice preparation where the grains remain separate and other ingredients are mixed through, rather than being layered and baked, as in a biryani. Pulao is a popular accompaniment to a banquet table or an everyday curry. It serves as the Indian equivalent of a risotto or paella.

South Indians, in particular, are rice eaters. It's the staple grain of their diet and a table is incomplete without the central rice dish, everything else being considered a condiment to the rice. In Kerala, grains are soaked overnight to slightly ferment before being ground, along with soaked white lentils (split urad dal), to make a paste that is transformed into steamed *idli* (rice cakes), *appam* (rice pancakes) or *dosa* (a crisp breakfast pancake).

At an Indian market, rice varieties are displayed in open sacks or baskets and the discerning shopper will feel, smell and discuss the harvesting time with the vendor to determine the right rice for what they're cooking. Texture and aroma play a vital role in the decision of which rice to choose. There are innumerable varieties that often don't grace the shelves of our food stores in Australia. This can all become rather confusing, so to make things easier in this chapter, I've used rices that are readily available here.

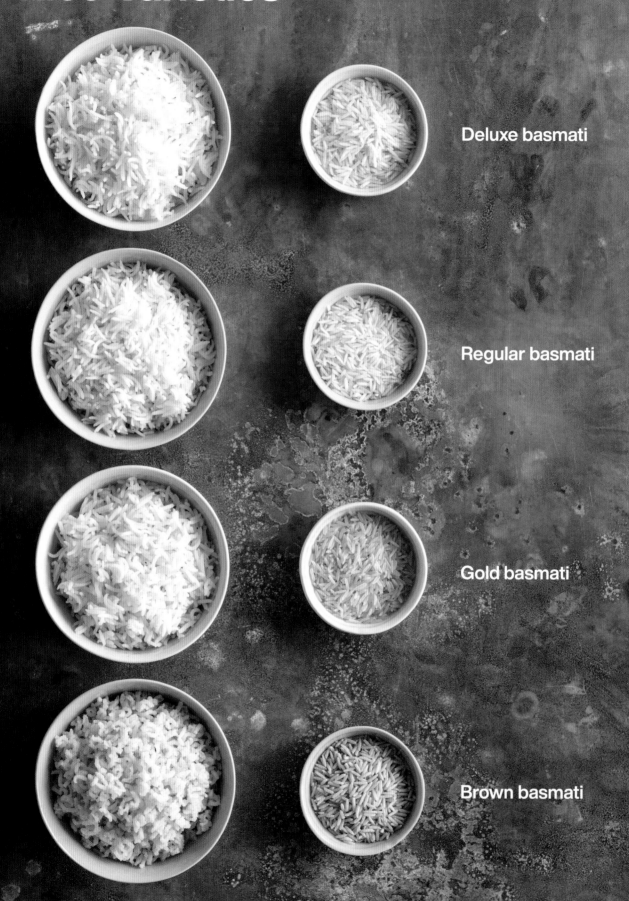

Rice Varieties

Deluxe basmati

Regular basmati

Gold basmati

Brown basmati

Himalayan
red rice

Kerala
short grain

Medium
grain rice

Rice Varieties

Basmati is a variety of long, slender-grain aromatic rice. It's geographically exclusive to select districts of India, Pakistan, Nepal and Bangladesh. More expensive than other rice varieties, it's considered the king of rice and is low in starch with a low glycaemic index. You'll find different grades of basmati in stores. I look for AAA grade, branded as 'premium deluxe' or 'aged rice', where the ageing allows the flavour to develop and the starch to reduce further, resulting in grains that stay separate during cooking and don't clump together. All grades of basmati grains have less calories than other rice varieties.

Regular basmati may not have the star quality of the deluxe grains or cost as much, yet these grains have the same characteristic uniformity of size and length and are silky to the touch. I use this when making pulao or when simply steaming to accompany a curry or other dishes.

Gold basmati can also be labelled as 'sella'. It's produced when raw rice is steamed then dried for milling. During the processing, the grains take on a golden hue. As a variety of basmati, it has a long grain and becomes fluffy and separated when cooked. Reliable brands in Australia are Taj King and Tilda, which are both widely available. I use gold basmati in some of my pulao and biryani recipes.

Brown basmati is highly nutritious with the bran, germ and endosperm intact. It's higher in protein and fibre because it's less refined and, as a result, is becoming a more popular choice these days. It can take slightly longer to cook than white rice.

Premium deluxe basmati is graded as such because the grains triple in size during cooking yet remain separate and are softer in texture than other long grain rice. It also doesn't require as much liquid during cooking. This is the rice you need when making a biryani.

Kerala short grain is sometimes labelled as 'idli' rice, the small grains of this variety are used for making the rice breads of the south or when a smaller, finer grain is required, such as for a breakfast rice porridge.

Medium grain rice is an Australian-grown rice that approximates the shorter, fatter grains of India's south. I use medium grain rice in my own home cooking. It can also be used in recipes that call for 'patna' rice, which is an everyday and more affordable rice in India

Red rice is a rustic rice grown in the coastal and desert regions of India. It's also a common grain used in the mountain regions of India and Bhutan, where it's often served with every meal and is sometimes referred to as 'patni' or 'village' rice. The grains are thick, short and a dusty, reddish-pink colour and you'll generally find it stocked at healthfood shops. Red rice is rich in nutrients with a nutty flavour and a pleasant chewy texture, making it an excellent accompaniment for spicy food, though it lacks the sophistication of basmati or other varieties.

Black Pepper and Cumin Brown Rice GF, V

I like to call this dish 'dirty rice' due to its murky brown colour. It's quick and easy to make and is given a sweet edge with caramelised onions and a kick of heat from the black pepper. I sometimes add cooked chickpeas or sprouted grains for a more substantial dish. Garnish it liberally with fried shallot slices, or you could use crispy fried onion rings, if you prefer.

Regardless of the cooking method, the result should yield fluffy, separate grains. It's important to soak the rice in plenty of cold water and rinse thoroughly until the water runs clear before cooking. This removes excess starch and ensures the grains remain separate when cooked. The general rule of thumb when cooking basmati rice is to use the ratio of 2:1 water to rice – the rice will absorb the water to yield soft, separate grains without becoming mushy or sticky.

Serves 4

1½ cups (300 g) brown basmati rice
75 g ghee
1 teaspoon black peppercorns, coarsely ground
2 teaspoons cumin seeds
2 red onions, finely diced
2 teaspoons ginger garlic paste, see recipe
  page 436
1 small green chilli, minced
¼ teaspoon ground cardamom
2 teaspoons sea salt flakes
3 tablespoons fried shallot slices, see Glossary

Wash the rice well under cold, running water until the water runs clear. Set aside to soak in cold water for 1 hour. Drain. Cook the rice in large pot of boiling water for 6 minutes or until al dente. Drain.

Melt the ghee in a large frying pan over medium heat. Add the pepper and cumin seeds and cook for 30 seconds or until fragrant. Add the onion and cook, stirring frequently, for 10 minutes or until starting to caramelise. Add the ginger garlic paste, chilli and cardamom and cook a further 2 minutes. Add the cooked rice and stir to thoroughly coat the grains. Cooking for 2–3 minutes. Add the salt and stir to combine. Top with fried shallot slices to serve.

**Masterclass step-by-step
Black Pepper and Cumin
Brown Rice ➔**

1

Wash the rice well under cold, running water until the water runs clear.

2

Soak in cold water for 1 hour.

3

Cook the rice in a large pot of boiling water for 6 minutes.

Drain the rice.

5

Melt the ghee in a large frying pan over medium heat.

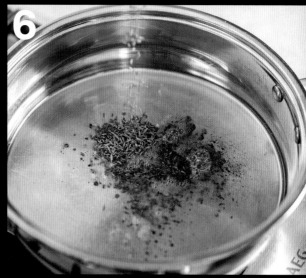

6

Add the pepper and cumin seeds and cook for 30 seconds or until fragrant.

7

Add the onion and cook, stirring frequently, for 10 minutes.

8

Add the ginger garlic paste, chilli and cardamom and cook for 2 minutes.

9

Add the rice.

10

Stir to coat the grains and cook for 2–3 minutes.

11

Add the salt and stir to combine.

12

Top with fried shallot to serve.

Saffron Chicken Biryani GF

A fragrant, celebratory rice dish made luxurious with the addition of saffron. This dish is bejewelled with sultanas and almonds and perfumed with rosewater, taking it to a whole other level. I make this for a grand occasion when there's something special to celebrate. Its layered flavour is the reward for the effort involved.

Serves 6

600 g free-range chicken thigh fillets, cut into
    4 cm cubes
2½ cups (500 g) premium deluxe basmati rice
2 teaspoons sea salt flakes
1 cinnamon stick
3 cloves
20 g ghee
1 brown onion, finely diced
2 tablespoons ginger garlic paste, see recipe
    page 436
4 small red chillies, minced
100 g saffron butter, plus extra for brushing,
    see Glossary
1 scant teaspoon rosewater
2 tablespoons ghee, extra
2 tablespoons sultanas
2 tablespoons flaked almonds
2 tablespoons fried shallot slices, see Glossary

YOGHURT MARINADE
1 teaspoon coriander seeds, roasted and ground
1 teaspoon cumin seeds, roasted and ground
250 ml thick plain yoghurt
60 g almond meal
¼ teaspoon ground cardamom
1 teaspoon chilli powder
½ teaspoon freshly ground black pepper
¼ teaspoon ground cloves
1 teaspoon nigella seeds
¼ teaspoon ground nutmeg
1 cinnamon stick
2 teaspoons sea salt flakes

To make the yoghurt marinade, place all the ingredients in a large bowl and mix thoroughly to combine. Add the chicken, cover and refrigerate for 2 hours to marinate.

Wash the rice several times until water runs clear. Drain and place in a saucepan with 2 teaspoons salt, the cinnamon, cloves and 6 cups (1½ litres) cold water. Set aside to soak for 1 hour.

Bring the rice to the boil and cook, covered, over low heat for 5 minutes or until rice is half-cooked. Remove from the heat, strain to remove excess water and discard the whole spices. Return rice to the pan, cover and set aside.

Preheat the oven to 160°C. Melt the ghee in a large, heavy-based pan over medium–low heat. Add the onion, ginger garlic paste and chilli and cook for 2–3 minutes or until slightly coloured. Increase heat to medium, add the chicken with the yoghurt marinade and cook for 3 minutes. Add 150 ml water, cover with lid, reduce heat to low and cook for 5 minutes or until the chicken is half-cooked. Remove pan from the heat and discard the cinnamon stick.

To assemble the biryani, brush a large, ovenproof pan or baking dish with 1 tablespoon of the saffron butter. Spread half the cooked rice over the base of the pan, dot with another 2 tablespoons of the saffron butter and sprinkle over half of the rosewater. The idea in adding the butter like this is that some of the rice grains will become yellow during final cooking, but it should not be a uniform saffron colour all over. Spoon the chicken mixture over the rice and top with the remaining rice. Dot rice with the remaining 2 tablespoons saffron butter and sprinkle with the remaining rosewater. Cover with a tight-fitting lid and bake for 30 minutes. Remove from the oven and allow to rest, without removing the lid, for 10 minutes.

While the biryani is resting, heat the extra ghee in a small frying pan over medium heat. Add the sultanas and flaked almonds and cook for 3 minutes or until crisp.

To serve, mix together the rice and the chicken and spoon the biryani onto a large platter. Top with fried shallots, almonds and sultanas. Serve immediately.

Prawn and Mussel Biryani GF

Biryanis from the coastal town of Thalassery in Kerala, once home to the early spice traders, differ to the Mughal versions of the north in that they cook with seafood rather than meat. Muslim traders settled here centuries ago and the classic biryani preparation was adapted to make use of the abundant seafood. The rice is different, too. The grains of the south are shorter and thinner and don't require the same amount of cooking time. At home, I use either gold or regular basmati rice for this recipe. As a dish, it starts out as two separate preparations and comes together as one when layered and baked in the same pot.

Serves 6

TO ASSEMBLE
30 g butter
½ teaspoon garam masala
2 tablespoons chopped coriander
1 tablespoon chopped mint

SEAFOOD
500 g large raw prawn meat, peeled and deveined
½ teaspoon ground turmeric
½ teaspoon freshly ground black pepper
½ teaspoon Kashmiri chilli powder
1 teaspoon sea salt flakes
1 kg mussels, washed
1 tablespoons vegetable oil
2 tablespoons ghee
2 white onions, finely chopped
2 tablespoons fresh curry leaves
2 tablespoons ginger garlic paste, see recipe
    page 436
1 teaspoon ground fennel seeds
1 teaspoon garam masala
½ teaspoon Kashmiri chilli powder
1 teaspoon turmeric powder
2 medium tomatoes, finely chopped
1 teaspoon salt
2 teaspoons lemon juice
2 tablespoons chopped coriander
1 tablespoon chopped mint

RICE
2 cups (400 g) gold basmati rice
2 tablespoons ghee
20 fresh curry leaves
2 small red onions, finely sliced
1 teaspoon freshly ground black pepper
1 cinnamon stick
10 black peppercorns
6 cloves
6 green cardamom pods
2½ teaspoons sea salt flakes
1 teaspoon lemon juice

To prepare the rice, wash the rice well under cold, running water until the water runs clear. Set aside to soak in a bowl of cold water for 30 minutes. Drain.

Melt the ghee in a large, heavy-based saucepan with a lid over medium heat. Add 10 of the curry leaves and cook for 30 seconds or until aromatic. Add the onion, black pepper, cinnamon, peppercorns, cloves and cardamom with ½ teaspoon of the salt and cook, stirring occasionally, until softened. Increase heat slightly and cook, stirring, for a further 3 minutes or until golden. Add the drained rice and stir well, cook for 2 minutes or until any excess water has evaporated and the rice is coated in the oil. Add 750 ml water to the pan, taste and season with the remaining 2 teaspoons salt. The water should be a little salty or the rice will be flavourless. Add the lemon juice and remaining curry leaves, bring to the boil, cover and reduce heat to low. Cook, undisturbed, for 6 minutes before testing a grain of rice. If rice is al dente, remove from heat and set aside for 10 minutes. Spoon onto a baking tray to allow the rice to cool quickly and ensure it doesn't overcook. Keep the saucepan on-hand for the final assembly.

To prepare the seafood, cut each prawn in half crosswise. Place prawn meat in a bowl with the turmeric, black pepper, chilli powder and salt and toss to coat. Set aside while you cook the mussels.

Steam the mussels in a covered frying pan over high heat until they open. Refresh under cold water. Remove mussels from their shells, discarding shells, and snip off their beards. Set aside.

Heat the oil and ghee in a non-stick frying pan over medium heat. Add the onion and cook for 6 minutes or until softened and golden. Reduce heat to low, add the curry leaves and ginger garlic paste and cook for 1 minute or until fragrant. Add the ground spices, tomato and salt and cook for 3 minutes. Add 2 tablespoons hot water and continue to cook for 5 minutes or until the tomato has softened and released some oil. Taste at this point, the flavour should be harmonious, if not, cook a little longer, adding some water if it's too dry. But be sure to cook down to a paste before the next step.

Add the seasoned prawns to the pan and cook for 2 minutes. Add the mussels and lemon juice with another 2 tablespoons hot water and stir to combine. Once it starts to simmer, remove from heat. Check seasoning for balance and adjust with salt, if necessary. Stir through the chopped coriander and mint.

Preheat oven to 180°C. To assemble the biryani, rub half the butter over the base of the reserved saucepan. Spread half the rice over the base of the saucepan and sprinkle with the garam masala and half the chopped coriander and mint. Spoon over the prawn and mussel mixture and cover with the remaining rice. Dot the rice with the remaining butter, broken into little pieces. Cover the pot with a tight-fitting lid and bake for 25 minutes. Remove from oven and set aside to rest, without removing the lid, for 15 minutes. Remove lid and sprinkle the biryani with the remaining coriander and mint. Spoon the rice and seafood onto a large serving plate, mixing the layers slightly, and serve immediately.

Pictured overleaf

Prawn and Mussel
Biryani

Masala Eggplant
Biryani

Masala Eggplant Biryani GF, V

Anyone who knows me knows that I'm a sucker for eggplant. It's my favourite vegetable to cook with and I find endless ways of preparing the many different varieties we have available to us. Spices work wonders with eggplant, it's so compatible with a wide array of flavours. Like any biryani, this is a laborious process – a real labour of love. Essentially, this is one of my favourite eggplant curries layered with fragrant rice to make for a special occasion. It's important to use the small, egg-shaped eggplants with striped, mauve-purple skin. If you're time-poor, you can serve the eggplant as a curry in its own right, simply with steamed rice or flaky parathas, rather than making the full biryani.

Serves 8

2½ cups (500 g) regular basmati rice
2 green cardamom pods
1 clove
1 small cinnamon stick
1 bay leaf
2 teaspoons sea salt flakes
3 tablespoons fried shallot slices, see Glossary
1½ tablespoons chopped coriander
1½ tablespoons chopped mint
2 tablespoons lemon juice
2 tablespoons melted ghee

EGGPLANT CURRY
8 x 80 g small round (egg-shaped) eggplants
1 teaspoon sea salt flakes
2 tablespoons vegetable oil
1 teaspoon black mustard seeds
12 fresh curry leaves
½ teaspoon ground cumin
1 tablespoon ground kasoori methi
   (dried fenugreek leaves), see Glossary
½ cup (125 ml) tamarind puree
3 tablespoons thick plain yoghurt
2 teaspoons sea salt flakes

MASALA BASE
2 cloves
1 cinnamon stick
1 teaspoon cumin seeds
5 green cardamom pods, cracked
1 tablespoon coriander seeds
½ teaspoon fenugreek seeds
2 tablespoons white sesame seeds, toasted
5 tablespoons dried shredded coconut, lightly
   toasted
2 tablespoons vegetable oil
2 brown onions, diced
3 tomatoes, seeded and diced
1 tablespoon ginger garlic paste, see recipe
   page 436
3 teaspoons chilli powder
1 teaspoon ground turmeric
½ teaspoon ground cinnamon
¼ teaspoon ground cardamom
1 teaspoon sea salt flakes
1 tablespoon brown sugar

To prepare the rice, wash the rice well under cold, running water until the water runs clear. Set aside to soak in a bowl of cold water for 30 minutes. Drain and set aside.

To prepare the eggplants, cut each eggplant into quarters from the base, cutting ⅔ of the way through the centre and leaving the eggplant intact at the stem. Lightly salt the inside of each eggplant along the cut surfaces and set aside to drain in a colander for 30 minutes. Wipe excess water and salt from the eggplants with a paper towel. Don't wash the eggplants as this makes the flesh too porous. Set aside.

To prepare the masala base, place the whole spices in a frying pan over low heat and dry roast for 1 minute or until fragrant. Remove from the heat and toss with the toasted sesame seeds to combine. Allow to cool before grinding with the toasted coconut to a fine powder in a spice grinder. Set aside.

Heat the oil in a heavy-based saucepan over medium–high heat. Add the onion and cook for 3 minutes or until softened. Add the tomato and cook for a further 5 minutes or until tomato starts to break down. Stir through the ginger garlic paste and cook for 2–3 minutes. Add the ground spices, salt and sugar and cook for a further 1 minute. Remove from heat and allow to cool for 10 minutes.

Place the onion mixture and the coconut spice mix in a food processor and blend to make a thick paste. This masala can be made a couple of days ahead and stored in the fridge until ready to use. Stuff each eggplant liberally with the masala paste, pushing the eggplants back into shape once the stuffing is added. Set aside.

To prepare the curry sauce, heat the oil a frying pan large enough to fit the eggplants snugly over medium heat. Add the mustard seeds and curry leaves and once they start to pop, stir in the cumin and kasoori methi. Cook for 30 seconds before adding the stuffed eggplants to the pan in a single layer. Add the tamarind and when simmering, stir in the yoghurt with 100 ml

water. Reduce heat to low, cover with a lid and cook, stirring occasionally and turning eggplants halfway through, for 15 minutes or until eggplants are soft. Add a little extra water if the sauce dries out too much. It should cling to the eggplants without being too wet. Sprinkle with salt and set aside.

To cook the rice, place 3 litres water in a large pot with the cardamom, clove, cinnamon and bay leaf and bring to the boil. Add the rice and cover with a lid, reduce heat to medium and cook for 5 minutes or until rice is parboiled (the grains should still have a chalky centre). Drain, discarding spices. Season with salt and stir to combine.

Preheat oven to 160°C. To assemble the biryani, spread half the rice over the base of an oiled 27 cm-round, cast-iron casserole pot. Spoon over half the curried eggplant and sprinkle with half the fried shallots and chopped herbs. Top with remaining eggplant curry and cover with remaining rice. Drizzle over the lemon juice and ghee, cover with a lid and bake for 30 minutes. Remove from oven and allow to rest, without removing the lid, for 10 minutes. Remove lid and sprinkle with the remaining fried shallots and chopped herbs. Spoon onto serving plates, scooping from the base upwards for a mixture of the curry and rice layers.

Pictured previous spread

Hyderabadi Lamb Biryani _{GF}

Kacchi gosht ki biryani is the most noted biryani peculiar to the Nizam's royal palace kitchens in Hyderabad. *Kacchi* means raw, and here, unlike with other biryanis, the meat and its marinade are layered into the rice uncooked. It is typically made with goat or mutton, but lamb or hogget are equally suitable. The cooking pot is sealed with a rope of bread dough, in a technique known as *dum*-style, where the meat and rice cook in their own steam. The seal is not broken until the biryani is ready to serve. You can get the same effect by wrapping a foil collar around the lid and sealing it onto the pot. It's important to use green, under-ripe papaya as the enzymes act as a meat tenderiser while marinating.

Serves 6

100 g green papaya, peeled, seeded and diced
4 tablespoons ginger garlic paste, see recipe page 436
2 tablespoons Kashmiri chilli powder
½ teaspoon ground cardamom
3 teaspoons sea salt flakes
1 kg boneless lamb shank (or leg meat), cut into large 4 cm pieces
4 small green chillies, finely sliced
2 teaspoons garam masala
500 g thick plain yoghurt, plus extra, to serve
½ cup chopped mint leaves
½ cup chopped coriander leaves
1 cup fried shallot slices, see Glossary
1 teaspoon green cardamom pods, cracked
1 teaspoon black cumin seeds
1 teaspoon cloves
1 cinnamon stick
½ teaspoon saffron threads
150 g ghee
4 cups (800 g) premium deluxe basmati rice
1 tablespoon rosewater

GRAM SALT
2 teaspoons toor dal (yellow split lentils)
2 teaspoons split urad dal (white lentils)
4 teaspoons sea salt flakes

To make the gram salt, place both dals in a frying pan over low heat and cook for 4 minutes or until nutty and aromatic. Allow to cool before grinding with the salt to a fine powder in a spice grinder. Set aside.

Place the papaya in a food processor and blend to make a smooth puree. Place puree in a large bowl with the ginger garlic paste, chilli powder, cardamom and salt and mix to combine. Add the lamb, rubbing the paste thoroughly into the meat, cover and refrigerate for 4 hours to marinate.

Place the green chilli, garam masala, yoghurt, half the mint and coriander, and half the fried shallot slices in a large bowl and mix to combine. Add to the lamb and mix until combined. Set aside.

Place 4 litres of water in a large saucepan and bring to the boil. Add the whole spices, saffron, 100 g ghee and 2 teaspoons of the gram salt (reserve the remainder for other use) with the rice and cook over medium heat for 5 minutes or until the rice is parboiled. Strain and spread out onto a large tray. Set aside to dry for 30 minutes.

Place half the lamb and the yoghurt marinade into a heavy-based casserole pot and smooth the surface. The meat should cover the base of the pot evenly. Cover with half the rice. Repeat both layers, finishing with the rice. Cover with a tight-fitting lid and seal the edges with a rope of dough or folded foil collar. Place pot over low heat and cook for 1 hour and 15 minutes. Remove from heat and set aside to rest for 20 minutes before removing the lid and seal. The residual heat will complete the cooking to perfection.

Once the lid has been removed, drizzle with the rosewater and remaining melted ghee. Scatter with the remaining chopped herbs and fried shallot and spoon onto plates, ensuring an even mix of meat and rice. Serve with raita or yoghurt.

Vegetable Biryani GF, V

You could lush this up a little by adding cubes of paneer to the vegetables when you're ready to layer with the rice. Although biryani is traditionally made with meat or fish, a vegetable-based biryani is good to have in your repertoire for non-meat eaters and to celebrate the bounty of the earth. It's an idea that is gaining traction as we shift our focus to a more plant-based diet for all manner of ethical reasons.

Serves 6

4 cups (800 g) regular basmati rice
100 ml milk
1 teaspoon saffron threads
½ small cauliflower, cut into florets
100 ml vegetable oil
2½ teaspoons sea salt flakes
2 teaspoons black mustard seeds
1 teaspoon cumin seeds
½ teaspoon asafoetida
3 red shallots, finely sliced
2 small red chillies, finely sliced
1 red capsicum, seeds removed, cut into
   2 cm dice
2 tablespoons ghee
2 garlic cloves, finely sliced
200 g small oyster mushrooms
2 teaspoons ground coriander
½ teaspoon chilli powder
½ teaspoon ground cardamom
½ teaspoon garam masala
175 g thick plain yoghurt
1 tablespoon lemon juice
1 cup shelled fresh or frozen green peas
2 tablespoons unsalted butter
2 tablespoons chopped coriander leaves
2 tablespoons fried shallot slices, see Glossary

To prepare the rice, wash the rice well under cold, running water until the water runs clear. Set aside to soak in a bowl of cold water for 30 minutes. Drain, place rice in a large saucepan with enough water to cover and bring to the boil. Cook for 5 minutes until parboiled. Drain and spread rice onto a baking tray to cool and dry.

Place the milk and saffron in a small saucepan over low heat until lukewarm or temperature reaches 37°C. Remove from heat and set aside for 30 minutes to allow the saffron to infuse.

Preheat oven to 200°C. Place the cauliflower, 2 tablespoons oil and ½ teaspoon salt in a baking tray lined with baking paper and toss to coat. Roast for 20 minutes or until golden. Remove from oven and set aside. Reduce oven temperature to 180°C.

Heat remaining oil in wide-based pan over medium heat. Add the mustard seeds, cumin seeds and asafoetida and cook for 30 seconds or until they start to pop. Add the shallot, chilli and capsicum and cook, tossing over the heat, for 30–40 seconds or until softened.

In a separate frying pan, melt the ghee over medium–high heat. Add the garlic and mushroom and cook for 4 minutes or until softened and starting to colour. Season with salt and pepper.

Add the garlic mushrooms and the roasted cauliflower to the capsicum mixture and stir to combine. Mix to combine the ground spices with the yoghurt, remaining 2 teaspoons salt and lemon juice and add to the vegetables. Return to low heat and cook for 1 minute to heat through. Remove from heat and stir through the peas.

Rub the butter over the base of a cast-iron casserole pot and spread with ⅓ of the rice. Drizzle with ⅓ of the saffron milk and spoon half the vegetables over the rice to make an even layer. Repeat layers, finishing with a final layer of rice and drizzling with the remaining saffron milk. Cover with tight-fitting lid and bake for 40 minutes. Remove from oven and allow to rest, without removing lid, for 10 minutes. To serve, gently mix the rice and vegetable layers together and spoon onto plates. Scatter with the chopped coriander and fried shallots.

Smoked Fish and Egg Red Rice Pulao GF

This makes a wonderful breakfast or supper dish using the deliciously nutty red rice, which you can buy from healthfood stores or some Indian grocers. I prefer to use hot-smoked rainbow trout, readily available at good fishmongers, but you can use any smoked fish. Or, if so inclined, you can grill a fresh salmon or ocean trout fillet and flake the fish into pieces to fold through the rice.

Serves 4

4 eggs
1 cup (200 g) Himalayan red rice
2 tablespoons ghee
1 red onion, finely diced
2 teaspoons minced ginger
2 teaspoons curry powder
400 ml chicken or vegetable stock
½ teaspoon sea salt flakes
½ teaspoon freshly ground black pepper
1 whole hot-smoked rainbow trout
zest of ½ lemon, minced
1 tablespoon lemon juice
4 green shallots, finely sliced
3 tablespoons chopped parsley
2 tablespoons chopped coriander
1 tablespoon chopped mint
2 tablespoons fried shallot slices, see Glossary
¼ teaspoon chilli oil

Cook the eggs in boiling water for 5 minutes. Allow to cool before peeling and cutting into quarters. Set aside.

Wash the rice well under cold, running water until the water runs clear. Set aside to soak in a bowl of cold water for 30 minutes. Drain.

Melt the ghee in a frying pan over high heat. Add the onion and cook for 4 minutes or until softened. Add the ginger and curry powder and cook for 2 minutes or until fragrant. Add the drained rice and toss to coat grains with the onion mixture. Add the stock, stirring to combine, and bring to the boil. Reduce heat to low, cover with a lid and cook for 10 minutes or until rice is tender and liquid has been absorbed. Season with salt and pepper. Flake the smoked fish into large pieces, discarding the skin and bones.

To assemble the pulao, stir the lemon zest and juice, green shallots, herbs and fried shallots through the rice. Add the flaked fish and gently toss to combine, taking care not to break up the fish too much. Spoon onto plates and arrange egg on top. Drizzle with chilli oil to serve.

Gunpowder Chicken Rice GF

Gunpowder is a hero ingredient in the food of the south, particularly Bangalore, Karnataka and Hyderabad, where it is used as a seasoning and also to flavour pickles and chutneys. This spice blend is a gentle but fiery alchemy, which includes the star ingredients Kashmiri chilli, black pepper, coriander seeds, ground ginger, cinnamon and amchur. The gunpowder lends this dish a real punch. I buy mine from Herbie's Spices (available online in Australia and New Zealand).

Serves 4

2 cups (400 g) basmati rice
100 g ghee
1 teaspoon cumin seeds
1 teaspoon brown mustard seeds
20 fresh curry leaves
1 red onion, finely diced
1 tablespoon ginger garlic paste, see recipe
　page 436
5 small green chillies, minced
250 g chicken thigh fillet, sliced into thin strips
1 tablespoon gunpowder spice mix, see Glossary
700 ml chicken stock
1 cup (250 ml) coconut milk
¼ cup (60 ml) tamarind puree
1 teaspoon sea salt flakes
1 cup shredded baby spinach leaves
2 tablespoons freshly chopped coriander leaves
1 tablespoon roasted cashews, roughly chopped

Wash the rice well under cold, running water until the water runs clear. Set aside to soak in a bowl of cold water for 30 minutes. Drain.

Melt the ghee in a wide-based saucepan over medium heat. Add the cumin seeds, mustard seeds and curry leaves and cook for 30 seconds or until they start to pop. Add the onion and cook for 5 minutes or until softened and just starting to colour. Add the ginger garlic paste and chilli and cook for a further 2–3 minutes. Add the chicken, sprinkle with half the gunpowder spice mix and stir to combine. Immediately stir in the rice and cook for 2 minutes. Add the stock, coconut milk and tamarind puree and bring to the boil. Reduce heat to low, cover and cook for 10 minutes or until most of the liquid has been absorbed. Remove the lid and stir through the salt, shredded spinach and coriander. Fluff up the rice with a fork and sprinkle with the cashews and remaining gunpowder spice mix to serve.

Vegetable and Nut Pulao GF, V

The legacy of the Mughal Empire left us with beautifully crafted dishes, such as this one, where the rice is studded with diced vegetables and nuts to give a bejewelled appearance. It is a complete meal in itself, a typical one-pot number to add to your repertoire.

Serves 6

¼ cup (60 ml) vegetable oil
½ teaspoon cumin seeds
1 teaspoon black mustard seeds
1 brown onion, finely diced
2 small green chillies, minced
2 teaspoons minced fresh ginger
1 teaspoon ground turmeric
2 teaspoons sea salt flakes
200 g cooked potato, cut into 2 cm dice
1 cup cooked cauliflower florets
1 large carrot, cooked and diced
1 tablespoon currants
12 cherry tomatoes, halved
½ cup fresh or frozen green peas
2 cups cooked basmati rice
1 tablespoon lime juice
2 tablespoons melted ghee
2 hard-boiled eggs, grated
2 tablespoons roasted cashews, chopped
1 tablespoon pistachios, chopped
1 tablespoon flaked almonds, lightly toasted
2 tablespoons boondi (puffed lentils), see
  Glossary
2 tablespoons chopped coriander leaves

Heat the oil in a large frying pan or heavy-based pot over medium heat. Add the cumin and mustard seeds and cook for 20 seconds or until they start to pop. Add the onion, chilli and ginger, stir to combine and cook for 5–6 minutes or until softened and starting to colour. Reduce heat to low, add the turmeric and salt and cook for a further 1 minute. Add the cooked vegetables, currants, tomato and peas, stir to combine and cook for 2 minutes. Stir through the cooked rice, cover and cook for 5 minutes. Add the lime juice, check for seasoning and adjust with extra salt, if necessary. Remove from heat and stir through the melted ghee, grated egg, nuts, boondi and coriander leaves to serve.

Cashew Pulao DF, GF, V

This is a popular and simple rice preparation I collected during my travels through the Himalayas. It complements any number of vegetable dishes.

Serves 4

1 cup (200 g) gold basmati rice
3 tablespoons vegetable oil
1 red onion, finely sliced
1 teaspoon nigella seeds
½ cup raw cashews, soaked in cold water
  for 30 minutes and drained
½ teaspoon sea salt flakes

Wash the rice well under cold, running water until the water runs clear. Set aside to soak in a bowl of cold water for 30 minutes. Drain.

Heat the oil in a frying pan or wok over medium heat. Add the onion and nigella seeds and cook for 3 minutes or until onion is softened. Add the softened cashews and cook for 5 minutes or until onion is caramelised. Add the rice and stir to coat the grains. Add 2 cups (500 ml) water and bring to the boil. Reduce heat to low, cover and cook for 12 minutes or until water has been absorbed and the rice is cooked. Season with salt and serve hot.

Cardamom and Onion Pulao GF, V

This flavoursome, aromatic rice partners well with myriad dishes. It's an everyday pulao that's quick to prepare and makes a great addition to your repertoire.

Serves 4

1 cup (200 g) basmati rice
4 tablespoons ghee
2 brown onions, finely sliced
3 cloves garlic, minced
1 teaspoon nigella seeds
seeds from 3 green cardamom pods, ground
1 bay leaf
1 cinnamon stick
4 cloves
1 teaspoon sea salt flakes
½ teaspoon freshly ground black pepper
2 tablespoons fried shallot slices, see Glossary

Preheat oven to 180°C. Wash the rice well under cold, running water until the water runs clear. Set aside to soak in a bowl of cold water for 30 minutes. Drain.

Melt half the ghee in a wide, heavy-based, ovenproof pan over medium–high heat. Add the onion and cook for 5 minutes or until it starts to colour. Add the garlic and cook for a further 2–3 minutes. Add the spices and stir to combine. Add the rice and stir to coat with the spices and ghee. Add 2 cups (500 ml) water, cover, transfer to the oven and bake for 15 minutes or until all the liquid has been absorbed and the rice is cooked. Season with salt and pepper. Remove the whole spices and stir through the remaining ghee to gloss up the rice. Scatter with the fried shallots and serve immediately.

Saffron Rice GF, V

With its luxurious, golden appearance, this is a great accompaniment to meat curries, such as the mutton korma (see page 276) and other dishes that complement its vibrant colour and heady aroma.

Serves 6

2 cups (400 g) gold basmati rice
3 teaspoons sea salt flakes
½ teaspoon saffron threads
75 g ghee

Wash the rice well under cold, running water until the water runs clear. Set aside to soak in 2 litres of cold water mixed with 2 teaspoons of salt for 30 minutes. Drain.

Grind the saffron in a mortar and pestle and place in a small bowl with 2 tablespoons hot water. Set aside to soak for 20 minutes to allow it to infuse. Rinse the rice again under cold running water and drain.

Melt the ghee in a wide-based pan over medium heat. Add the drained rice and stir to coat the grains with the ghee. Add the remaining 1 teaspoon salt and stir to combine. Reduce heat to low, add 4 cups (1 litre) boiling water, the water should sizzle as it hits the pan. Cover and simmer for 15 minutes or until the rice is cooked, fluffy and the liquid has been absorbed. Make 4 indents into the rice with a knife and divide the saffron infusion between them. Cover pan with lid, remove from heat and set aside for 10 minutes without stirring. Fluff the rice gently with a fork. You should have 2 colours of rice, white and yellow, rather than a uniform colour. Serve immediately.

Lemon Rice DF, GF, V

This tangy rice can be served with coconut curries, grilled meats or a vegetable salad. Sometimes I just stir a pickle through the rice for an instant snack. Day-old cooked and cooled rice is best for this recipe.

Serves 6

1 tablespoon vegetable oil
½ teaspoon brown mustard seeds
1 teaspoon chana dal (split chickpeas), dry-roasted and coarsely ground
12 fresh curry leaves
2 tablespoons raw peanuts, roughly chopped
1 teaspoon fresh ginger, minced
2 green chillies, finely chopped
¼ teaspoon ground turmeric
3 cups cooked basmati rice
2 tablespoons lemon juice
1 teaspoon sea salt flakes
2 tablespoons chopped coriander leaves

Heat the oil in a frying pan over medium heat. Add the mustard seeds and cook for 30 seconds or until they start to pop. Add the ground chana dal, curry leaves, peanut, ginger and green chilli and cook for 3 minutes. Stir through the turmeric and immediately add the cooked rice, stirring to combine. Cook, stirring continuously, for 2–3 minutes or until warmed through. Add the lemon juice and salt to taste and toss to combine. Top with chopped coriander to serve.

Tamarind Rice DF, GF, V

Rice is given a tangy, spicy edge with the addition of tamarind. Commonly served as an offering and given to pilgrims in the Shiva temples of Tamil Nadu, this is a popular accompaniment to any south Indian meal. Try it with grilled or roasted fish and a crunchy vegetable salad.

Serves 4

1 cup (200 g) basmati rice
3 teaspoons sea salt flakes
2 tablespoons vegetable oil
1 teaspoon black mustard seeds
12 fresh curry leaves
1 small white onion, finely diced
½ teaspoon dried chilli flakes
½ teaspoon ground fenugreek seeds
4 tablespoons tamarind puree
1 tablespoons tomato puree (not paste)
2 teaspoons brown sugar

Soak the rice in cold water for 20 minutes. Drain and rinse. Bring 2 cups (500 ml) water to the boil in a saucepan. Add the washed rice and 1 teaspoon salt, cover with a lid, reduce heat to low and cook for 10 minutes or until rice is soft. Drain and set aside.

Heat the oil in a frying pan over medium heat. Add the mustard seeds and cook for 30 seconds or until they start to pop. Add the curry leaves and cook for 30 seconds. Add the onion, increase heat to high and cook for 5 minutes or until golden. Add the chilli flakes and ground fenugreek and cook for 1 minute or until fragrant. Add the tamarind puree, tomato puree and sugar, bring to a simmer and stir through the cooked rice. Cook, stirring continuously, for 5 minutes or until rice is thoroughly coated with the tamarind base. Season rice with the remaining 2 teaspoons salt and serve hot.

Curd Rice GF, V

You may see this recipe also called 'yoghurt rice'. The yoghurt is hung overnight to remove excess whey, forming a thick curd, which is cooked into the rice with a few gentle, aromatic flavours. It makes an excellent accompaniment to roasted or grilled meats or fish, a vegetable thoran and dry-style dishes without any gravy or sauce. It's typical of the Tamil diet because of its cooling and digestive properties.

Serves 4

1 cup (200 g) basmati rice, washed and drained
1 tablespoon ghee
1 teaspoon brown mustard seeds
4 fresh curry leaves
1 pinch of asafoetida
1 teaspoon minced ginger
1 small green chilli, minced
275 g fresh curd (hung yoghurt), see Eggs and Dairy page 110
2 teaspoons sea salt flakes

Fill a large saucepan with 2 cups (500 ml) water and bring to the boil. Add the rice, cover with a lid and cook for 12–15 minutes or until rice is soft and fluffy and most of the water has been absorbed. Drain rice to remove any excess water, return to the pot and set aside.

Melt the ghee in a small frying pan over medium heat. Add the mustard seeds and cook for 30 seconds or until they start to pop. Add the curry leaves, asafoetida, ginger and chilli, reduce heat to low and cook for 1 minute or until fragrant. Add the curd and salt and cook for 1 minute or until heated through but not bubbling. Mash the cooked rice slightly to break the grains and stir through the curd mixture until rice is evenly coated. Served warm or at room temperature.

Tomato Rice <small>GF, V</small>

Tomatoes, along with chillies, were introduced to India by early Portuguese settlers and both became staple ingredients throughout the country. This particular dish originates in Goa, where the Portuguese ruled for several centuries. I like to serve it with fish or chicken cooked in yoghurt. Cucumber raita also makes a lovely accompaniment to this rice.

Serves 4

1¼ cup (250 g) gold basmati rice
60 g ghee
½ teaspoon fennel seeds
1 cinnamon stick
1 tablespoon ginger garlic paste, see recipe
   page 436
1 teaspoon ground cumin
2 teaspoons ground coriander
½ teaspoon ground turmeric
pinch of ground cloves
¼ teaspoon ground cardamom
¼ teaspoon Kashmiri chilli powder
150 ml fresh tomato puree (from 2 small,
   ripe tomatoes)
1 teaspoon sea salt flakes
1 teaspoon caster sugar
2 tomatoes, seeded and diced
4 green shallot tops, finely sliced
1 tablespoon chopped mint

Wash the rice gently under cold, running water until the water runs clear. Set aside to soak in cold water for 30 minutes. Drain.

Melt the ghee in a large frying pan over medium heat. Add the fennel and cinnamon and cook for 30 seconds or until fragrant. Add the ginger garlic paste and cook for 30–40 seconds or until softened. Add the rice and stir to combine, before adding 1½ cups (375 ml) boiling water. Cover with a lid, reduce heat to low and simmer for 10 minutes or until rice has absorbed the water. Stir through the ground spices, tomato puree, salt and sugar, cover, and cook for a further 8 minutes or until all the liquid has been absorbed and the rice is cooked. Stir through the diced tomato, green shallot and mint to serve.

Rice Porridge DF, GF, V

This popular, porridge-like breakfast dish called *uppitta*, *or upma* in local dialect, is typical of Kerala. It's very easy to digest and doesn't sit heavily in the gut, making it a staple in the Ayurvedic diet. There are other regional versions made with semolina, too. Ask for broken rice at your Indian grocer or you may find it at Asian food stores that stock it for congee, a similar Asian breakfast porridge. If you can't find broken rice, you can make it by lightly pounding whole, medium-grain rice in a mortar and pestle, then passing through a sieve to remove any fine rice powder – it's the broken grains you're after here. Cooking broken rice means the grains don't remain separate during cooking, they break down and form that magical, comforting porridge consistency.

Serves 4

2 cups (400 g) broken rice
⅓ cup (80 ml) vegetable oil
1 teaspoon black mustard seeds
2 tablespoons split urad dal (white lentils), washed
16 fresh curry leaves
2 small green chillies, minced
⅛ teaspoon asafoetida
¾ cup raw peanuts, soaked in cold water for 20 minutes, drained
1 teaspoon ground cumin
1 teaspoon freshly ground black pepper
4 tablespoons grated fresh coconut
1 teaspoon minced ginger
30 ml lemon juice
2 teaspoons sea salt flakes
1 tomato, seeded and finely diced
2 tablespoons chopped coriander
2 green onions, finely sliced

Preheat oven to 160°C. Place the rice in a baking dish and bake for 20 minutes to warm through. Set aside.

Heat the oil in a large, heavy-based pot over medium heat. Add the mustard seeds and cook for 30 seconds or until they start to pop. Add the dal and cook for 1 minute or until it starts to colour. Add the curry leaves and chilli and cook for 10 seconds. Add the asafoetida, peanuts, cumin and pepper and cook, stirring to thoroughly combine, for a further 1 minute. Add 6 cups (1½ litres) water to the pot, increase heat to high and bring to the boil. Once boiling, add the rice and reduce heat to medium–low. Cook, continuing to stir so rice doesn't clump together, for 4 minutes or until the rice returns to a simmer and bubbles appear on the surface. Stir in the coconut and ginger. Cover with a lid and cook a further 6–8 minutes or until much of the water has been absorbed and the rice has a porridge-like consistency. Remove from the heat, add the lemon juice, salt, tomato, coriander and green onion and stir to combine. Serve warm.

Prawn Kedgeree GF

An age-old comfort dish using two staple grains, rice and lentils, this recipe is common throughout India and popularised by the British, who changed the spelling from *khichadi* to kedgeree. It can be made soupy with the addition of extra liquid for a nourishing and calming dish cooked for children and people convalescing. I've glamorised this humble dish with the addition of prawns and cook it so it has a similar texture to risotto.

Serves 6

1 cup (200 g) regular basmati rice
120 g toor dal (yellow split lentils)
100 g ghee
1 cinnamon stick
2 bay leaves
2 cardamom pods, cracked
4 cloves
1 brown onion, finely diced
2 tablespoons ginger garlic paste, see recipe
　page 436
1 small green chilli, minced
½ teaspoon freshly ground black pepper
3 teaspoons sea salt flakes
600 g raw prawn meat, peeled, deveined
　and butterflied
1 teaspoon ground turmeric
1 teaspoon ground cumin
12 fresh curry leaves
2 tomatoes, seeded and diced
1 tablespoon coriander leaves

Wash the rice and the dal separately. Soak in separate bowls of cold water for 30 minutes. Drain.

Melt 50 g of the ghee in a wide-based pan over medium heat. As the ghee melts, add the whole spices and fry for 1 minute or until starting to colour. Add the onion and cook for 5 minutes or until softened. Add the ginger garlic paste, chilli and pepper and stir to combine. Add the drained rice and dal and stir to coat in the onion mixture. Add 6 cups (1½ litres) boiling water and 2 teaspoons salt, cover and cook over medium–low heat for 15 minutes or until rice and dal are cooked and much of the water is absorbed. If it's too dry, just add a little extra hot water. It should be the consistency of a risotto. Remove from heat and discard the whole spices.

Meanwhile, season the prawns with the turmeric, cumin and remaining 1 teaspoon salt. Melt the remaining 50 g ghee in a frying pan over high heat. Once it starts to sizzle, add the curry leaves and the seasoned prawns and cook, tossing over the heat, for 2 minutes or until prawns start to colour. Add the tomato and cook for 30 seconds. Add the prawns to the hot rice and stir until thoroughly combined. Check seasoning and garnish with coriander to serve.

Dal and Lentils

Dal (or *dhal*) is often translated as lentils, but actually refers to a split version of a number of lentils, peas, kidney beans and so on. If a pulse is split in half, it is a dal. For example, split mung beans are mung dal. A stew or soup made with any kind of pulse, whole or split, is known as dal. The lentil is an edible legume from a bushy annual plant known for its lens-shaped seeds that grow in pods, usually with two seeds in each. As a food crop, its importance cannot be underestimated in India. With the world's largest number of vegetarians, lentils take pride of place in a meatless diet, providing necessary protein and nutrition.

Dal is also the common name in India for a dish made of split lentils, peas or beans with a texture that can vary from thin and soupy to a thick puree and everything in between. A staple accompaniment to rice and roti, dal is very easy to cook, is nutritious and sustaining, and is endlessly versatile. A meal is considered incomplete if dal is not served, even at the humblest table. Dal is consumed with robust enthusiasm and the methods for its preparation vary between states and regions. It seems that the repertoire for dal alone is inexhaustible, adapted by cooks everywhere.

Dal is a dish that can successfully be made in enormous quantities, such as at weddings and other festivals when feeding huge numbers of people is required. I am always amazed when I visit a Sikh temple to watch the cooks ply their vast vats in the *langars* (kitchens), cooking for the many thousands of people that are served every day. The langar is a place of equality and lies at the centre of Sikh teaching. Eschewing the Hindi caste system, the langar allows people to sit and eat together regardless of social status, religion, caste, colour, age or gender. Dal is at the centre of this daily routine; it's the food of the people. It's something that can be prepared and enjoyed without much expense, making it a real leveller.

Being a dried ingredient with a long shelf life, dal is a pantry essential. Easy to store and even easier to cook, you can have four or five different types in your cupboard and be able to turn out a variety of delicious dishes. A pressure cooker is an essential piece of equipment in the Indian kitchen and one that is used frequently to cook dal, as it hastens the cooking time and uses much less fuel – a precious commodity for many. A pressure cooker is a thrifty investment, and interestingly, one that is making something of a comeback in today's kitchen, where there is an emphasis on tools for time-poor cooks.

When cooking dal, it's useful to know how to recognise the different types by their name, colour and shape. See my guide on the following page to learn your toor dal from your masoor dal.

Urad dal is black when whole, called black gram, and is used extensively in the cooking of the north. When split and hulled, the lentils appear creamy-white and are used more in the cooking of the south.

Toor dal is hulled and split small, yellow lentils that cook more quickly than chana dal (split chickpeas, see below) because they're softer. Toor dal is typical in southern cooking.

Masoor dal is split red lentils. They're soft, cook quickly and change colour to dusty yellow when cooked.

Mung dal is referred to as green gram when whole. It's small, oval and olive-green in appearance with a stronger flavour than the split version. When soaked in water for a couple of days, it sprouts and can be used in salads or soups for texture. Sprouted lentils are readily available these days at reputable vegetable purveyors and at many farmers markets. The hulled split lentils are green and white and cook more quickly than the whole dal. Mung dal is low in fat and very high in protein, it's considered one of the best plant-based sources of protein.

Chana dal is split chickpeas, sometimes called Bengal gram. It's the most widely known and used lentil in India.

Kala chana is small, whole black chickpeas with an earthier and more robust flavour than the kabuli (white) variety. Used in the cooking of the north, you'll likely only find these at a specialist Indian grocer.

Kabuli chana is whole yellow chickpeas and the ones we are most familiar with in Western cooking. When picked, the peas are soft and green before being left to dry. They are a prized ingredient during winter when they are harvested.

Rajma is dried, whole red kidney beans, prepared in the same manner as any other dal and often combined with black urad lentils when making *dal makhani* (buttery black dal, see recipe page 318) or other dal preparations in the northwest regions of India.

Buttery Black Dal GF, V

Dal makhani enriched with butter and cream, is a staple from the Punjab and northwest regions and a signature on just about every Indian menu anywhere in India, or the world for that matter. Traditionally served with meat kebabs and roti, it's the most acclaimed of dal preparations with a deeply satisfying, earthy flavour. I have also seen the dal cooked with a mix of black urad lentils and red kidney beans (*rajma*). To do this, you would simply adjust the quantity of dal to accommodate the inclusion of the beans and the emphasis is always on the buttery character of the dal – both versions are authentic.

Serves 8

1½ cups (300 g) whole black urad dal, soaked in
   cold water overnight
2 teaspoons vegetable oil
300 ml tomato puree (blend 3 ripe tomatoes)
2 tablespoons ginger garlic paste, see recipe
   page 436
¼ teaspoon asafoetida
2 teaspoons Kashmiri chilli powder
3 teaspoons sea salt flakes
150 g unsalted butter
150 ml cream
2 teaspoons crushed kasoori methi
   (dried fenugreek leaves), see Glossary
2 small green chillies, finely sliced
½ teaspoon garam masala

Drain the urad dal and rinse with cold water until the water runs clear. Transfer to a large pot with 6 cups (1½ litres) water and bring to the boil over medium–high heat. Reduce heat to medium and cook, stirring occasionally, for 1 hour or until the lentils have split and are slightly broken in appearance. Drain, transfer to a food processor and pulse briefly to form a coarse mash. Return to the pot with the oil and mash until smooth. Add the tomato puree, ginger garlic paste, asafoetida, chilli powder and salt with ½ cup (125 ml) water and stir to combine. Reduce heat to low and cook, stirring occasionally, for 30 minutes or until thickened. Stir in the butter and cream and cook for a further 10 minutes or until the dal looks rich and glossy. Add the kasoori methi, green chilli and garam masala and stir to combine, adjust the seasoning if necessary. Serve hot.

**Masterclass step-by-step
Buttery Black Dal →**

1

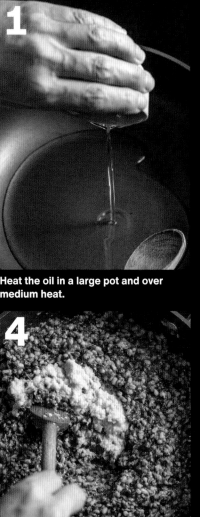

Heat the oil in a large pot and over medium heat.

2

Add the boiled and mashed urad dal.

3

Add the tomato puree.

4

Add the ginger garlic paste.

5

Add the asafoetida.

6

Add the Kashmiri chilli powder.

7

Add the salt.

8

Add the water and stir to combine. Reduce heat to low and cook, stirring occasionally, for 30 minutes.

9

Stir in the butter.

10

Add the cream.

11

Stir to combine.

12

Cook for 10 minutes or until dal looks rich and glossy.

13

Add the kasoori methi and stir to combine.

14

Add the green chilli and stir to combine.

15

Add the garam masala and stir to combine. Serve hot.

Breakfast Dal GF, V

Pongol is a nutritious breakfast dish and one I became familiar with when travelling through southern India, especially during the Sanskrit festival. The dal has a porridge-like consistency with a gentle pepperiness. It's light and easy to digest, making it an important dish in the Ayurvedic diet. Serve with a fresh coconut chutney.

Serves 4

1 cup (200 g) short grain rice
⅔ cup (125 g) split mung dal (green lentils)
1 teaspoon ground turmeric
20 roasted cashews, roughly chopped
1 teaspoon sea salt flakes
2 tablespoons ghee
12 fresh curry leaves
1 teaspoon cumin seeds
½ teaspoon cracked black pepper
1 tablespoon minced or grated ginger
2 small green chillies, minced
½ teaspoon asafoetida
1 tablespoon lime juice
2 tablespoons shredded fresh coconut
2 tablespoons chopped coriander leaves

Using a mallet or a mortar and pestle, pound the rice to crack the grains. Place rice in a frying pan over medium heat and dry roast until warmed through. Remove from pan and set aside. Place the mung dal in the same pan and dry roast for 4 minutes or until starting to colour. Place the rice and dal in a large saucepan over medium heat with 1 litre water and the turmeric and bring to the boil. Reduce heat, cover with a lid and simmer for 25 minutes or until the dal and rice are soft. The mixture should have a porridge-like consistency. Add the chopped cashews and salt and stir to combine.

Meanwhile, melt the ghee in a frying pan over medium heat. Add the curry leaves, cumin, black pepper, ginger and green chilli and cook for 30 seconds or until just starting to pop. Add the asafoetida and lime juice and cook for a further 10 seconds. Add to the dal with the coconut and stir to combine. Scatter with chopped coriander leaves to serve.

Spiced Chickpea Dal v

Chole bhatura is a Punjabi staple that makes use of humble pantry ingredients. *Chole* is a chickpea curry served with puffed *bhatura* bread, a dish that has been widely embraced in other regions of India. The dal preparation can vary across districts depending on its blend of spices and this version was my favourite breakfast during my travels through Sikkim staying in village houses.

Serves 8

1½ cups (250 g) dried chickpeas, soaked in cold
   water overnight, drained
¼ cup (60 ml) vegetable oil
3 small red onions, finely diced
2 tablespoons ginger garlic paste, see recipe
   page 436
2 small green chillies, minced
3 tomatoes, diced
2 teaspoons ground turmeric
1 teaspoon Kashmiri chilli powder
2 teaspoons ground coriander
1 teaspoon ground cumin
½ teaspoon chaat masala
2 teaspoons sea salt flakes
150 g thick plain yoghurt
3 tablespoons chopped coriander leaves
1 tablespoon lemon juice
2 tablespoons fried shallot slices, see Glossary
6 bhatura breads, see Breads page 388

Cook the chickpeas in large pot of boiling water for 45 minutes or until soft. Drain, reserving 50 ml of the cooking water. Place 1 cup chickpeas (leave the rest whole) and the reserved water in a food processor and blend to form a puree. Set aside.

Heat the oil in a frying pan over medium heat. Add the onion and cook for 4 minutes or until softened. Add the ginger garlic paste and green chilli and cook for 30 seconds or until coloured. Add the tomato and cook for 4 minutes or until softened. Mix the ground spices together in a small bowl and add to the onion and tomato mixture. Stir to combine and cook for 2 minutes or until fragrant. Add the whole chickpeas, chickpea puree and salt, stir to combine and cook for 2–3 minutes. Add the yoghurt and simmer gently for a further 5 minutes. Remove from heat and stir through the coriander leaves and lemon juice. Scatter with the fried shallots and serve with hot bhatura bread.

Pumpkin and Coconut Dal DF, GF, V

I use the softer textured Japanese kent pumpkin for this dal, but any other pumpkin is suitable, you may just need to vary the cooking time slightly depending on the density of its texture. Although stocks are not part of the Indian vernacular, I have adopted the Western practice and use vegetable stock when cooking this dal, rather than water, because it adds a real boost of flavour.

Serves 6

6 x 3 cm-thick wedges Japanese kent pumpkin, skin on
½ cup (125 ml) olive oil
1 teaspoon sea salt flakes
½ teaspoon freshly ground black pepper
½ teaspoon ground turmeric
1 onion, finely chopped
1 tablespoon ginger garlic paste, see recipe page 436
2 teaspoons minced fresh turmeric
2 cups (400 g) masoor dal (red lentils), rinsed under cold running water, drained
2 cups (500 ml) hot vegetable stock or hot water
300 ml coconut milk
3 baby cucumbers (cukes), quartered lengthwise and diced
100 g green beans, cut into 1 cm sticks, blanched
2 small green chillies, finely sliced
2 tablespoons coconut flakes, lightly toasted
2 tablespoons roasted cashews, roughly chopped
2 tablespoons coriander leaves, roughly chopped
25 ml lime juice
½ teaspoon nigella seeds, toasted
¼ teaspoon chaat masala

Preheat oven to 220°C. Line a baking tray with non-stick baking paper. Toss the pumpkin with ¼ cup (60 ml) oil and season with salt, pepper and ground turmeric. Place onto the prepared baking tray in single a layer and roast for 20 minutes or until tender. Set aside and keep warm.

Meanwhile, heat the remaining ¼ cup (60 ml) oil in a deep frying pan over medium–high heat. Add the onion and cook, stirring, for 2 minutes or until softened. Add the ginger garlic paste and turmeric and cook for 2 minutes or until fragrant. Stir in the masoor dal and cook for 1 minute to combine. Add the hot stock (or water) and the coconut milk and bring to the boil. Reduce heat to medium and simmer, stirring occasionally, for 10 minutes or until lentils are cooked. Because the lentils are soft, they will start to lose their shape. Don't worry, this is how they should be – it forms a porridge-like consistency.

Spoon the dal into serving bowls and top with a wedge of pumpkin. Place the baby cucumber, beans, green chilli, coconut flakes, cashew, coriander leaves, lime juice and nigella seeds in a bowl, season with chaat masala and toss to combine. Scatter salad over the pumpkin and dal to serve.

Cauliflower Dal GF, V

This vegetable dal is prepared in two parts then combined together to give textural contrast. It's a dish I like to serve with grilled fish or with a simple rice pulao. It also makes a great addition to a picnic hamper as it transports well and can be eaten at room temperature with bread or pappadams.

Serves 8

2 cups (400 g) mung dal (green lentils), soaked in cold water for 30 minutes, drained
1 tablespoon chopped ginger
3 long green chillies, chopped
2 ripe tomatoes, chopped
50 g ghee
4 shallots, finely sliced
4 garlic cloves, sliced
1 tablespoon brown mustard seeds
1 tablespoon ground turmeric
4 tablespoons coriander leaves, roughly chopped
2 tablespoons fried curry leaves

CAULIFLOWER
120 g ghee
2 teaspoons brown mustard seeds
3 shallots, finely sliced
2 long green chillies, finely sliced
2 garlic cloves, finely sliced
200 g cauliflower florets
2 tablespoons fresh curry leaves
1 teaspoon sea salt flakes
1 teaspoon roasted ground coriander seeds

Place 2 litres of water in a large pot and bring to the boil. Add the mung dal and cook for 2 minutes, using a spoon to remove any impurities from the surface. Drain and set aside.

Place the ginger, chilli and tomato in a blender and process to form a paste. Melt the ghee in a saucepan over medium heat. Add the shallot and garlic and cook for 3 minutes or until starting to colour. Add the mustard seeds and turmeric and cook for 1 minute or until fragrant. Add the chilli and tomato paste, stir and cook for a further 1–2 minutes or until fragrant. Add the mung dal, reduce heat to low and simmer, stirring occasionally, for 40 minutes or until softened.

While the dal is cooking, prepare the cauliflower. Melt the ghee in a frying pan over medium heat. Add the mustard seeds and cook for 30 seconds or until they start to pop. Add the shallot, chilli and garlic and cook for 2 minutes or until softened. Add the cauliflower and cook for 8 minutes or until crisp and golden. Add the curry leaves and cook for 1 minute. Season with salt and ground coriander seeds.

To serve, stir the coriander leaves through the cooked dal, scatter over the fried cauliflower and garnish with the fried curry leaves.

Dal Fry GF, V

This is a typical Nepali lentil preparation popular in everyday Sikkimese cooking, which uses less spice than other regions of India. You could spice it up more by adding ground coriander, cumin and turmeric, if you wish. It makes a great addition to the shared table along with other contrasting dishes.

Serves 6

1 cup (180 g) chana dal (split chickpeas), soaked in cold water for 2 hours, drained
2 tablespoons ghee
1 black cardamom pod, cracked
2 bay leaves
2 small green chillies, minced
2 small red onions, diced
2 small tomatoes, diced
1 teaspoon sea salt flakes
2 tablespoons chopped coriander leaves

Cook the chana dal in large pot of boiling water over medium high heat for 20 minutes or until soft. Drain and set aside.

Melt the ghee in a frying pan or wok over medium heat. Add the cardamom, bay leaves and chilli and cook for 2 minutes or until fragrant. Add the onion and tomato and cook for 7–8 minutes or until coloured. Add the cooked dal and mash roughly with the back of a spoon, taking care not to break it down too much. Add 2/3 cups (160 ml) water and the salt and bring to the boil. Simmer for a further 2–3 minutes. Remove from heat and stir through the chopped coriander to serve.

Tomato Dal DF, GF, V

Tamaata pappu is a common vegetarian dish of the Andhra region, which I came across while staying in Hyderabad. With a gentle tangy flavour, it can be served with steamed rice or roti and a spicy mango or lime pickle. I find it also makes a great accompaniment to roasted root vegetables.

Serves 4

1 cup (180 g) toor dal (yellow split lentils), washed and soaked for 30 minutes, rinsed
300 g ripe tomatoes, chopped
2 long green chillies, sliced
3 garlic cloves
2 tablespoons vegetable oil
1 teaspoon cumin seeds
1 teaspoon black mustard seeds
1 white onion, finely diced
2 tablespoons fresh curry leaves
2 teaspoons minced ginger
1 teaspoon ground turmeric
1 teaspoon ground coriander seeds
1 teaspoon chilli powder
1 teaspoon sea salt flakes
2 teaspoons sambar powder, see Soups page 58
2 tablespoons chopped coriander leaves

Place the toor dal in a saucepan over medium–high heat with 2 cups (500 ml) water. Cover and cook for 25–30 minutes or until the dal is soft and the water has been absorbed. Remove from heat and mash the dal a little with a large fork, without making it a smooth paste. Set aside.

Place the tomato, green chilli and garlic in a food processor and blend to form a puree. Set aside.

Heat the oil in a frying pan over medium heat. Add the cumin and mustard seeds and cook for 30 seconds or until they start to pop. Add the onion and cook for 4 minutes or until softened. Add the curry leaves and ginger and cook for 2 minutes. Stir through the turmeric, ground coriander and chilli powder and cook for 1 minute. Add the tomato puree with ½ cup (125 ml) water, stir to combine and cook, stirring occasionally, for a further 15 minutes. Stir through the mashed dal, season with salt and sambar powder, reduce heat to low and simmer for 6–8 minutes. Remove from heat and stir though the coriander to serve.

Gujarati Spiced Dal DF, GF, V

A typical addition to a vegetarian thali plate, this dal relies on pantry staples and quick preparation. Serve it for lunch with flatbread and a tangy pickle or as an accompaniment to grilled meat or fish.

Serves 4

1 cup (200 g) toor dal (yellow split lentils), washed and soaked for 30 minutes, rinsed
2 tablespoons vegetable oil
1 onion, finely diced
2 tablespoons grated fresh coconut
$2/3$ cup coriander leaves
1 teaspoon cumin seeds
1 teaspoon brown mustard seeds
2 teaspoons white poppy seeds
1 tablespoon fresh curry leaves
1 teaspoon ginger garlic paste, see recipe page 436
4 small green chillies, minced
1 tomato, seeded and finely diced
1 teaspoon ground turmeric
1 teaspoon chilli powder
1 teaspoon ground coriander
½ teaspoon caster sugar
2 teaspoons sea salt flakes

Place the toor dal in a saucepan over medium–high heat with 2 cups (500 ml) water, cover and cook for 10–12 minutes or until the dal is soft and the water has been absorbed. Set aside.

Heat a frying pan over high heat. Add 1 tablespoon of the oil, onion and coconut and cook for 5 minutes or until starting to brown. Transfer to a blender with half the coriander leaves and blend to a coarse paste. Set aside.

Wipe out the frying pan with paper towel and return to medium heat. Add the remaining oil, cumin, mustard and poppy seeds and cook for 30 seconds or until they start to pop. Add the curry leaves, ginger garlic paste and green chilli and stir to combine. Add the onion coconut paste and tomato, stir to combine and cook for 1 minute. Add the turmeric, chilli powder and ground coriander and stir to combine. Add the cooked dal, sugar and salt, stir and cook for a further 5 minutes. Serve hot, garnished with the remaining coriander leaves.

Vegetable Dal DF, GF, V

Light and healthy in texture and taste and easy to digest, this recipe comes from an Ayurvedic retreat I have visited in Karnataka and is perfect to cook when you're feeling a little under the weather, convalescing or needing some essential nourishment. You can use a mixture of vegetables (carrot, green peas, corn, beans, cauliflower and broccoli florets, turnip or kohlrabi) to stir through the dal. Just be sure to cut everything to uniform dice, about the same size as green peas, so they cook evenly together.

Serves 4

½ cup (40 g) toor dal (yellow split lentils)
½ teaspoon sea salt flakes
½ teaspoon ground turmeric
2 tablespoons vegetable oil
1 teaspoon cumin seeds
½ red onion, finely diced
1 small green chilli, finely sliced
2 garlic cloves, crushed
2 tomatoes, seeded and diced
pinch of asafoetida
1 cup cooked diced vegetables (such as carrot, peas, cauliflower)
1 tablespoon chopped coriander leaves
2 teaspoons lime juice

Heat a frying pan over medium heat. Add the toor dal and toast for 2–3 minutes, stirring to keep an even heat. Wash and rinse the toasted dal and place in a saucepan over medium heat with 1½ cups (375 ml) water (the ratio is 3 times water to dal), salt and turmeric. Cover with a lid and cook for 12–15 minutes or until soft.

While the dal is cooking, heat a frying pan over medium heat. Add the oil and cumin seeds and cook for 30 seconds or until they start to pop. Add the onion, green chilli and garlic and cook, stirring occasionally, for 4–5 minutes or until softened and starting to brown. Add the tomato and cook for a further 2 minutes.

Whisk the cooked dal with the remaining cooking liquid and add to the tomato mixture. Cook for 2 minutes, season with asafoetida and cook for a further 1 minute. Stir through the cooked vegetables, chopped coriander and lime juice to serve.

Yellow Dal with Garlic and Spinach GF, V

Typical of the Rajasthani region, *dal palak* is easy to prepare. Its final flavour comes from the *tarka* (tempered spices), in this case, cumin seeds and dried chillies fried in ghee until sizzling and poured over the cooked dal. I sometimes use warrigal greens in place of spinach, as I have an abundance of them in my garden and they make an excellent substitute, giving a very Australian character to the dish. This dal can be served with barbecued meats, a variety of fresh salads and flatbread and makes a great addition to a picnic hamper.

Serves 4

3 tablespoons ghee
2 teaspoons cumin seeds
1 red onion, finely diced
2 garlic cloves, minced
1 teaspoon minced green chilli
1 teaspoon ground turmeric
1 teaspoon sea salt flakes
1 cup (100 g) chana dal (split chickpeas), soaked, rinsed and drained
1 cup chopped spinach
4 small dried chillies

Melt 1 tablespoon of ghee in a saucepan over medium heat. Add 1 teaspoon cumin seeds and cook for 30 seconds or until they start to pop. Add the onion and cook for 3 minutes or until softened and pink. Add the garlic, green chilli, turmeric and salt and stir to combine. Add the chana dal and stir thoroughly to coat in the spices. Stir in 2 cups (500 ml) water, cover and cook for 20 minutes or until the dal is soft and most of the water has been absorbed without the mixture being dry. Add a splash more water, if required.

Meanwhile, heat 1 tablespoon ghee in a frying pan over medium heat. Add the spinach and cook for 2 minutes or until just wilted. Add the spinach to the dal and stir to combine. Heat the remaining 1 tablespoon ghee in a frying pan over medium heat. Add the remaining 1 teaspoon cumin seeds and dried chillies and cook for 30 seconds or until sizzling. Pour the cumin and chilli over the spinach dal to serve.

Mixed Lentil Dal GF, V

A nourishing dal recipe that is flavoursome, wholesome and healthy for the body. I like to serve it with a simple pulao topped with chopped mint.

Serves 4

2 tablespoons chana dal (split chickpeas)
3 tablespoons masoor dal (red lentils)
2 tablespoons split mung dal (green lentils)
1 tablespoon split urad dal (white lentils)
1 teaspoon sea salt flakes
½ teaspoon ground turmeric
2 teaspoons ginger garlic paste, see recipe page 436
2 teaspoons ground coriander
1 teaspoon ground cumin
½ teaspoon dried chilli flakes
pinch of ground cloves
¼ teaspoon ground cinnamon
¼ teaspoon freshly ground black pepper
2 tablespoons ghee
1 red onion, chopped
½ teaspoon amchur (dried mango powder)
½ teaspoon powdered black salt, see Glossary
½ cup sprouted lentils (mung beans or mixed lentil sprouts)
2 tablespoons chopped coriander leaves

Place all the dals in a bowl, cover with cold water and set aside to soak for 30 minutes. Rinse in a colander until water runs clear. Drain and transfer to a saucepan over medium heat with 3 cups (750 ml) water, salt and turmeric. Cook, covered, for 25 minutes or until soft and water is mostly absorbed. The cooked lentils should be a little slushy (like a loose porridge). Remove from heat and mash lightly with a fork. Set aside.

Place the ginger garlic paste, ground coriander, cumin, chilli, cloves, cinnamon and black pepper in a bowl with 1 tablespoon water and mix to make a paste. Set aside.

Melt the ghee in a frying pan over medium heat. Add the onion and cook, stirring occasionally, for 4 minutes or until softened and starting to colour. Add the ginger garlic spice paste, stir to combine and cook for 3 minutes or until fragrant. Add the amchur and black salt with the cooked lentils and stir to combine. Add ¾ cups (180 ml) water and simmer for 5–6 minutes or until reduced slightly. Stir through the sprouted lentils and garnish with coriander leaves to serve.

Green Dal GF, V

A quick and easy dal recipe to make, I sometimes serve this with steamed green beans tossed through toasted breadcrumbs or chopped nuts for added crunch.

Serves 6

1½ cups (300 g) split mung dal (green lentils), soaked in cold water for 1 hour, drained
1 garlic clove, sliced
1 teaspoon ground turmeric
150 g English spinach leaves, stalks removed
150 g rainbow chard (or silver beet) leaves, stalks removed
4 tablespoons ghee
1 tablespoon ginger garlic paste, see recipe page 436
3 small green chillies, minced
½ teaspoon ground cumin
½ teaspoon chilli powder
1 teaspoon ground coriander
2 tomatoes, seeded and diced
1 teaspoon sea salt flakes
3 tablespoons chopped coriander leaves
1 tablespoon garam masala
3 tablespoons fried shallot slices, see Glossary

Place the mung dal in a large pot of boiling water with the sliced garlic and ½ teaspoon turmeric and cook for 10–12 minutes or until tender. Drain and set aside.

Blanch the spinach and chard leaves in boiling water for 15 seconds. Drain, squeeze out excess moisture and roughly chop. Set aside.

Melt the ghee in a large frying pan over medium heat. Add the ginger garlic paste and green chilli and cook, stirring, for 20 seconds or until softened. Add the cumin, chilli powder, coriander and remaining ½ teaspoon turmeric and cook for 20 seconds or until fragrant. Add the tomato and cooked lentils and cook, stirring to combine, for 3 minutes. Add the chopped green leaves and cook for a further 2 minutes or until any liquid has evaporated and the greens have become paste-like. Stir in the salt, coriander leaves and garam masala and remove from heat. Top with fried shallots to serve.

White Dal GF, V

I collected this *urad mogar* dal recipe from a local family when travelling through the Rajasthani desert. It makes a terrific accompaniment to a goat curry, grilled meats or a vegetable thali and shows the incredible versatility of lentil preparations.

Serves 6

1 cup (200 g) split urad dal (white lentils), soaked for 15 minutes in cold water, drained
2 teaspoons fennel seeds
2 teaspoons coriander seeds
1 teaspoon ground cumin
2 teaspoons sea salt flakes
3 tablespoons vegetable oil
1 bay leaf
1 cinnamon stick
1 black cardamom pod, cracked
2 whole cloves
¼ teaspoon peppercorns
3 large dried chillies
¾ cup onion puree (blend 1 white onion)
1 tablespoon sliced garlic
200 g fresh curd (hung yoghurt), see Eggs and Dairy page 110
3 tablespoons fried shallot slices, see Glossary

Place the urad dal in a large saucepan over high heat with 1 litre water, the fennel seeds, coriander seeds, cumin and 1 teaspoon salt. Cook for 15 minutes or until tender. Drain and set aside.

Heat the oil in a frying pan over medium heat. Add the bay leaf, cinnamon, cardamom, cloves, peppercorns and chillies and cook for 30 seconds or until fragrant. Add the onion puree and cook for 3 minutes or until golden. Add the garlic and cook for a further 1 minute. Stir in the curd and the remaining 1 teaspoon salt and cook until mixture boils. Reduce heat to low and cook for 10 minutes or until all the liquid has evaporated and the oil has separated. Add the dal and half the fried shallots and stir to combine. Transfer to a serving plate and scatter with the remaining fried shallots to serve.

Dal Butter GF, V

This comes from my friend and colleague, Adelaide chef Emma McCaskill, who draws on her British-Indian heritage with imagination and flair. The cooked dal is blended and whipped in a food processor or blender with butter to make the most unctuous condiment for paratha or roti, in much the same way as you would make a liver pâté. You're after a rough ratio of 60 g dal to 40 g of butter, so it's beautifully silky. I slather it on a baguette and add shredded cooked chicken (spiced, of course) to make a perfect sandwich. It also makes an ideal partner for wood-grilled meat kebabs.

Serves 6

2 tablespoons vegetable oil
½ brown onion, peeled and finely chopped
2 cm piece fresh ginger, peeled and finely chopped
1 clove garlic, crushed
½ teaspoon ground cumin
½ teaspoon ground coriander
1 teaspoon ground turmeric
½ cup (90 g) masoor dal (red lentils), rinsed until water runs clear
1 teaspoon sea salt flakes
125 g salted butter, diced

Heat the oil in a saucepan over medium heat. Add the onion, ginger and garlic and cook for 5–7 minutes or until onion is translucent. Add the cumin, coriander and turmeric and cook for 2–3 minutes or until fragrant. Add the masoor dal, stir to coat in the spiced onion, and cook, stirring constantly to prevent sticking, for 3–4 minutes. Add 4 cups (1 litre) water, making sure the lentils are covered, and increase heat to high. Bring to the boil and cook for 10 minutes. Reduce heat to low and cook, stirring to prevent sticking, for a further 30 minutes or until the lentils have absorbed most of the water and dal has the consistency of thick porridge. Season with salt, remove from heat and allow to cool for 20–30 minutes.

Place the cooled dal in a food processor and blend, adding butter gradually, until smooth. It should have a similar consistency to apple puree. Check seasoning and set aside in an airtight container in the fridge overnight. The consistency will thicken when refrigerated. Serve cold or at room temperature with paratha.

Minced Lamb, Tomato and Green Bean Dal DF, GF

Keema dal is a more substantial dish that could easily be served on its own as a main dish along with some bread or rice and a raita salad. You can replace the lamb with minced chicken, if you prefer.

Serves 4

1 cup (180 g) green gram (whole mung beans), washed and soaked for 1 hour, drained
2 teaspoons sea salt flakes
½ teaspoon ground turmeric
120 g green beans, cut into 5 mm sticks
2 tablespoons vegetable oil
1 white onion, finely diced
½ teaspoon freshly ground black pepper
½ teaspoon ground cinnamon
1 tablespoon minced ginger
400 g minced lamb shoulder
½ teaspoon chilli powder
16 oven-roasted cherry tomatoes, see Glossary
2 tablespoons lime juice
1 teaspoon garam masala
pinch of asafoetida
½ cup chopped mint leaves
½ cup chopped coriander leaves
3 tablespoons curry dressing, see Salads page 90
2 tablespoons fried curry leaves

Place the green gram, 1 teaspoon salt and the turmeric in large pot of boiling water over medium heat and cook for 25 minutes or until tender. Add the bean sticks and cook for a further 2 minutes. Drain and set aside.

Heat the oil in a frying pan over medium heat. Add the onion, pepper and cinnamon and cook for 4–5 minutes or until starting to brown. Add the ginger and cook for 1 minute or until fragrant. Add the lamb mince and cook, stirring to break up the meat and mix with the onion, for 2 minutes. Add ¾ cups (180 ml) water, remaining 1 teaspoon salt and chilli powder and stir to combine. Reduce heat to low, cover with a lid and simmer for 15 minutes or until mince is tender. Using a spoon, carefully remove any fat from the surface. Add the cherry tomato, lime juice, garam masala and asafoetida and cook for a further 2 minutes. Add the chopped herbs, cooked dal and green beans and stir to combine. Stir through the curry dressing and top with fried curry leaves to serve.

Pickles and Chutneys

Indian cuisine is a tapestry of diverse flavours and textures, which can be attributed to the vast array of condiments that accompany a meal, such as fresh sauces, raita, dips, relishes, soothing chutneys and piquant pickles. No Indian meal is complete without them. Even meals at their most simple (such as at a Sikh temple) will include rice, dal and pickle. Fly on any Indian airline and the in-flight food will always include a little packet of pickle, regardless of the time of day.

An age-old ritual that makes the most of the season's bounty, the ancient art of preserving food goes back thousands of years, when vegetables were preserved in salt to extend their shelf life. Modern-day pickles carry on that tradition with a more complex layering of flavours, ranging from hot and tangy to aromatic, fragrant and spicy. Pickling is considered an art form. It's a discipline that belongs to expert home cooks and communities involved in small-scale production. Pickling honours every region and ensures that the vast cultural heritage of India remains intact. As I've discovered, there are many experts across the country that have added weight to the importance of preserving food and bringing diversity to the table, so this chapter is a tribute to their collective voices.

Known as *achars* in India, vegetable or fruit pickles add a piquancy and kick to everyday meals. They're the heart and soul of home cooking and an early childhood taste memory for all Indians. Techniques and the finished products vary between regions, each one having its specialty. There are many variations influenced by the souring agent used to make the pickle, be it amchur, tamarind, buttermilk, vinegar or lemon juice. Pickles have the honour of making rice, bread and dal more appetising and are essential condiments on a thali plate. Even a modest tiffin will feature a dollop of chutney or pickle to accompany the rice and dal. Faced with infinite preparations from India, where every family has their favourite, I've included my most trusted, tried and true recipes that are staples in my own pantry.

To distinguish between the different types of condiments I have covered in this chapter, pickles (achars) are cooked and stored in preserving jars to use throughout the year. Not only made with fruit or vegetables, they sometimes feature fish or shellfish in coastal regions. Whereas chutneys (*chatni*) are made with fruit, herbs, nuts or vegetables and are served fresh (uncooked) upon being made. They're not meant to be stored and are best eaten the same day to keep their vibrancy. Chutneys usually bring a cooling effect and occasionally a gentle sweetness to food, whether it's tempering the spicy heat of a curry or adding piquancy to fried snacks, pastries, dosas and barbecued kebabs, fish or meats.

Pickles and chutneys add depth and new dimensions to food. Expand your repertoire and capture the abundance of the season by distilling its essence. Enjoying delicious condiments at the table is the ultimate reward for due diligence in the kitchen.

Eggplant Pickle DF, GF, V

Given my undying love for eggplant (or *brinjal*), this pickle is a constant in my pantry as it makes a great flavour companion and is incredibly versatile. Sometimes, I just add a generous dollop to steamed rice with a fried egg for an instant supper.

Makes 800 g

4 x 300 g purple eggplants, peeled and diced into
    2 cm cubes
1 teaspoon table salt
2 cups (500 ml) vegetable oil
½ cup (125 ml) mustard oil
1 tablespoon black mustard seeds
1 tablespoon fennel seeds
1 tablespoon cumin seeds
½ cup fresh curry leaves
120 g ginger garlic paste, see recipe page 436
1 tablespoon Kashmiri chilli powder
1 tablespoon ground turmeric
160 ml white vinegar
3 tablespoons tamarind puree
220 g soft brown sugar
2 tablespoons sea salt flakes

Sprinkle the eggplant with table salt and set aside to drain in a colander for 30 minutes. Squeeze out excess moisture and rub dry with a cloth. Don't use water to rinse the eggplant, as the flesh will become mushy.

Heat the vegetable oil in a deep-fryer or large saucepan until temperature reaches 180°C. Add the eggplant in small batches and fry for 4 minutes or until golden. Set aside to drain on paper towel.

Heat the mustard oil in a large frying pan over medium heat. Add the mustard, fennel and cumin seeds with the curry leaves and cook, being careful not to burn, for 30 seconds or until fragrant. Stir in the ginger garlic paste and cook for 2 minutes. Add the ground spices and cook for 30 seconds. Stir through the vinegar, tamarind, sugar and salt and cook for 5 minutes. Add the fried eggplant, reduce heat to medium–low and cook for a further 5 minutes or until liquid has reduced and mixture has become sticky. Pour into sterilised glass jars and seal with tight-fitting lids. Store in the refrigerator for up to 1 month.

Masterclass step-by-step Eggplant Pickle ➔

1

Sprinkle the eggplant with table salt and set aside
to drain in a colander for 30 minutes.

2

Squeeze to remove excess moisture
and rub dry with a cloth.

3

Fry the eggplant in small batches for
4 minutes or until golden.

4

Heat mustard oil in a frying pan over medium heat. Add
the seeds and curry leaves and cook for 30 seconds.

5

Add the ginger garlic paste and cook
for 2 minutes.

6

Add the ground spices and cook for
30 seconds.

7

Stir through the vinegar.

8

Stir through the tamarind.

9

Add the sugar and salt.

10

Cook for 5 minutes.

11

Add the eggplant.

12

Reduce heat to medium-low and cook for 5 minutes or until sticky and reduced.

Chilli Mango Pickle DF, GF, V

There's nothing better than exploring pickle shops around India and tasting their wares. For me, each place is defined by its distinctive flavours. This recipe is a taste memory I collected from Mysore. It has a gentle explosion of heat and is wonderful served on a thali plate or with myriad vegetable preparations. You can even stir it through steamed rice for an easy and quick flavour fix.

Makes 500 g

2 tablespoons vegetable oil
1 red onion, minced
2 garlic cloves, crushed
1 teaspoon garam masala
4 green cardamom pods, cracked
2 small red chillies, minced
2 tablespoons fresh curry leaves
300 ml apple cider vinegar
1 Granny Smith apple, peeled, cored and
    finely diced
3 green or under-ripe mangoes, peeled and
    finely diced
330 g brown sugar

Heat the oil in a large frying pan over medium heat. Add the onion, garlic, garam masala, cardamom, chilli and curry leaves and cook, stirring regularly, for 5 minutes or until softened. Add the vinegar and apple and cook for 6 minutes or until softened. Add the mango and sugar and cook for 5 minutes or until sugar has dissolved. Reduce heat to low and simmer for 30 minutes or until liquid has evaporated. Pour the hot pickle into hot, sterilised glass jars and seal with tight-fitting lids. Keep for up to 1 year. Refrigerate after opening.

Tomato Kasundi Pickle DF, GF, V

This Bengali mustard pickle has been part of my repertoire for a few decades now. It makes a terrific accompaniment to grilled or baked fish, is great tossed through pasta or noodles, or simply served as a condiment on a cheese sandwich.

Makes 600 g

1 tablespoon brown mustard seeds
160 ml malt vinegar
1 tablespoon chopped fresh ginger
6 garlic cloves
8 small red chillies, minced
100 ml mustard oil
1 tablespoon cumin seeds, toasted and ground
½ teaspoon ground cloves
2 teaspoons ground turmeric
1 kg ripe tomatoes, peeled and roughly chopped
50 g brown sugar
1 tablespoon sea salt flakes

Heat a frying pan over low heat. Add the mustard seeds and vinegar and cook for 5 minutes, taking care not to evaporate the vinegar. Set aside to cool.

Place the mustard seed vinegar, ginger, garlic and chilli in a food processor and blend until a smooth paste forms.

Heat the oil in a heavy-based frying pan over medium–low heat. Add the ground spices and cook for 15 seconds or until just fragrant. Add the mustard paste and tomato, stir to combine and cook, stirring occasionally, for 45 minutes or until the tomato has broken down. Add the sugar and salt, stir to combine and cook for a further 5 minutes. Taste and adjust seasoning, if necessary. Transfer to a food processor and pulse briefly to form a coarse paste. Pour into sterilised glass jars and seal with tight-fitting lids. Store in the pantry for up to 1 month. Refrigerate once opened.

Cauliflower Pickles DF, GF, V

In many cultures, it's a much-loved custom to make good use of the season's plentiful vegetables by pickling the harvest, and India is no exception. This tangy cauliflower pickle makes a wonderful partner to charcuterie or cheese and, in a more traditional way, I serve it with raita and roti (making an ideal pairing for a picnic), or as an accompaniment to grilled or roasted fish and meat.

Makes 1 litre

500 g cauliflower, cut into florets
2 tablespoons table salt
3 tablespoons vegetable oil
5 garlic cloves, finely sliced
2 tablespoons finely shredded ginger
10 small red chillies, thinly sliced
2 teaspoons black mustard seeds
1 teaspoon cumin seeds
1 teaspoon ground turmeric
½ teaspoon Kashmiri chilli powder
2 cups (500 ml) apple cider vinegar

Place the cauliflower in a colander, sprinkle with 1 teaspoon salt, cover with a lid and set aside at room temperature for 5 hours. This allows the cauliflower to soften slightly. Tip cauliflower out onto a dry cloth and rub off any excess liquid or salt. Don't rinse the cauliflower in water. Set aside.

Heat the oil in a wide-based pot over medium heat. Add the garlic, ginger and chilli and cook for 45 seconds or until softened but not coloured. Add the spices, stir to combine and cook for a further 30 seconds or until fragrant. Add the vinegar with the remaining salt, bring to the boil and simmer for 3 minutes. Remove from heat, add the cauliflower and stir to combine. Spoon into a 1 litre sterilised glass jar, making sure the cauliflower is covered with the liquid, and seal with a tight-fitting lid. Allow to cool before storing in the refrigerator until ready to serve. Enjoy these pickles within 2 weeks of making.

Date and Lime Pickle DF, GF, V

This is a fruit pickle that uses the traditional lime pickle as its base, so this gives you a double recipe. You can make the lime pickle and use it on its own or give it another dimension by adding fresh dates. Make sure you have the lime pickle already made and set aside before you begin to make the date pickle.

Makes 2 litres

1 kg fresh dates, pitted and diced
80 g jaggery or palm sugar, shaved
1¼ litres water
2 teaspoons sea salt flakes
½ cup (125 ml) strained lime juice
75 ml apple cider vinegar

LIME PICKLE
1 teaspoon fenugreek seeds
1 cup (250 ml) vegetable oil
50 g large red chillies, halved lengthwise
1 tablespoon table salt
2 teaspoons brown mustard seeds
1 teaspoon ground turmeric
½ teaspoon amchur (dried mango powder)
¼ teaspoon asafoetida
12 limes, cut lengthwise into 8 wedges

To make the lime pickle, place the fenugreek seeds in a frying pan over low heat and cook until fragrant. Remove from heat.

Heat ½ cup (125 ml) of the vegetable oil in a frying pan over medium heat. Add the chilli and cook for 5 minutes or until softened. Remove with a slotted spoon and reserve the oil from pan. Place the chilli, dry-roasted fenugreek seeds and half the salt in a mortar and pestle and pound to form a paste. Set aside.

Heat the remaining ½ cup (125 ml) vegetable oil in a frying pan over medium heat. Add the mustard seeds, turmeric, amchur and asafoetida and cook for 20 seconds or until fragrant. Reduce heat to low, add the lime wedges and remaining salt, cover and cook for 15 minutes or until softened. Remove from heat and allow to cool.

Add the pounded chilli mixture to the lime mixture with the reserved chilli oil and stir to combine. Spoon into sterilised glass jars and seal with tight-fitting lids. Store in the pantry for 1 month before using. Makes 6 cups (1½ litres). Keep for up to 1 year. Refrigerate after opening.

To make the date and lime pickle, place all ingredients with 600 g of the lime pickle in a saucepan over low heat and bring to a simmer. Cook, stirring occasionally, for 8 minutes or until sugar has dissolved. Continue to cook gently for a further 15 minutes before removing from heat. Spoon into sterilised glass jars and seal with tight-fitting lids. Store for 2 weeks in the pantry before using. Keep for up to 1 year. Refrigerate after opening.

Pickled Mussels DF, GF

Mussels are prolific in the daily catch at the fishing port of Thalassery in northern Kerala. The small fishing boats pull up onto the sand each morning and the fishermen unload their catch, their nets filled with an abundant supply of mussels that feature prominently in many of the local dishes. This is a traditional pickle of the Mappila (Muslim) cuisine of the region, it makes an ideal accompaniment to bread or rice and can be used as a condiment for grilled fish or a vegetable dal, along with a fresh curd. I sometimes toss it through pasta or noodles for an added kick of flavour.

Makes 500 g

25 g small dried chillies
400 ml white vinegar
1 teaspoon white poppy seeds
15 g golden raisins (or sultanas)
1 tablespoon tamarind puree
25 g jaggery or palm sugar
3 tablespoons sesame oil
1 teaspoon black mustard seeds
600 g mussels (in shell)
½ teaspoon ground turmeric
2½ teaspoons sea salt flakes
15 fresh curry leaves
2 teaspoons minced ginger
3 small green chillies, split lengthwise
2 small garlic cloves, minced
½ teaspoon white sugar

Place the dried chillies and vinegar in a blender and blend to form a smooth paste. Place the poppy seeds, raisins, tamarind and jaggery in a mortar and pestle and grind to form a paste. Mix to combine with the chilli vinegar. Set aside.

Heat 1 tablespoon of the sesame oil in a frying pan over low heat. Add the mustard seeds and the chilli vinegar paste and bring to the boil. Once boiling, remove from heat, cover, and set aside to cool for 5 hours or overnight at room temperature.

Steam the mussels open, gently remove from their shells, discarding shells, and snip off their beards. Mix to combine the turmeric with ½ teaspoon salt and rub into the mussels. Heat the remaining 2 tablespoons sesame oil in a frying pan over low heat. Shallow fry the mussels for 2 minutes or until crisp. Remove from the pan and set aside.

In the same pan, add the curry leaves, ginger and green chilli and cook for 30 seconds or until crisp and fragrant. Remove from the pan and set aside.

Add the fried mussels, curry leaf mixture and the garlic to the vinegar paste and mix well. Stir through the sugar and the remaining 2 teaspoons salt. Pour into a large sterilised glass jar, seal with a tight-fitting lid and store in the refrigerator for 3 days before using. Keep refrigerated for up to 1 month.

Pickled Prawns DF, GF

Balchao is my favourite relish from Goa, where it is served as a condiment with snacks and seafood at restaurants and the food shacks that line the beaches. I like to stir this relish into fried rice or toss it through rice noodles with leafy greens. Make the masala paste first and store any leftover in a sealed jar in the fridge for later use. Remember to start making the relish at least one week before you intend to use it, as it needs time for the flavours to blend together and develop.

Makes 375 g

⅓ cup (80 ml) vegetable oil
3 garlic cloves, minced
2 tablespoons fresh curry leaves
6 red shallots, finely sliced
2 teaspoons dried shrimp, ground to a floss
1 kg small school (or harbour) prawns, peeled and
　 deveined (yields 400 g peeled prawn meat)
1 teaspoon sea salt flakes

RED MASALA PASTE
100 g long red chillies, chopped
1 tablespoon ginger garlic paste, see recipe
　 page 436
1 teaspoon ground cinnamon
1 teaspoon ground cloves
1 teaspoon freshly ground black pepper
½ teaspoon ground turmeric
½ teaspoon ground cumin
100 ml fermented coconut vinegar

To make the red masala paste, place all the ingredients together in food processor and blend to make a loose and smooth paste. Set aside.

Heat 2 tablespoons oil in a frying pan over medium heat. Add the garlic and cook for 15 seconds or until softened. Add the curry leaves and cook for 15 seconds or until they start to pop. Add the shallot and cook for 3 minutes or until golden. Stir in 5 tablespoons of the red masala paste with the shrimp floss and cook for 15 minutes or until the mixture binds together. Remove from heat and set aside to cool. Spoon into a sterilised glass jar and seal with a tight-fitting lid. Refrigerate for 1 week.

One week later, complete the relish. Heat the remaining 2 tablespoons oil in a frying pan over high heat. Add the prawns and cook for 1 minute or until they change colour. Add the masala pickle with 50 ml water, just enough to loosen the mix, and cook for a further 3 minutes. Remove from heat, season with salt and serve at room temperature. Keeps well in the fridge for up to 1 month.

Coconut Chutney DF, GF, V

Coconut is used in a huge variety of preparations in the southern and coastal regions of India and is an important element of Hindu food rituals. I like to serve this fresh chutney with grilled fish, steamed rice or vegetable pastries.

Makes 160 g

1 teaspoon chana dal (split chickpeas)
1 teaspoon split urad dal (white lentils)
150 g grated fresh coconut
2 small green chillies, minced
1 teaspoon sea salt flakes
1 tablespoon vegetable oil
1 teaspoon black mustard seeds
6 fresh curry leaves
¼ teaspoon ground cumin
2 teaspoons tamarind puree

Soak both dals in cold water for 3 hours. Drain and set aside.

Place the coconut, chilli and salt in food processor and blend to make a fine paste. Keep in the bowl of the food processor.

Heat the oil in a frying pan over medium heat. Add the mustard seeds with both the softened dals and cook for 30 second or until they start to pop. Add the curry leaves and cumin and cook for 30 seconds or until starting to colour. Stir the mixture into the coconut paste in the food processor and blend with the tamarind puree until combined. Set aside at room temperature until ready to serve.

Coriander Coconut Chutney DF, GF, V

This is a Goan-style, coconut-based chutney that's typically served with fried snacks, vadas or steamed idli. If I have any left over, I use it as a spread on sandwiches. It's best served within two days of being made to maximise its freshness.

Makes 250 g

2 red shallots, quartered
½ teaspoon vegetable oil
100 g shredded or grated fresh coconut
½ teaspoon sesame oil
4 tablespoons chopped coriander leaves
2 small green chillies, chopped
1 teaspoon sea salt flakes
1 teaspoon ginger garlic paste, see recipe
   page 436
1 tablespoon tamarind puree
1 teaspoon black mustard seeds
¼ teaspoon freshly ground black pepper
½ teaspoon ground cumin
¼ teaspoon ground turmeric
pinch of asafoetida

Heat a frying pan over high heat. Add the shallot and vegetable oil and cook for 2 minutes or until softened. Set aside to cool.

Place the coconut, sesame oil, coriander, chilli and salt in a food processor or blender and blend to make a smooth puree. Add the cooled shallots, ginger garlic paste, tamarind and spices and blend to form a coarse paste. Refrigerate until ready to serve.

Mint Chutney DF, GF, V

A wonderful accompaniment to fried snacks, kebabs and meats cooked in the tandoor, this fresh, zingy chutney is best served the day it's made. It's an ideal option for those looking for a dairy-free condiment.

Makes 150 g

70 g mint leaves
2 small green chillies
2 teaspoons minced ginger
1 tablespoon lime juice
1 tablespoon caster sugar
1 teaspoon sea salt flakes
¼ teaspoon freshly ground black pepper
2 teaspoons sunflower oil

Place all the ingredients together in a food processor or blender and blend to make a smooth paste. Refrigerate until ready to serve.

 left

Green Mango Chutney DF, GF, V

This fresh and vibrant chutney is the ideal condiment to serve with vegetable pakoras or fritters. It's perfect to make when green mangoes are plentiful. I sometimes serve it with cheddar or other aged cheese, as it contrasts and balances the flavours beautifully. Try adding it next time you make a ham sandwich.

Makes 400 g

2 cups tightly packed mint leaves
1 cup coriander leaves
4 small green chillies, finely sliced
2 green mangoes, peeled and diced
    (yields 350 g)
1 tablespoon lime juice
2 teaspoons sea salt flakes
2 teaspoons caster sugar
1 teaspoon ground cumin

Place the mint, coriander, chilli, green mango and lime juice in a food processor or blender and blend to make a smooth paste. Add the salt, sugar and cumin and mix to combine. This chutney is best served the day it is made to capture its vibrant freshness.

 right

Mint Yoghurt Chutney GF, V

An essential staple, *podina* is a yoghurt-based chutney typically enjoyed with fried snacks and tandoori-grilled meats from street vendors, both in restaurants and at home. If you can find it, try to use buffalo yoghurt as it gives a delicious tanginess and rich creaminess to the chutney.

Makes 200 ml

40 g mint leaves
25 g coriander leaves
2 small green chillies, chopped
1 garlic clove, chopped
1 teaspoon minced ginger
1 red shallot, finely diced
1 tablespoon caster sugar
2 teaspoons sea salt flakes
1 teaspoon lime juice
150 g thick plain yoghurt

Place the mint, coriander, chilli, garlic, ginger, shallot, sugar, salt and lime juice in a food processor or blender with 1 tablespoon water and blend until a smooth paste forms. Transfer to a bowl and stir through the yoghurt until completely smooth. Don't add the yoghurt to the other ingredients in the blender as this won't give the proper consistency. Serve immediately.

left ➡

Tamarind Chutney DF, GF, V

Thanks to its savoury-sweet flavour combination this deliciously piquant chutney is a versatile condiment to add to your table.

Makes 350 g

400 g dried tamarind pulp
2 tablespoons vegetable oil
1 tablespoon sesame oil
4 small red chillies, finely sliced
1 tablespoon minced fresh ginger
1 teaspoon brown mustard seeds
1 teaspoon cumin seeds
1 tablespoon fresh curry leaves
2 teaspoons sea salt flakes
1 teaspoon ground turmeric
1 tablespoon chilli powder
50 g brown sugar
¼ teaspoon asafoetida
1 teaspoon chaat masala

Soak the tamarind in 2 cups (500 ml) warm water for 30 minutes. Use your fingers to loosen the pulp. Squeeze the pulp and press through a sieve to make a thick puree, discard solids. You'll need 400 ml puree to continue. Set aside.

Heat both the oils in a heavy-based pan over low heat. Add the chilli, ginger, mustard and cumin seeds and cook for 30 seconds or until they begin to pop and become fragrant. Add the curry leaves, salt, turmeric and chilli powder and cook for 1 minute or until fragrant, taking care not to burn the mixture. Add the tamarind puree, increase heat to medium–high and bring to the boil. Cook for 15 minutes or until mixture has reduced to less than half its volume and has a sauce-like consistency. Add the sugar, asafoetida and chaat masala, mixing well to avoid lumps, and return to the boil. Once boiling, remove from heat and allow to cool. Refrigerate until required. Keep refrigerated for up to 2 weeks.

right ➡

Green Chilli Chutney DF, GF, V

This herb chutney has a decent kick of chilli and is typical of the Punjab region. It's a mandatory condiment to serve with fried fish nuggets (see Snacks page 41), but is also a great accompaniment to *chaat* (savoury snacks) and fried snacks or stirred through vegetables and rice for a flavour boost.

Makes 180 g

40 g mint leaves
20 g coriander leaves
8 small green chillies, chopped with seeds
4 garlic cloves
100 g tomatoes, seeded and chopped
25 g fresh ginger, peeled and chopped
1 teaspoon amchur (dried mango powder)
1 teaspoon lime juice
1 teaspoon sea salt flakes

Place all the ingredients together in a small food processor or blender and blend to make a smooth paste. Check the seasoning and balance with salt or lime, if necessary. Enjoy the same day it's made.

Ginger Chutney DF, GF, V

This chutney dances on the palate. It has lovely lingering hot and sour flavours that make it all the more delicious when served with grilled vegetables or a vegetable curry, as a condiment to a salad, or with roti and raita.

Makes 300 g

2 tablespoons vegetable oil
1 teaspoon black mustard seeds
1 brown onion, finely diced
1 cup (250 ml) tamarind puree, see Glossary
3 small dried chillies, broken into pieces and
    soaked in cold water for 1 hour to soften
1 small red chilli, minced
90 g fresh ginger, minced
75 g jaggery or palm sugar
2 teaspoons sea salt flakes
2 tablespoons shredded coriander leaves

Heat the oil in a saucepan over medium heat. Add the mustard seeds and cook for 30 seconds or until they start to pop. Add the onion and cook for 5 minutes or until softened. Stir in the tamarind, softened chilli, fresh chilli, ginger, jaggery and salt with 150 ml water and reduce heat to low. Cook for 45 minutes or until chutney has thickened. Allow to cool before stirring through the coriander.

Tomato Chutney DF, GF, V

I collected this deliciously fresh Bengali relish after enjoying it served with steamed *momos* (dumplings). It makes a great accompaniment to just about anything that needs that little bit of embellishment. Try it with cheese, especially an aged cheddar or gruyere, or as a condiment on a charcuterie plate to extend it beyond its Indian context.

Makes 300 g

1 teaspoon mustard oil
½ teaspoon panch phoran, see Glossary
250 g tomatoes, chopped
2 teaspoons sea salt flakes
1 tablespoon finely shredded ginger
½ teaspoon chilli powder
1 tablespoon seedless raisins (or sultanas), soaked in water, strained
3 tablespoons white sugar

Heat the mustard oil in a frying pan over medium heat. Add the panch phoran and cook for 30 seconds or until it stops spluttering. Add the tomato and stir well to coat with the spices. Add the salt and mix to combine. Cover and simmer on low heat for 10 minutes. Add the ginger, chilli and raisins and stir to combine. Stir in the sugar with 1 cup (250 ml) water and cook for 10 minutes or until tomato is cooked and the chutney is thickened. Season with extra salt, if necessary. Allow to cool at room temperature before serving cold as a condiment.

Spiced Plum Chutney DF, GF, V

This is a wonderful accompaniment to a light curry and rice, imparting lovely sweetness and tanginess all at once. Make it in late summer or early spring when plums are in season, at their peak ripeness and full-flavoured.

Makes 700 g

500 g blood (or other red) plums, quartered and stones removed
1 teaspoon ginger garlic paste, see recipe page 436
2 small red chillies, sliced
1 teaspoon minced orange zest
100 ml red wine vinegar
100 g caster sugar
1 cinnamon stick
½ teaspoon ground cinnamon
½ teaspoon ground cardamom
½ teaspoon allspice
½ teaspoon freshly ground black pepper
½ teaspoon Kashmiri chilli powder
1 teaspoon sea salt flakes

Place the plum in a saucepan over medium heat with the remaining ingredients and bring to the boil. Reduce heat to low and simmer gently, uncovered and stirring frequently, for 30 minutes or until chutney has thickened. Discard the cinnamon stick. Spoon into hot, sterilised glass jars with tight-fitting lids and seal immediately. Keeps for up to 1 month. Refrigerate after opening.

Pineapple Chutney DF, GF, V

I've been enthralled watching the guys at the cavernous Mechua fruit market in Kolkata as they work with long, razor-sharp knives to deftly remove the skins and eyes from ripe pineapples, which are sold to make juice or cut into chunks (a wonderful convenience for home cooks).
On further investigation, I found the pineapple also makes a delicious sweet-and-sour chutney. In Kerala, pineapple appears in countless forms and makes a fabulous pachadi relish to serve with grilled river fish.
Be sure to use very ripe pineapples for the best flavour. Unlike most other chutneys that are best eaten the day they're made, this one keeps very well stored in a sealed jar in the fridge for up to one week.

Makes 500 g

1 large ripe pineapple (yields 900–950 g cut fruit)
100 g jaggery or palm sugar
100 g caster sugar
3 tablespoons sultanas
½ teaspoon Kashmiri chilli powder
½ teaspoon dried chilli flakes
2 teaspoons minced ginger
1 teaspoon sea salt flakes
2 tablespoons vegetable oil
2 teaspoon panch phoran, see Glossary

Remove peel and eyes from pineapple, cut into quarters lengthwise and slice off the core from each piece. Cut the pineapple flesh into 1 cm dice.

Place the pineapple in a large saucepan over low heat with the jaggery, sugar, sultanas, chilli powder and flakes, ginger and salt and cook, stirring frequently, for 6–8 minutes or until the sugar is dissolved and starting to caramelise. Add 400 ml water and simmer for 20 minutes or until the pineapple starts to break down. Continue to cook, stirring and adding a splash of water if it becomes a little dry, for a further 30 minutes or until the mixture has the consistency of thick jam and coats the back of a spoon. Taste and adjust with sugar or salt, if necessary – the balance needs to be just right. Remove from heat.

Heat the oil in a small frying pan over low heat. Add the panch phoran and cook for 30 seconds or it starts to pop. Pour the mixture over the chutney and stir to thoroughly mix. Serve at room temperature or spoon into hot, sterilised glass jars with tight-fitting lids and seal immediately. Keeps refrigerated for up to 1 week.

Breads

An everyday necessity that can also signify celebratory and festive occasions, there's a vast variety of breads throughout India. The repertoire is diverse and regardless of where you are, bread in some form will make an appearance at the table. More often than not, breads are unleavened, cooked on a *tawa* pan (a concave cast-iron pan or plate) or in a tandoori oven and are designed to be eaten immediately while still warm. It was during British rule that Western-style bread using yeast was introduced and baked in home kitchens along with the indigenous flatbreads. This is when the ubiquitous, pillowy-soft white buns (*pav* or *pao*) became a fixture, especially as a popular street food snack such as *pav bhaji* (vegetable curry with soft bun) or *bun maska* (a bun served with butter).

In the north, bread is an essential staple served with every meal. It often replaces rice (which is the staple crop in the south), as this is where wheat and other grains grow in abundance. Breads can be made with wheat, barley, corn, chickpea, semolina, sorghum or millet flour, depending on the region, each yielding a different density and flavour. In the south, rice and white (split urad) dal are soaked in water overnight to ferment before being ground to create the pancake-like batters for *idli*, *appam*, *akki*, *pathiri* and *dosa*.

These are included in the broad repertoire along with the unleavened breads *roti* or *chapati* cooked on the tawa; *paratha*, *bhatura* and the Bengali *luchi* that are layered with ghee and pan-fried; deep-fried *puris* that puff up and become hollow when cooked; and the leavened breads, *naan* and *kulcha*, that are baked in an oven. The difference between the latter being the type of flour used – wholemeal for naan, which is also leavened with yoghurt, and the finer textured plain (or *maida*) flour for kulcha, which is a staple of the Punjab region.

Traditionally, whole grains are ground on a heavy stone slab, but in these modern times and for the increasingly time-poor cook, ready-ground flours are available. The local *atta* flour, sometimes labelled chapati flour, is a stone-ground wholemeal (or wholewheat) flour ideal for breadmaking, yielding the required pliable texture. The other common refined flour made from wheat is *maida*, which has a finer texture and is used for making cakes, pastries and some softer flatbreads, such as the Punjabi bhatura. Lentils and split peas can also be ground to make flour, often used for savoury breakfast pancakes (*pesar attu* or *chilla*) or for making pappadams.

As for any breadmaking, the quality of the flour and ingredients, along with the ambient temperature of your kitchen, especially with leavened bread, are determining factors in the outcome. You need to adopt an instinctive feel for the dough to get the best result minus the stress. Making Indian breads requires varying levels of skill, so start with the easy ones and go from there.

Parathas v

This pan-fried flatbread with its flaky layers is one of India's most popular breads. This recipe takes its lead from the Malabar paratha (*parotta*) of the south, where the dough is made with a strong bread flour and has a finer texture than its northern relative, *lachha* paratha from the Punjab. There, wholemeal flour gives a slightly denser texture, but both versions are made luscious with the liberal use of ghee. Be aware that using plain flour will not give the best results, leaving the dough too soft and without the required body. The flaky characteristic of this bread is achieved through the folding and pleating of the dough, creating layers that puff and expand during cooking. Don't be shy about using ghee and oil as the suppleness of the paratha is dependent on it for its flakiness.

Makes 12

500 g white bread (strong) flour, plus extra
    for dusting
pinch of bicarbonate of soda
1 teaspoon caster sugar
2 teaspoons sea salt flakes
70 g melted ghee, plus extra for drizzling
2 tablespoons milk
150 ml vegetable oil

Sift the flour, bicarbonate of soda, sugar and salt into a large bowl and mix to combine. Make a well in the centre and add 2 tablespoons melted ghee and the milk. Add 1 cup (250 ml) water. Using your hands, gradually draw the flour into the centre of the well and mix until a sticky dough forms.

Rub a little vegetable oil into your hands to make it easier to work with the dough. Turn dough out onto a bench and knead for 3–4 minutes or until pliable, smooth and elastic. If it feels sticky, incorporate a little extra flour and if it feels too dry, add a little extra water. Cover the dough with plastic wrap and set aside to rest for 20 minutes.

Roll dough to flatten slightly. Divide the dough into 12 even-size pieces and roll each piece into a ball on a lightly floured surface. Using your hands, flatten each ball into a disc. Use a rolling pin to make 2 mm-thick, 20 cm rounds (the thinner the better). Brush with the remaining melted ghee and dust very lightly with flour. Rub a little more oil into your fingers to work with the dough. There are different ways of folding the dough to achieve the required flakiness. I suggest starting at the top and folding concertina-style to make narrow pleats approximately 15 mm-wide. Going back and forth, over and under to create the layers. Then, starting at one end, roll the pleated dough length around itself into a round, tucking the other end under the round to secure. It should resemble a spiralled knot. Use your hand to press the top of the knot to flatten to approximately 3 cm-thick. Use a rolling pin to flatten to a 16–18 cm round. Place on a tray lined with baking paper until ready to cook. Repeat with remaining dough.

Heat a non-stick frying pan over medium–high heat. Drizzle with oil and slide 1 paratha into the pan, drizzle over a little more oil and fry for 2 minutes or until the paratha starts to puff up. Turn, drizzle with more oil and fry on the other side for a further 1 minute, the paratha should continue to puff up. Move the paratha around in the pan as it cooks to ensure all the surfaces have even access to heat. When golden and cooked and you can't see any raw dough, drizzle with melted ghee and remove from the pan. Fluff up the sides of the paratha by gently tapping the sides, a bit like clapping your hands with the paratha in the middle, to accentuate the flaky layers. Stack on a plate and cover with foil to keep warm while you cook the remaining parathas. Serve immediately.

Masterclass step-by-step Parathas ➜

1

Sift the flour, bicarbonate of soda, sugar and salt.

2

Make a well in the centre.

3

Add 2 tablespoons melted ghee.

4

Add the milk and 1 cup (250 ml) water.

5

Using your hands, drag the flour into the centre to form a sticky dough.

6

Knead for 3–4 minutes until pliable, smooth and elastic.

7

Set aside to rest for 20 minutes.

8

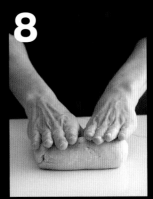

Roll to flatten slightly.

9

Divide dough in half.

10

Divide each half into 6 to make 12 even-size portions.

11

Roll each piece into a ball.

12

Using your hands, flatten each ball into a round.

13

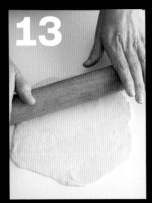

Use a rolling pin to make 2 mm-thick, 20 cm rounds.

14

Brush with melted ghee.

15

Dust very lightly with flour.

16

Start at the top of each round.

17

Fold, concertina-style, to make 15 mm pleats.

18

Fold back and forth, over and under to make layers.

19

Continue folding until all the dough is pleated.

20

Starting at one end, roll the pleated dough around itself.

21

The dough will take a snail shape.

22

Keep rolling until you reach the end.

23

Tuck the end underneath to secure.

24

It should resemble a spiralled knot.

25

Use your hand to flatten into a 3 cm-thick round.

26

Use a rolling pin to make a 16–18 cm round.

27

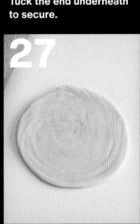

Repeat with remaining dough.

28

Slide 1 paratha into the pan

29

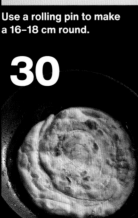

Drizzle with oil and cook for 2 minutes or until puffed.

30

Turn, drizzle with more oil and fry for 1 minute.

31

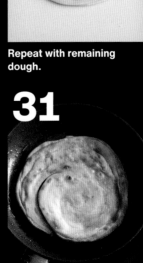

Move the paratha around in the pan to cook evenly.

32

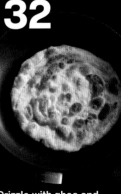

Drizzle with ghee and remove from pan

Stuffed Parathas v

Chur chur paratha is a crisp and flaky layered flatbread stuffed with crumbled fresh cheese, spices and herbs. It's a bread I have eaten many times, usually for a late breakfast snack when trawling through the food alleyways of Old Delhi. More recently, I've watched chef Manish Mehrotra prepare them at Indian Accent, his restaurant in Delhi, for the launch of my second edition of *Tasting India*. I like to serve this flatbread with black dal and mint yoghurt chutney. When cooking these parathas, they require more ghee than regular parathas to make them crispy, so don't be alarmed at the quantity, this is what makes them deliciously appealing and moreish.

Serves 8

400 g wholemeal flour
75 g rice flour
1 teaspoon sea salt flakes
200 g melted ghee
plain flour, for dusting

CHUR CHUR STUFFING
80 g cottage cheese (or crumbled paneer)
2 green onions, finely sliced
1 tablespoon chopped coriander leaves
1 tablespoon chopped mint leaves
2 small green chillies, minced
2 teaspoons kasoori methi (dried fenugreek leaves), see Glossary
½ teaspoon Kashmiri chilli powder
½ teaspoon ground ginger
¼ teaspoon chaat masala
¼ teaspoon freshly ground black pepper
1 teaspoon sea salt flakes

To make the bread dough, sift the flours and salt into a large bowl, add 1 tablespoon ghee and mix to combine. Add ½ cup (125 ml) water and mix to combine. Add another ½ cup (125 ml) water and transfer the dough to a lightly floured surface. Knead for 2–3 minutes or until smooth and pliable, but not sticky or soft. Cover with a damp cloth and rest for 20 minutes.

To make the chur chur stuffing, place the cheese in a bowl and mash. Add the green onion, herbs, spices and salt and mix to combine. Set aside.

Once the dough has rested, knead for a further 1 minute and divide into 8 even-size pieces. Roll each piece into a ball and roll each ball out on a lightly floured surface to make 18 cm-rounds. Brush the entire surface of the rounds with a little melted ghee. Spoon the cheese mixture into the centre of each round and fold in the sides to cover the stuffing completely, effectively making an envelope to conceal the stuffing. Be sure there are no open corners for the stuffing to escape. Sprinkle with plain flour and roll out again to make 3 cm-thick, 16 cm-rounds. Press lightly to ensure the dough does not split and expose the stuffing.

Heat a non-stick frying pan over medium heat. Drizzle the pan with ghee and slide in a paratha, drizzle extra ghee on top and fry for 30 seconds. Turn, drizzle with more ghee, and fry for a further 30 seconds. Repeat this process, flipping and drizzling with ghee until the paratha is crisp and golden. Hold the paratha in your hands and press the edges to crush slightly. Stack on a plate and cover with foil to keep warm while you cook the remaining parathas. Serve immediately.

Curry Crackers v

I've been making these crackers for many years. Filled with spice, they're a nod to my Indian pantry, rather than being anything that I've seen cooked in India. They're great to serve with pickles and condiments and, being a similar texture to lavosh, they make a wonderful accompaniment to hard cheeses, such as cheddar, gruyère or pecorino. I've used spelt flour as I love the texture it produces. It's an ancient grain that's nutritious and easier to digest than wheat, so is a suitable flour to use for those who are gluten intolerant, but not strictly coeliac.

Serves 6

3 tablespoons unsalted butter
½ small white onion, minced
2 teaspoons ginger garlic paste, see recipe
 page 436
1 teaspoon ground cumin
2 teaspoons ground coriander
2 teaspoons ground turmeric
½ teaspoon Kashmiri chilli powder
300 g spelt flour
1 teaspoon sea salt flakes

Melt the butter in a frying pan over medium heat. Add the onion and ginger garlic paste and cook for 4 minutes or until softened. Add the ground spices and cook for 1 minute. Remove from heat and set aside to cool for 5 minutes.

Preheat oven to 180°C. Place the flour and salt in a food processor. Add the onion mixture and blend until it resembles coarse breadcrumbs. Slowly add ½ cup (125 ml) water and blend until the dough comes together but is not sticky. Add a little extra water if it looks dry or a little extra flour if it feels too wet. It should have the same texture as pasta dough.

Transfer dough to the bench and divide into thirds. Roll each piece into a long, 4 mm-thick length (you can use a pasta machine). Cut each length into 8 cm lengths, trim the edges and prick with a fork. Arrange in a single layer on baking trays lined with baking paper and bake for 20–25 minutes or until crisp. Allow to cool. Store for up to 1 week in an airtight container.

Pappadams DF, GF, V

Making your own pappadams is so satisfying and the result beats any packet version hands down. It's important to crush or grind the spices before mixing into the dough, as they will cause the dough to tear when it's rolled through the machine if left whole. They will keep perfectly in an airtight container for up to four days after being fried, so you can prepare them ahead to have ready to serve with a curry or other dish.

Serves 8–10

250 g white urad dal flour
100 g chickpea (besan) flour
30 g rice flour
1 teaspoon ground ajwain seeds, see Glossary
1 teaspoon brown mustard seeds, crushed
1 teaspoon ground fennel
1 teaspoon freshly ground black pepper
25 g sea salt flakes
2 cups (500 ml) vegetable oil, for deep-frying

Place all the ingredients together in a food processor and mix to combine. Slowly add enough cold water (approximately 170 ml) to make a firm dough. You're looking for the same texture as pasta; the dough should not be wet or sticky. Transfer dough to the bench and knead until smooth and there are no lumps. Divide into 12 even-size pieces. Run each through a pasta machine, starting at the widest setting and decreasing the thickness with each roll until each has gone through the third thinnest setting. I have found the thinner settings cause the dough to rip. Hang the sheets over a dowel (or clean broomstick handle) and allow to air dry for 1 hour or until semi-dry. Using a knife, cut each sheet into 10 cm lengths.

Heat the vegetable oil in a deep-fryer to 170°C. Fry the sheets, a few at a time, making sure they don't stick together, for 3–4 minutes or until golden and crisp. Drain on paper towel and store in an airtight container until ready to use.

Roti v

This flatbread is straightforward and easy, making it a good place to begin when setting out to gain confidence with your breadmaking. Roti is the generic name given to flatbread with regional variations made with wheat, maize, sorghum, millet, rice and so on, depending on the grains being farmed. This particular recipe is a little more lush than chapati with the addition of milk and egg giving a softer result. This same dough is also used to make *roomali* or handkerchief bread, where the dough is stretched by hand until it resembles tissue-thin cloth. It's a highly skilled technique that requires lots of practice and a deft hand. Roomali is cooked on a convex metal pan, which looks like an upturned wok sitting over a stack of hot coals, whereas roti or chapati are cooked on a dry tawa pan or skillet.

Makes 12

50 ml vegetable oil, for greasing
100 g melted ghee

DOUGH
500 g wholemeal flour, plus extra for dusting
½ cup (125 ml) water
½ cup (125 ml) milk
1 egg, lightly beaten
½ teaspoon sea salt flakes
1 teaspoon caster sugar
1 tablespoon vegetable oil

To make the dough, place all the ingredients in a stand mixer fitted with a paddle attachment and blend until a soft, sticky dough forms. Add a little extra water if the dough looks or feels a little dry. Turn out onto a floured surface and knead for 10 minutes or until smooth, elastic and shiny. Place in a lightly oiled bowl, cover with a damp cloth and set aside to rest for 20 minutes.

Roll the dough into a long cylinder, cut into 12 even-size pieces and roll into balls. Pour oil into a flat tray and add dough balls, turning each to coat. Cover with plastic wrap and set aside to rest for a further 1 hour.

On a lightly oiled surface, roll each ball into a 20 cm-rounds. Using greased hands, stretch each disc in a circular motion until very thin, pulling gently outwards from the top centre as you go. When dough is wafer-thin, dab lightly all over with melted ghee. Fold the opposite sides into the centre to overlap. Fold in the remaining 2 sides to make an envelope, trapping air under the folds. Roll again into a flat square.

Heat a frying pan, tawa or flat grill over high heat. Brush the pan with ghee and cook roti, one at time and adding more ghee as needed, for 2–3 minutes or until golden and crisp. Flip and cook on the other side for a further 2–3 minutes. Stack on a plate and cover with a cloth or foil to keep warm while you cook the remaining roti. Serve immediately.

Millet Roti DF, GF, V

Bajia (millet) flour gives this roti a denser texture. It's a good bread to cook if you want to keep it gluten-free and is typical of the hot, dry regions where these grains grow. If you'd like to embellish the bread with a richer flavour, you could use ghee instead of oil.

Makes 12

1 cup (150 g) millet flour
½ teaspoon sea salt flakes
1 tablespoon chopped coriander leaves
⅛ teaspoon Kashmiri chilli powder
½ teaspoon ginger garlic paste, see recipe
 page 436
2 teaspoons minced red onion
¼ cup (60 ml) vegetable oil

Mix the flour, salt, coriander, chilli powder, ginger garlic paste and red onion together in a bowl and gradually add ½ cup (125 ml) water, mixing with your hands to form a firm dough. The dough should not stick to your hands. Divide dough into 12 even-size pieces and roll each piece into a ball. Using a rolling pin, flatten each ball to make a round 15 cm round.

Heat a pan, tawa or flat grill over medium–high heat or flame. Add 1 teaspoon of oil and cook each bread, one at a time and adding more oil as needed, for 1 minute each side or until crisp and golden. Stack on a plate and cover with cloth or foil to keep warm while you cook the remaining roti. Serve immediately.

Chapati V

Chapati and roti are almost identical, and either name is often used to describe this style of bread. However, chapati, which is prepared everyday by the billions throughout India, is the most basic of unleavened breads. It's essentially flour and water, making it a little firmer or chewier than roti, which has milk and egg added to soften it.

Makes 10

300 g wholemeal flour, plus extra for dusting
2 teaspoons sea salt flakes
¼ cup (60 ml) sunflower oil or vegetable oil
170 ml warm water
2 tablespoons melted ghee

Place the flour and salt in a bowl and mix to combine. Add the oil and water and use your hands to mix together, adding a little more water, if the dough feels too dry. Turn out onto a floured surface and knead for 2–3 minutes. The dough should feel soft but not sticky. Cover with a dry cloth and set aside to rest for 30 minutes.

Divide the dough into 10 even-size pieces and roll each into a ball. Roll each on lightly floured surface to make 5 mm-thick, 12 cm rounds.

Heat a frying pan or flat grill over medium–high heat. Cook the breads, one at a time, for 2 minutes or until bubbles appear on surface and the bread starts to puff up. Turn and cook on the other side, pressing down with a spatula to ensure even cooking, for a further 1 minute or until golden brown. Remove from pan, cover with a cloth to keep warm and continue to cook the remaining breads. Brush the bread with ghee while hot and serve warm.

Garlic Naan ᵥ

Introduced to India by the Mughals a few centuries ago, this defining bread of the north is leavened with yeast and softened with yoghurt and milk before being stretched into its classic teardrop shape. It's then slapped onto the inside wall of a hot tandoor oven to quickly bake. I find the best way to cook this bread without access to a clay tandoor oven is to sit a large, unglazed clay tile (or pizza stone) at the base of a hot oven and cook the bread directly on that, as you would pizza.

Makes 8

1 tablespoon active dried yeast
1 teaspoon caster sugar
150 ml lukewarm milk
500 g white bread (strong) flour
2 teaspoons sea salt flakes
2 tablespoons thick natural yoghurt
¼ cup (60 ml) melted ghee
2 garlic cloves, crushed
1 teaspoon nigella seeds
2 tablespoons unsalted butter, softened

Place the yeast and sugar in a bowl and mix to combine. Add the milk and set aside to bloom for 15–20 minutes or until small bubbles appear on the surface. This is what activates the yeast before it's added to the flour. Sift the flour and salt into a large bowl and stir through the yoghurt and the yeast mixture. Turn out onto the bench, and using your hands, knead for 3–4 minutes or until a smooth and pliable dough forms. Place the dough in a lightly oiled bowl and cover with a damp cloth. Set aside in a warm place for 3 hours or until the dough has doubled in volume.

Transfer the dough onto the bench and divide into 8 even-size pieces. Roll each piece into a ball and place, spaced apart, on a flat tray so they don't stick together. Set aside, uncovered, to prove for a further 10–15 minutes.

Place a large clay tile (or flat baking tray) in the oven and preheat to 230°C. Roll each dough ball into a flat 5 mm-thick rounds. Pull one end of each round to stretch and form a teardrop shape. Drizzle with the melted ghee and transfer to the hot clay tile to bake for 4–5 minutes or until cooked through with scorch marks and bubbles appearing on the surface.

Mix the crushed garlic and nigella seeds with the softened butter and spread a little over the naan. If making one at a time, keep the cooked naan on a plate covered with cloth or foil to keep warm while you bake the rest. If baking on a flat tray, you can probably make 2–3 at a time. Serve immediately.

Potato-stuffed Kulcha v

Travelling with a Sikh friend in the Punjab, I became smitten with their *kulcha*, a flaky bread stuffed with potatoes or paneer, onions and spices and cooked on the walls of a scorching hot tandoor oven. It's so popular (and addictive) it's eaten for breakfast, lunch and dinner. Crisp on the outside and soft within, it's packed with distinct flavours and textures. Eating them fresh on a bustling street with a cup of masala chai is one of my most cherished breakfast memories. Given that Western kitchens don't have a tandoor oven, you can cook the bread on a clay tile (or pizza stone) in the oven. They're also equally good cooked on a barbecue, or as I have done here, in a heavy-based cast-iron pan. The Sikhs are champions in their liberal use of butter and cream, with many dairy-rich dishes coming from this region, so be sure to brush these with a little butter before serving.

Makes 10

2 cups (300 g) plain flour, plus extra for dusting
1 teaspoon caster sugar
1 teaspoon sea salt flakes
½ teaspoon baking powder
2 tablespoons ghee
100 g unsalted butter, softened

POTATO STUFFING
700 g potatoes, boiled and peeled
½ red onion, finely diced
2 tablespoons melted ghee
½ teaspoon ajwain seeds, see Glossary
2 teaspoons ground coriander
½ teaspoon ground cumin
½ teaspoon garam masala
½ teaspoon chilli powder
½ cup chopped coriander leaves
1 long green chilli, minced
1 teaspoon sea salt flakes

To make the dough, mix the flour, sugar, salt and baking powder together in a bowl. Add the ghee and 150 ml water and, using your hands, bring together to form a dough, adding a little extra water if the dough is too dry. It's important to gauge the feel of the dough; it should be moist and pliable without sticking to your hands and will soften as it's kneaded. Knead on a lightly floured surface for 2–3 minutes. Divide into 10 even-size pieces and roll each into a ball. Place on a flat tray covered with a clean cloth and set aside to rest for 1 hour.

While the dough is resting, make the stuffing. Place all the ingredients in bowl and, using your hands, break down the potatoes into a coarse mash. Combine until the mixture is quite smooth. Divide the stuffing into 10 even-size portions.

Assemble the breads on a lightly floured bench. Using a rolling pin, flatten each piece to a 5 mm-thick, 24 cm-round. Brush with a little butter and divide the filling between the rounds, spreading it over the dough and leaving the edges clear. Starting at the edge closest to you, begin to roll the dough over, as you would a Swiss roll, until you have a rope-like length. Pull the ends of the dough to elongate and spiral the dough around itself to make a coil, tucking in the ends. Press down with your hand to flatten the coil back into a round, sprinkle with a little flour and roll gently to make a 16–18 cm round, being careful to keep the filling from escaping, but don't worry if it does split a little. Cover with a cloth while you form the remaining breads.

Heat a cast-iron frying pan over high heat. Place a bread round in the pan and cook for 1 minute, brush with a little butter, and turn with a spatula. Cook on the other side for a further 1 minute. Continue to flip the bread for 4–5 minutes, brushing with butter each time, until the bread is crisp and golden. Swirl a little butter over the surface of the bread. Transfer to a plate and cover with a cloth to keep warm while you cook the remaining breads. Serve hot.

Puri v

Known as *puri* (or *poori*), this crispy, golden, deep-fried and unleavened flatbread made with wholewheat (or wholemeal) flour is one of the most common breads in north India. Much like a chapati or roti, it's the deep-frying in hot oil that makes it magically puff up and give a thoroughly decadent texture. Nobody ever eats just one! In Bengal, you'll find it by the name of *luchi*, where it's generally fried in ghee rather than oil. And in the south from Goa to Kerala, *vadappam* is a puri made with rice flour that's kneaded into a dough with hot water and seasoned with cumin.

Makes 10

270 g wholemeal flour, plus extra for dusting
½ teaspoon sea salt flakes
2 tablespoons ghee
2 cups (500 ml) vegetable oil, for deep-frying

Place the flour and salt in a bowl. Using your fingers, rub the ghee into the flour and gradually add enough water, about ½ cup (125 ml), to form a firm dough. Transfer the dough to the bench and knead for 4 minutes or until the dough is silky, soft, and does not stick to your hands. Place the dough in a lightly oiled bowl, cover with a damp cloth and set aside to rest for 30 minutes.

Roll the dough into a rope-like length and cut into 10 even-size pieces. Roll each piece into a ball, making sure there are no cracks in the dough. Roll each ball out on a lightly floured surface to make a flat 12 cm round. Use a 11 cm-round pastry cutter to cut smooth, even edges. Separate each puri with a piece of baking paper and stack on top of each other.

Heat the oil in a wok over high heat to 180°C. Fry the puri, 2 at a time, for 2 minutes, pressing down with a slotted spoon until they puff up and gently splashing hot oil over as they cook. Flip and cook on the other side for a further 2 minutes or until golden. Remove from the oil with a slotted spoon and drain on paper towel. Serve immediately while hot and puffed.

Bhatura v

At the heart of Punjabi cooking, I find this puffed, deep-fried bread dangerously addictive. Typically served with *chole*, a chickpea dal, one is never enough. Adding semolina with the flour gives the bread a crisper texture.

Makes 10

200 g white bread (strong) flour
100 g wholemeal flour
50 g semolina
2 tablespoons thick natural yoghurt
1 teaspoon baking powder
1 teaspoon sea salt flakes
1 teaspoon caster sugar
2 cups (500 ml) vegetable oil, for deep-frying
melted ghee, for greasing

Place both flours, semolina, yoghurt, baking powder, salt and sugar in the bowl of a stand mixer fitted with a dough hook and mix to combine. Add 100 ml warm water and knead for 7–10 minutes or until a soft batter forms. Leave the dough in the bowl and cover with a clean damp cloth. Set aside for 1 hour or until risen slightly.

Divide dough into 10 even-size pieces and roll into golf ball-size balls. Place the balls on a flat tray, cover with cloth and set aside to rest for a further 30 minutes.

Heat the oil in a wok or large saucepan over medium–high heat to 180°C. Grease your hands with a little melted ghee (or oil) to stop the dough from sticking and press each ball onto the bench to flatten. Pull dough upwards with your fingers, stretching into a longer shape (similar to making naan). Take the dough and slap it between your hands. Once the dough has been stretched, it needs to be cooked immediately.

One at a time, carefully slide the stretched dough into the hot oil. Fry, pressing down with a spoon (this helps the bread to puff up), for 90 seconds or until golden. Flip and cook, spooning over hot oil over as it cooks, for a further 90 seconds or until puffed. Remove with a mesh spoon and drain on paper towel. Serve immediately while hot and puffed.

Dosa DF, GF, V

Made with fermented rice and white dal, this is the same batter used to make steamed *idli*. But *dosa* is a pan-fried, crisp pancake. When folded over a spicy ginger potato mix, it's called *masala dosa*, and is perhaps the most popular breakfast dish of India. Serve your dosa with coconut chutney and dal. Dosa loses its crispness very quickly, becoming limp and soggy, so it must be served as soon as it's made.

Serves 6

60 g split urad dal (white lentils)
½ teaspoon fenugreek seeds
200 g idli (short grain) rice
1 teaspoon sea salt flakes
vegetable oil, for brushing

Rinse the split urad dal and soak in cold water with the fenugreek seeds for 4 hours. Wash and soak the rice in a separate bowl of cold water for the same time.

Drain the rice, reserving ½ cup (125 ml) of the water. Place the rice in a food processor with the reserved water and blend to form a paste. Drain the dal, reserving ⅓ cup (80 ml) of the water. Blend the dal in a food processor with the reserved water to form a paste.

Mix both pastes together in a large bowl. It should be of pouring consistency, similar to a crepe batter. If too thick, add a little extra water. Add the salt and stir to combine. Cover with a cloth (not plastic wrap) and set aside overnight to allow the batter to ferment and increase in volume. The surface will be bubbled from the slow fermentation.

Heat a flat 22 cm frying pan over medium–high heat and brush with oil. Pour a ladleful of the batter into the pan, swirling to cover the base of the pan with a thin layer of batter. Working in a circular motion, use the back of the ladle to help spread the batter to the edges. When the surface starts to bubble, flip the dosa over with a spatula and cook on the other side for 1 minute or until golden. Remove from the pan and cover with a cloth or foil to keep warm while you cook the remaining dosa.

If you're adding a filling to the dosa, spoon it onto the uncooked surface, fold over to enclose and serve. In this instance, don't flip the dosa. Serve immediately.

Green Chilli Dosa v

Similar to a crepe, these savoury dosa are very easy to make and can be served with all manner of things, such as curry, dal or braised vegetables. I sometimes partner them with a salad of flaked smoked trout, cucumber, shredded coconut, coriander, sliced red onion and watercress, dressed with lime juice and a little oil.

Makes 6

1 cup (160 g) wholemeal flour
50 g rice flour
15 g minced fresh ginger
1 long green chilli, finely chopped
1 teaspoon cumin seeds
2 teaspoons sea salt flakes
1½ teaspoons ghee

Sift both flours into a bowl and add the ginger, chilli, cumin and salt. Whisk in 450 ml water to form a batter the same consistency as a pancake batter. Cover with a cloth and set aside for 1 hour.

Heat 1 teaspoon of ghee in a non-stick frying pan over medium–high heat. As soon as it has melted, swirl in 2 tablespoons of the dosa batter, enough to coat the base of the pan, and cook for 3 minutes or until crisp. Flip the dosa over with a spatula and cook on the other side for a further 1 minute. Transfer to a plate, cover with cloth to keep warm and repeat with remaining batter and ghee. Serve immediately.

Rice Flour Bread DF, GF, V

Pathiri is a breakfast bread made like a pancake with rice and coconut, both of which are staple ingredients of the Malabar coast and find their way into many of the region's dishes. Lightly textured, it makes the ideal accompaniment to savoury mince ramped up with a splash of chilli and spice, chicken curry or fried eggs with a tangy chutney.

Makes 12

1 teaspoon cumin seeds
100 g grated fresh coconut
2 red shallots, finely diced
½ teaspoon sea salt flakes
400 g rice flour, plus extra for dusting
2 teaspoons coconut oil

Place the cumin seeds in small frying pan over low heat and toast for 2 minutes or until fragrant and starting to colour. Allow to cool before grinding to a powder. Place the coconut, shallot, ground cumin and salt in a food processor and blend to make a paste. Set aside.

Place 1 cup (250 ml) water in a saucepan and bring to the boil. Stir in the rice flour and immediately add the coconut paste, stirring vigorously with a wooden spoon until the dough comes together. Brush a little coconut oil onto the bench. Transfer the dough to the bench and, while still hot, knead to form a smooth dough. The dough should be moist but not sticky. Working with wet hands, roll the dough into 12 even-size balls. Cover with a damp cloth while you work so the dough doesn't dry out. Brush a little more oil onto the bench. Using an oiled rolling pin, flatten each ball to make 3 mm-thick, 20 cm-rounds. It should be thin like a crepe, the thinness of the dough is more important than the diameter, but do be careful not to roll too thin or it will break in the pan – it's a fine balance. Dust the top with a little extra rice flour to help with rolling.

Heat a tawa or non-stick frying pan over medium heat. Place a round, rolled side-down, in the pan (this helps it to puff up) and cook for 2 minutes. Take care not to brown the bread too much, you're after a pale, slightly golden colour and crisp edges. Flip and cook on the other side for a further 2 minutes or until cooked through. Stack on a plate covered with a cloth to keep warm while you cook the remaining rounds. Serve immediately.

Steamed Rice Cakes DF, GF, V

A staple of the south, *idli* is served for breakfast from Pondicherry across to Kochi, usually with sambar and coconut chutney. If you don't have the traditional dome-shaped idli moulds, you can easily use egg poaching cups that will sit on a steamer tray. The batter is the same as the dosa, but steaming produces a different texture.

Makes 12

60 g split urad dal (white lentils)
200 g idli (short grain) rice
½ teaspoon brown mustard seeds
1 teaspoon sea salt flakes
vegetable oil, for brushing

Rinse the dal and soak in cold water for 4 hours. Wash and soak the rice in a separate bowl of cold water for the same time.

Drain the rice, reserving ½ cup (125 ml) of the water. Place in a food processor with the reserved water and blend to form a paste. Drain the dal, reserving ⅓ cup (80 ml) of the water, and blend with reserved water to form a paste.

Mix both pastes together in a large bowl. It should be of pouring consistency, same as a crepe batter. If too thick, add a little extra water. Add the mustard seeds and salt and stir to combine. Cover with a cloth (not plastic wrap) and set aside overnight to allow the batter to ferment and increase in volume. The surface will be bubbled from the slow fermentation.

Brush 12 idli moulds (or egg holders or cupcake moulds) with oil and fill with batter. Place on a steamer tray, cover with a lid and steam over gently boiling water for 15 minutes or until firm and puffed. Remove from the steamer and cool for a couple of minutes before removing from their moulds. Serve warm. They can be resteamed gently when ready to serve.

Rice Appams DF, GF, V

Crisp rice and coconut pancakes made with a light batter left to ferment overnight before being cooked, these are essential for the Keralan breakfast table. Appams really need to be cooked in a special bowl-shaped, deep-sided *appa chatti* pan to get the best result. You can buy the pan from Indian specialty grocers or kitchenware stores. A small *kadhai* (deep pot) is a fair alternative. It's best to start this process the day before to give the batter time to ferment. Serve for breakfast with a wet curry (vegetable, fish or mutton) or with egg roast (see page 127).

Makes 24

600 g uncooked short grain rice
½ cup grated fresh coconut
⅛ teaspoon active dried yeast
1 cup cooked short or medium grain rice
½ teaspoon bicarbonate of soda
1 teaspoon white sugar
1 teaspoon sea salt flakes
vegetable oil, for brushing

Soak the rice in water for 5 hours. Drain, place in a food processor with the coconut, yeast and cooked rice and blend to form a smooth, thick batter. Add the bicarbonate of soda, sugar and salt and set aside to ferment for 8 hours or overnight.

Heat an appa chatti pan (see above) or kadhai over medium heat and brush with oil. Pour a ladleful of batter into the pan and immediately swirl over the heat so the edges become lacy and the batter sets in the middle. Cover the pan with a lid and leave to steam for 2 minutes or until cooked through and the edges are crisp. Gently lift the appam from the pan and place on a plate. Stack and keep covered while you cook the remaining appams. Serve immediately.

Sweet Flatbread ᵥ

Puran poli is a stuffed sweet bread from Mumbai and Maharashtra. It's made during the Diwali festival, where sweets play an integral role in the celebrations and rituals.

Makes 20

400 g chana dal (split chickpeas), soaked in cold water for 4 hours, drained
400 g shaved jaggery (or palm sugar)`
1 teaspoon ground cardamom
¼ teaspoon saffron threads, powdered
¼ teaspoon freshly grated nutmeg
2 cups (300 g) plain flour, plus extra for dusting
½ teaspoon ground turmeric
¼ cup (60 ml) vegetable oil, plus extra for brushing
melted ghee, to serve

Cook the softened dal in boiling water for 30 minutes or until soft. Drain well and spread out on a flat tray lined with a dry cloth and leave to dry for 20 minutes.

Heat a frying pan over medium heat. Add the jaggery and dried dal and cook, stirring continuously to prevent burning, for 10 minutes or until the sugar has completely dissolved. Mash into a soft paste, add the cardamom, saffron and nutmeg and mix thoroughly. Roll into 20 even-size balls and set aside.

To make the dough, mix the flour, turmeric and oil with ¾ cup (185 ml) water in a large bowl to make a very soft, sticky dough. Knead well in the bowl, adding a little extra oil if necessary, until dough is smooth.

Brush your hands with a little extra oil, pinch off some dough and flatten into an 8 cm-round, palm-size round. Place a ball of jaggery mixture in the centre and fold the dough over to enclose the paste completely. Press the edges to seal. Repeat with the remaining dough and paste until you have 20 pieces.

Roll each out on a lightly floured surface to make 2 cm-thick, 15 cm rounds. This can get tricky as the paste may try to slide out, so sprinkle lightly with flour as you roll and continue to press gently to ensure the filling remains enclosed.

Heat a dry grill or tawa pan over medium heat. Cook each round for 2–3 minutes. Turn and cook for a further 2–3 minutes or until golden. Remove from pan and brush both sides with ghee while still hot. Serve immediately.

Kashmiri Fried Sweet Bread v

A sweet treat considered sacred by Kashmiri Pandits, this part-bread, part-biscuit *roth* is essentially a chapati bread deep-fried in oil or ghee, depending who makes it. It's both luscious and filling, making it fitting for a festival celebration.

Makes 12

180 g caster sugar
600 g wholemeal flour, plus extra for dusting
120 g ghee, softened
seeds from 1 black cardamom pod, ground
12 raw almonds
600 ml vegetable oil, for deep-frying
2 tablespoons white poppy seeds
2 tablespoons icing sugar, sifted

Place 600 ml water in saucepan over high heat with the sugar and boil for 2 minutes or until a light syrup forms. Allow to cool.

Place the flour, ghee, cardamom and cooled sugar syrup in a large bowl and knead to make a firm dough. Roll the dough out on a lightly floured surface to 1 cm-thick. Using an 8 cm-round cutter, cut out 12 rounds and prick the surface in a couple of places with a fork. This prevents the breads from puffing up too much during cooking. Press an almond into the centre of each round.

Heat the oil in a wok or deep saucepan over medium–high heat to 170°C. Fry the rounds, one at a time, for 3 minutes or until golden. Drain on paper towel. Sprinkle with poppy seeds and dust with icing sugar. Serve warm.

Savoury Breakfast Pancake GF, v

Besan chilli, a savoury breakfast pancake made with chickpea (or gram) flour, is something you'll find in Bengal and Assam. It's typically served with sweet tamarind chutney and I like to add a dollop of yoghurt as well.

Makes 4

1 tablespoon vegetable oil
2 tablespoons melted ghee
tamarind chutney, to serve, see Pickles and
    Chutneys page 362

PANCAKE BATTER
1 cup (150 g) chickpea (besan) flour
¼ teaspoon caraway seeds
¼ teaspoon ground turmeric
½ teaspoon sea salt flakes
1 tablespoon finely diced red onion
1 teaspoon ginger garlic paste, see recipe
    page 436
2 tablespoons finely diced tomato
1 tablespoon chopped coriander leaves

To make the pancake batter, place the ingredients together in bowl and mix with 150 ml water to make a batter the same consistency as pancake batter.

Heat a non-stick frying pan over medium heat. Brush with oil and pour in 2 cm of batter to coat the base of the pan. You're after the same thickness as a pancake or a flapjack. Cook for 3 minutes or until golden and bubbles appear on the surface. Flip pancake and cook on the other side for a further 1 minute. Place on a plate and cover with a cloth to keep warm while you cook the remaining batter. Cut pancakes into quarters, drizzle with melted ghee and serve with tamarind chutney and yoghurt.

Desserts

As our finale to the spiced world of Indian cooking, this chapter is focused on all things sweet. For some of these recipes, I've blended familiar flavours and some traditional preparations and given them a more modern and Western aesthetic. For others, I've remained true to tradition.

So much of the Indian diet is based on dairy. Milk, butter, ghee, yoghurt, cream and buttermilk are used liberally across every region, providing essential moisture and flavour to food. It's pretty much impossible to find a dessert that doesn't have any dairy, apart from cut fruit (for which no one needs a recipe), making things a little difficult for the sweet-toothed lactose intolerant or vegan person.

Festivals, religious ceremonies and family celebrations are marked with the sharing of sweets. Right across the country, there are designated sweet shops serving traditional sweetmeats, such as *barfi*, *ladoo*, *rasgulla*, *rasmalai*, *mithai*, *sandesh*, *halwa* and *rabri* to name the most popular and widely available. These treats range from fried delights akin to dumplings and doughnuts soaked in sugar syrups to a vast repertoire of milk-based confections. *Kulfi* is another popular dessert thought to have arrived to India by way of the Mughals. This frozen sweet is available from ice-cream parlours and is essentially an Indian ice-cream made with evaporated milk and set in conical vessels. It's wonderfully cooling on the palate after spicy food.

While Indians love their sweets (called *mitha*), it's not common for desserts to be made at home, instead, they're generally purchased from a specialty sweet shop and vary from region to region. However, it is Bengal and Gujarat that lead the way with their dazzling repertoire of all things sweet.

Traditional and contemporary desserts are devoured at every restaurant and have a cult following. There are now dedicated dessert restaurants and cafes in the larger cities that cater to the country's sugar cravings. Much experimentation takes place as chefs reinvent the classics and introduce new flavours and techniques, such is the importance of sweets in India.

Carrot Halwa, Coconut Yoghurt and Cashew Nougatine GF, V

This is one of India's classic desserts and is usually served on its own. Carrots, dusty-pink in colour, unlike their Western relative, are one of the most common vegetables throughout India. I have tasted many regional versions of halwa across India and this one from Rajasthan has become my favourite. Here, I've layered it in a stemless glass and dressed it up with yoghurt and a crunchy crumble for textural contrast. I have a preference for coconut yoghurt instead of dairy-based yoghurt – it makes such a delicious partner for the carrot. The halwa is at its best 30 minutes after being made, having had time to cool slightly. Don't serve it cold from the fridge, as this dulls the flavours and texture.

Serves 4

200 g coconut yoghurt

CARROT HALWA
2 tablespoons ghee
2 cups tightly packed finely grated carrot
   (about 3 large carrots)
125 g caster sugar
1 cup (250 ml) milk
½ cup (60 g) raw cashews, crushed
1 teaspoon ground cardamom

CASHEW NOUGATINE
120 g caster sugar
100 g roasted unsalted cashews, roughly chopped
20 g unsalted butter

To make the cashew nougatine, place the sugar and 2 tablespoons water in a small saucepan over high heat and cook, without stirring, for 5 minutes or until a caramel forms. When the caramel reaches a lovely golden colour, add the cashews and toss to coat. Stir in the butter and swirl until combined. Cook for a further 2 minutes and remove from heat. Pour onto a silicone baking mat or a flat tray lined with baking paper and set aside to cool and harden. Chop into small chunks the same consistency as a coarse crumble and set aside.

To make the carrot halwa, melt the ghee in a frying pan over low heat. As it melts, add the carrot and cook, stirring frequently, for 5 minutes or until softened. Stir in the sugar and cook for a further 3 minutes or until sugar is dissolved. Add the milk and cashews and cook for a further 15 minutes or until all the liquid has been absorbed. Add the cardamom and stir to combine. Set aside to cool for 30 minutes before assembling dessert.

To assemble, divide the carrot halwa between serving glasses and smooth the surface. Spoon over the yoghurt to completely cover the halwa, using the back of a spoon to make an even layer. Sprinkle with a 1 cm-thick layer of the crumbled nougatine and serve immediately.

**Masterclass step-by-step
Carrot Halwa ➔**

Make the cashew nougatine before beginning the carrot halwa.

1

Melt ghee in a frying pan over low heat.

2

Add the shredded carrot and cook, stirring, for 5 minutes or until softened.

3

Stir in the sugar and cook for 3 minutes or until dissolved.

4

Add the milk.

5

Add the crushed cashews and cook for 15 minutes or until liquid is absorbed.

6

Add the ground cardamom and stir to combine. Set aside for 30 minutes.

7

Spoon carrot halwa into serving glasses and smooth the top.

8

Spoon over the coconut yoghurt.

9

Sprinkle with a 1 cm-thick layer of nougatine and serve immediately.

Coconut and Jaggery Pancakes ᵥ

These feathery-light pancakes (or crepes) are a popular Indian sweet, known as *alle belle* in Goa, *mottayappam* in Kerala and *patishapta* in Kolkata. They're quick and easy to make and can be served as a breakfast treat or after curry and rice. To achieve the right texture, moisture content and flavour, the coconut must be fresh, not dried. They are best eaten as soon as they are made.

Serves 4

1 large egg, lightly whisked
⅔ cup (100 g) plain flour
50 g rice flour
1 tablespoon caster sugar
pinch of sea salt flakes
275 ml milk
vegetable oil, for brushing

COCONUT FILLING
125 g jaggery or palm sugar
250 g shredded fresh or frozen coconut,
    see Glossary
1 teaspoon ground cardamom
¼ teaspoon sea salt flakes

To make the coconut filling, place the jaggery in a small saucepan over high heat with 90 ml water and bring to the boil. Boil for 2 minutes or until a syrup forms. Reduce heat to low, stir through the coconut, cardamom and salt and cook for a further 5 minutes or until the coconut has absorbed the syrup and mixture feels sticky to the touch. Set aside.

To make the pancake batter, place the egg, both flours, sugar and salt in a food processor or stand mixer fitted with the paddle attachment and blend until combined. Add the milk and blend until a smooth batter forms.

Heat a non-stick frying pan over medium heat, brush with a little oil and pour in enough batter to coat the base of the pan. Cook for 2 minutes or until the pancake is set on top and golden underneath. Flip and cook the other side for a further 1 minute. Transfer to a plate, cover with a clean cloth and repeat until all batter is used.

Spoon some coconut filling lengthwise along one side of each pancake and gently roll over to enclose. Arrange pancakes on plates and scatter over any remaining coconut filling to serve.

Cardamom Doughnuts with Lemon Ginger Curd v

Doughnuts are universally loved, regardless of their origin. Stuffed with a tangy citrus curd and rolled in cardamom sugar, these have a distinctly Indian twist. It's impossible to stop at one!

Makes 30

7 g (1 sachet) active dry yeast
85 g caster sugar
⅓ cup (80 ml) lukewarm milk
400 g plain flour
3 large egg yolks
60 g unsalted butter, softened and cubed
1½ cups (330 g) caster sugar, extra
2 teaspoons ground cardamom
2 cups (500 ml) vegetable oil, for deep-frying

LEMON GINGER CURD
3 large egg yolks
60 g caster sugar
50 ml lemon juice, strained
1 tablespoon chopped ginger
½ teaspoon ground ginger
75 g cold unsalted butter, cubed

To make the lemon ginger curd, place the yolks and sugar in a heatproof bowl and whisk until light and fluffy. Add the lemon juice and chopped and ground ginger and stir to combine. Place the bowl over a bain-marie (water bath) over low heat and cook, stirring constantly, until thickened. Add the butter, one cube at a time, stirring each piece to incorporate before adding the next. The mixture should have thickened by the time the last piece of butter has been added. Remove bowl from the heat and strain mixture into another bowl, discard solids and stand bowl over ice to cool. Spoon the curd into a piping bag fitted with a small, round nozzle, tie to seal and refrigerate until ready to serve. This can be made the day before.

Place the yeast and 2 teaspoons (10 g) caster sugar, the milk and ⅓ cup (80 ml) lukewarm water in a bowl and stir to combine. Set aside in a warm place for 10 minutes or until frothy.

Place the flour and remaining 75 g sugar in a stand mixer fitted with a dough hook attachment. Add the yeast mixture and egg yolks and knead until combined. With the motor running, add the butter, one cube at a time, kneading well after each addition. Knead for a further 10 minutes or until the butter is completely incorporated and the dough is smooth and elastic. Transfer to a lightly greased bowl, cover and set aside in a warm place for 1 hour or until doubled in size.

Divide dough into 30 even-size pieces, roll into tight balls and place on a greased tray. Cover and set aside for 20 minutes or until slightly risen. Place the extra sugar and ground cardamom on a plate and mix to combine. Set aside.

Heat the oil in a wok or deep-fryer to 150°C. Fry the doughnuts, in batches, rolling in the oil as they cook, for 5 minutes or until cooked through and golden brown. Remove with a mesh spoon and drain on paper towel. While still warm, roll the doughnuts in the cardamom sugar until thoroughly coated. Prick the base of each doughnut with the tip of a small knife and pipe a little of the lemon ginger curd inside. Serve immediately.

Baked Sweet Yoghurt and Pomegranate GF, V

Known as *mishti doi* in Bengal, this sweet curd is a popular fixture on the breakfast table throughout India. It's the first treat I seek out when I'm there. Its silken, smooth texture is achieved through cooking the curd in clay cups, which it's also served in. The unglazed clay is essential for the success of this recipe – you just don't get the same result using anything else, as the porosity of the clay allows the curd to set properly. You can often find clay cups at specialty Indian grocers, homewares stores, or, failing that, find a ceramicist to make some for you. This is delicious served with chopped fruit – I just happen to love it with pomegranate.

Serves 6

½ cup (125 g) thick plain yoghurt
½ cup (125 ml) pouring cream
½ cup (125 ml) condensed milk
½ cup pomegranate seeds

Line a bowl with enough muslin cloth to overhang the sides. Pour the yoghurt into the centre of the cloth and tie the ends to secure. Hang over a bowl for 2 hours until the yoghurt has thickened.

Preheat oven to 150°C. Place the thickened yoghurt, cream and condensed milk in a saucepan over low heat and cook, stirring gently, for 8 minutes or until combined. Pour into small (80–100 g-capacity) clay cups until full and place on a flat tray. Bake for 8 minutes or until set. Remove from the oven and allow to cool slightly. Top with enough pomegranate seeds to cover the surface and serve.

Assamese Fried Rice Cakes GF, V

Tel pitha or fried rice cakes are typical of Assamese cooking. They're served for the Holi festival when sweets take centre stage, every region having its specialty to signify the celebration. They're a great treat to serve with afternoon tea and would be suitable for vegans, if served with an alternative to cream, such as coconut cream or coconut yoghurt. But they do require that addition of fat to make them delectable.

Serves 4

300 g short grain rice, washed
⅓ cup (75 g) caster sugar
1 teaspoon ground fennel
½ teaspoon bicarbonate of soda
2 cups (500 ml) vegetable oil, for deep-frying
½ cup (125 ml) pouring cream, whipped, to serve

Soak the rice in cold water for 2 hours and drain. Place the rice, sugar, fennel, bicarbonate of soda and about 1 tablespoon water (enough to make a thick paste) in a food processor or blender and blend until smooth. Working with wet hands, roll mixture into balls and press to slightly flatten into 5 cm-diameter patties.

Heat the oil in a wok or saucepan over high heat to 180°C. Fry the patties, in batches, on both sides until crisp and puffed. Drain on paper towel and serve warm with cream.

Pineapple Tarts with Cashew Cream v

I discovered this rather luscious dessert at a safari lodge in Assam, a region with an abundant supply of its two key ingredients – pineapple and cashews. You can make small individual tarts using 10 cm-round tart tins, otherwise, make one 20 cm tart to cut into slices.

Serves 6

CASHEW CREAM
2 cups (500 ml) thickened cream
12 g powdered gelatine, dissolved in ¼ cup
   (60 ml) hot water
200 ml condensed milk
125 g raw cashews, ground to a powder

SWEET PASTRY
120 g icing sugar
190 g plain flour
115 g unsalted butter, cubed
3 egg yolks
½ teaspoon vanilla extract

PINEAPPLE FILLING
1 ripe pineapple, peeled and cut into 1 cm dice
   (to yield 900 g)
90 g caster sugar
1 cinnamon stick
1 teaspoon ground cardamom
90 ml freshly squeezed orange juice, strained

To make the cashew cream, place 1 cup (250 ml) cream in small saucepan over low heat and bring to a simmer. Stir through the softened gelatine and set aside to cool. Stir gelatine mixture into the remaining cream with the condensed milk and cashew powder and mix until combined. Strain through a fine mesh sieve into a clean bowl. Cover and refrigerate for 2 hours or until set.

To make the sweet pastry, chill the bowl and blade of a food processor in the refrigerator. Once chilled, sift the icing sugar and flour into the bowl, add the butter and process until the mixture resembles fine breadcrumbs. Add the egg yolks and vanilla and process until the dough just comes together and looks crumbly. Take care not to overwork the pastry or it will become tough. Wrap the dough in plastic wrap and refrigerate for 2 hours or until chilled through.

Roll the pastry out on a cold, floured surface to 5 mm-thick. Using a 13 cm-round pastry cutter, cut 6 rounds from the pastry. Grease 6 x 10 cm-round tart tins (or 1 x 20 cm-round tart tin) and line each one with pastry, pressing down to ensure the pastry is evenly spread over the base and sides of the tin and the edges are smooth. Prick the pastry with a fork. Place the tart tins on a flat tray and refrigerate for 30 minutes.

Preheat oven to 160°C. Blind bake the tart shells for 11–12 minutes or until pale and golden. Allow to cool on a wire rack for 20 minutes before gently removing pastry shells from their tins.

To make the pineapple filling, place the pineapple, sugar, spices and orange juice in a frying pan over medium–high heat and cook, stirring frequently, for 10 minutes or until caramelised. Remove cinnamon stick and allow filling to cool slightly before pouring into the tart shells. Press down gently to smooth the surface. Set aside at room temperature for 15 minutes to allow to settle. Spoon the cashew cream over the pineapple tarts to serve.

Cardamom Rice Pudding and Saffron Pears GF, V

Kheer, as it's known in most of India, or *payasam* in Kerala, is a creamy and sweet rice pudding that goes right to the heart of comfort food. Many south Indian desserts begin with rice, vermicelli or tapioca, cooked with milk, sugar and spices. The gentle fragrance and flavour of the cardamom in the rice is the perfect foil for the saffron-bathed pears. I prefer to serve the rice while still warm as its flavour and texture are more pronounced.

Serves 6

SAFFRON PEARS
6 Josephine or William pears, peeled
600 g caster sugar
1 cup (250 ml) sweet dessert wine
   (moscatel or similar)
50 ml orange blossom water
2 mace blades
½ teaspoon saffron threads
½ vanilla bean, split lengthwise
zest of 1 orange, grated

CARDAMOM RICE PUDDING
250 g medium grain rice
25 g unsalted butter
1 litre full-cream milk
½ vanilla bean, split lengthwise
150 g caster sugar
¼ cup (60 ml) pouring cream
½ teaspoon ground cardamom

To make the saffron pears, cut the pears into balls using a 2.5 cm Parisienne cutter (melon baller). Place the sugar and 600 ml water in a wide-based saucepan over medium–high heat and bring to the boil. Add the remaining ingredients, return to the boil and cook for 3 minutes or until sugar has completely dissolved. Add the pear balls, reduce heat to low and simmer gently, stirring frequently to ensure pear cooks evenly, for 5 minutes or until pear is softened. Remove pan from the heat and set aside. Leave the pear in the syrup while you cook the rice pudding.

To make the cardamom rice pudding, wash the rice under cold, running water for 1 minute and drain. Melt the butter in a frying pan over low heat. Add the rice and stir to coat in the butter. Add the milk, vanilla and sugar and cook, stirring to combine, for 15 minutes or until rice has absorbed most of the milk and is fluffy. Add the cream and cardamom and stir until warmed through. Remove from heat and discard vanilla bean. The rice should have the consistency of risotto. If the rice is left to cool, it will become firm in texture, so it's best served within 10 minutes.

To serve, spoon the warm rice pudding into bowls, top with the pear and drizzle over the saffron syrup.

Saffron Rice Pudding with Grilled Apricots and Pistachio GF, V

Phirni is another traditional rice pudding. I collected this recipe on my travels in north India. It's really another variation to *kheer* or *payasam* (see recipe page 413), but this version has a porridge-like consistency because the rice grains are broken before being cooked. I've used rice here, as I prefer its texture, but it can also be made with broken wheat, sweet corn (coarse yellow polenta), millet or tapioca. Apricot orchards are common in the Himalayas and the fruit is a standard summer crop in Ladakh where it appears in many guises. If apricots aren't available, use mango or papaya, but don't cook these. I serve the rice with a fresh, tangy curd made from buffalo milk as the extra richness is the perfect foil for the rice. Labne would be equally successful as an accompaniment.

Serves 4

8 apricots, halved and stones removed
2 tablespoons brown sugar
2 tablespoons fresh buffalo or goat curd
    (hung yoghurt), see Eggs and Dairy page 110
1 tablespoon pistachios, slivered

RICE PUDDING
250 g medium grain rice
1 litre full-cream milk
100 g caster sugar
¼ teaspoon ground mace
½ teaspoon saffron threads
few drops of rosewater

To make the rice pudding, wash the rice under cold, running water for 1 minute and drain. Place in a food processor and pulse briefly, just enough to break the grains and make a coarse paste. Don't overwork the rice or it will become mushy.

Place the milk in a heavy-based saucepan over high heat and bring to the boil. When it starts to boil, stir in the rice paste, reduce heat to low and cook for 15 minutes or until the mixture has thickened and the rice is soft. Add the sugar and stir to dissolve. Cook for 3 minutes before stirring through the mace, saffron and rosewater. Remove from heat and set aside.

While the rice is cooking, prepare the apricots. Place the apricots cut-side up on a baking tray and sprinkle with the sugar. Cook under a preheated hot grill for 5 minutes or until the sugar has caramelised and the apricots have softened. You could also use a blowtorch to caramelise the sugar, if you have one.

Spoon the warm rice pudding into bowls, arrange 4 apricot halves on top of each bowl, spoon over the curd and scatter with pistachios to serve.

Rose Syrup Dumplings v

Gulab jamun is one of the definitive desserts of India and can be found on just about every menu across the country from street vendors to *dhabas* (humble cafes) and restaurants. These soft, warm dumplings are first fried then soaked in a sweet rosewater syrup. If you choose to decorate the dumplings with tiny flecks of silver leaf, be careful not to let your skin come into contact with the silver as it sticks to you rather than the food – it's a precarious and fickle task. I leave the silver leaf on its paper backing and then dab a small piece onto each dumpling, pulling my hand away to avoid anything larger being stuck to the dumpling.

Makes 24

¼ cup (35 g) self-raising flour
1 tablespoon fine semolina
100 g milk powder
½ teaspoon ground cardamom
30 g almond meal
30 g ground pistachios
½ cup (125 ml) full-cream milk, warmed
75 g ghee, melted
2 cups (500 ml) vegetable oil, for deep-frying
2 tablespoons chopped pistachios
1 sheet edible silver leaf (optional)

ROSE SYRUP
500 g caster sugar
5 green cardamom pods, cracked
½ teaspoon rosewater

Sift the flour, semolina, milk powder and cardamom into a large bowl. Add the almond meal and pistachios and stir to combine. Combine the warm milk and ghee in a jug and pour over the flour mixture. Using a wooden spoon, gradually incorporate the dry ingredients into the milk mixture and knead with your hands until a smooth dough forms. Cover the bowl with a cloth or plastic wrap and set aside to rest for 30 minutes.

Using wet hands, roll the dough into 24 small, even-size balls. Heat the oil to 170°C. To test the temperature of the oil, sprinkle some flour into the oil, if it sizzles, the oil is ready. Fry the balls, in batches, for 3 minutes or until golden brown. Remove from the oil with a slotted spoon and drain on paper towel.

To make the rose syrup, place the sugar, cardamom and 325 ml water in a large saucepan over medium heat and bring to the boil, stirring occasionally. Reduce heat to low and simmer for 5 minutes. Remove the cardamom pods and add the rosewater. Add the fried dumplings and simmer for 2–3 minutes, rolling them around in the pan so they absorb the syrup.

Remove the dumplings from the syrup, arrange on plates and sprinkle with chopped pistachios. Stick small flakes of silver leaf to the dumplings, if desired.

Jalebi and Pistachio Cream v

I am a sucker for a jalebi. It's perhaps my favourite Indian sweet snack, often bought from a street vendor when I'm in need of a sugar fix. This modern, sophisticated interpretation is tributed to my friend and colleague, chef Manish Mehrotra of Indian Accent in Delhi. He partners it with *rabri*, a thickened sweetened milk that is reduced to a creamy consistency, which he serves from a siphon that aerates the cream. Inspired by his clever presentation, which gives tradition a modern perspective, I have made a lighter-textured, easier-to-make pistachio cream that's piped onto the jalebi disc. The jalebi can be served on their own without the cream, if you would like to make them dairy-free.

Serves 8

¼ teaspoon saffron threads
1 cup (150 g) plain flour
1 tablespoon rice flour
¼ teaspoon baking powder
1 tablespoon fresh curd (hung yoghurt),
    see Eggs and Dairy page 110
350 g caster sugar
¼ teaspoon ground cardamom
3 teaspoons rosewater
2 cups (500 ml) vegetable oil, for deep-frying
120 g peeled pistachios, chopped to a fine crumb

PISTACHIO CREAM
75 g pistachio paste, see Glossary
⅓ cup (75 g) caster sugar
2 cups (500 ml) thickened cream

To make the pistachio cream, whisk the pistachio paste, sugar and cream in a stand mixer until combined and thick. Spoon into a piping bag fitted with a star nozzle (size 9) and tie the end to secure. Refrigerate until ready to serve.

To make the jalebi batter, place the saffron in a small frying pan over low heat and dry roast for 10 seconds. Allow to cool. Place in a mortar and pestle and grind to a powder. Add the saffron powder to a small glass with ¼ cup (60 ml) hot water and stir to combine. Place both flours, baking powder, curd and 90 ml warm water in a bowl and whisk until combined. Add 1 teaspoon of the saffron water and whisk until smooth. Cover bowl and set aside for 2 hours to ferment.

While the batter is fermenting, make the syrup. Place the sugar and 300 ml water in a saucepan over high heat and simmer, stirring to dissolve sugar, for 5 minutes. Add the cardamom and remaining saffron water and cook for 2 minutes. Turn off heat and add the rosewater.

To cook the jalebi, whisk the batter thoroughly and pour into a piping bag fitted with a small round nozzle (size 2). Twist and tie the end to secure. Heat the oil in a frying pan to 150°C. Test the temperature with a little batter, if it sizzles, the oil is ready. Making only 2 or 3 jalebi at a time, pipe the batter into the oil in a steady stream to form coils approximately 8 cm in diameter. Deep-fry for 2 minutes or until golden and crisp, turn and cook on the other side for a further 2 minutes. It sometimes takes a few goes to get this right, so don't despair. Remove jalebi with a mesh spoon and drain on paper towel for 1 minute. Once drained, add to the saffron syrup to soak for 5 minutes. Remove and place on a wire rack to remove excess syrup and dry out slightly.

To serve, place the jalebi on a plate and pipe the pistachio cream on top, forming a raised peak in the centre. Dust liberally with pistachio crumbs to lightly cover the surface of the cream. Serve immediately.

Green Tea Panna Cotta, Masala Chai Sauce and Cumin Shortbread v

This is my favourite treat from Glenburn Tea Estate near Darjeeling, where the elegance of their estate teas is woven into this dessert. It's a house signature that allows the flavour of the tea to shine through. Their chefs have adapted tradition and given a more Western interpretation and presentation. You can set the panna cotta into small pudding moulds then dip into hot water to turn out onto plates when serving. Otherwise, the easier option is to set them in glasses or small bowls from which they are served. It tastes exactly the same, either way.

Serves 6

PANNA COTTA
2 cups (500 ml) pouring cream
1 cup (250 ml) full-cream milk
2 tablespoons Darjeeling green tea leaves
125 g caster sugar
10 g gold strength gelatine leaves, softened
  in cold water and squeezed

MASALA CHAI SAUCE
1 cup (250 ml) pouring cream
1 tablespoon minced ginger
3 green cardamom pods, cracked
2 tablespoons Assam (black) tea leaves
⅓ cup (75 g) caster sugar

CUMIN SHORTBREAD
100 g unsalted butter, softened
50 g caster sugar
1 teaspoon cumin seeds, dry-roasted and ground
1 teaspoon sea salt flakes
3 teaspoons pouring cream
125 g plain flour, sifted

To make the panna cotta, heat the cream, milk, tea leaves and sugar in a saucepan over low heat for 5–6 minutes or until the tea is infused and the sugar is dissolved. Bring to a simmer, then remove from heat and set aside for 30 minutes to infuse.

Return milk mixture to low heat and bring to a gentle simmer. Add the softened gelatine and stir for 2 minutes or until dissolved. Remove from heat, strain through a fine mesh sieve and pour into small (150 ml-capacity) dariole moulds or bowls until ⅔ full. Cover with plastic wrap and refrigerate for 3 hours or until set.

To make the cumin shortbread, place the butter, sugar, cumin and salt in a stand mixer fitted with the paddle attachment and whisk until pale and creamy. Add the cream and whisk to combine, taking care not to overwork the dough. Fold in the flour until combined. Turn the dough out onto the bench and use your hands to bring the dough together. Wrap in plastic wrap and place in the fridge for 1 hour to chill until firm.

Roll the dough out on a bench to 4 mm-thick and cut into rounds using a 6 cm-round pastry cutter. Place the biscuits on a silicone baking mat or flat baking sheet lined with non-stick baking paper. Cut enough biscuits to ensure there are 2 per serve and reserve any extra shortbread dough for later use. It can be frozen for up to 1 month in a vacuum-sealed bag. Place the biscuits in the fridge for 30 minutes to chill. This prevents them from shrinking during baking.

Preheat oven to 170°C. Bake the biscuits for 10 minutes or until light golden and crisp. Remove from the oven and place on a wire rack to cool. Store in an airtight container until ready to serve.

To make the masala chai sauce, place the cream in a saucepan over medium heat and bring to the boil. Reduce heat to low, add the ginger, cardamom and tea leaves and stir to combine. Simmer for 2 minutes, add the sugar and stir to dissolve. Let the sauce cool for 10 minutes before straining. Place in the fridge to chill before using.

To turn out the panna cotta, dip each mould in hot water for 20 seconds to loosen, then invert onto serving plates. The panna cotta should slide out from the mould. Spoon over the masala chai sauce to make a 1 cm-thick layer and serve with the cumin shortbread.

Mango Cardamom Kulfi GF, V

Kulfi is a popular Indian iced confection traditionally made by reducing milk over very low heat for several hours until it evaporates, leaving a thick and creamy mixture. It's then flavoured with spices, fruit puree or nuts and frozen in small conical moulds. This recipe is a quick version that requires no cooking. I've used milks that have already been evaporated and condensed to approximate the same texture. To mould the ice-cream, I use conical pastry moulds. Line the inside with a piece of baking paper and, when frozen, remove from the mould but keep the paper wrapping on until ready to serve. This method makes it easy to remove the ice-cream from the mould and the paper can be peeled away when you're ready to eat. Insert a wooden skewer into the base of the frozen ice before serving.

Serves 6

400 ml thickened cream
1 x 395 ml tin condensed milk
1 x 375ml tin evaporated milk
500 g fresh mango puree
200 ml sugar syrup, see Glossary
1 teaspoon ground cardamom

Place the cream, condensed milk and evaporated milk in a large bowl. Add the mango puree, sugar syrup and cardamom and stir to combine. Pour into a freezer-proof container (or small metal conical moulds, if you have them) lined with baking paper, cover and freeze for 5 hours or overnight. If you have frozen the kulfi in conical moulds, insert a wooden skewer or ice-cream stick into the base before you unwrap the paper, so there is something to hold while eating.
If you don't have conical moulds, set the kulfi in a rectangular tray, then slice into squares when ready to serve.

Salted Caramel, Banana and Chocolate Crepes GF, V

There's a wonderful little place in Bandra, north Mumbai, called Suzette with a menu of crepes, sandwiches, snacks and fresh juices. Inspired by the creperies of France, this cafe with its relaxed vibe is a little slice of heaven amid the bustle of this turbo-charged city. Not at all Indian, nevertheless, the crepes are a sure-fire hit with locals. I have embellished these with my favourite combination of dark chocolate, salted caramel, banana and peanuts.

Serves 6

2 tablespoons unsalted butter
3 small ripe bananas, peeled and sliced
2 tablespoons roasted peanuts, crushed
1 tablespoon pure icing sugar, sifted

CREPE BATTER
2 large eggs
150 g caster sugar
¼ teaspoon ground cinnamon
250 g buckwheat flour
350 ml full-cream milk
pinch of sea salt flakes

SALTED CARAMEL SAUCE
150 g caster sugar
100 ml pouring cream
125 g unsalted butter, diced
½ teaspoon sea salt flakes

CHOCOLATE SAUCE
150 g dark couverture chocolate, chopped
½ cup (125 ml) pouring cream
30 g unsalted butter, cubed

To make the salted caramel sauce, place the sugar and 50 ml water in a medium saucepan over high heat and bring to the boil. Cook, without stirring, for 4–6 minutes or until temperature reaches 195°C on a sugar thermometer and caramel is a golden colour.

Meanwhile, place the cream in a separate saucepan over medium–low heat and bring to a gentle simmer, making sure the cream doesn't reach boiling point. The cream needs to be hot when the caramel is ready, so you need to coordinate these steps. When the caramel is ready, pour the hot cream into the caramel, taking care as it will splutter and expand, and stir to combine.

Reduce heat to medium–low, add the butter, a little at a time, and cook, stirring, until melted. Add the salt. When the butter is amalgamated into the sauce, set aside to cool. This can be made ahead of time and refrigerated in an airtight jar until ready to serve.

To make the crepe batter, place the eggs, sugar and cinnamon in a bowl and whisk for 2 minutes or until light and fluffy. Add ⅓ of the flour and whisk to combine. Add ⅓ of the milk and continue to whisk until mixture is smooth and there are no lumps. Repeat until all the flour and milk has all been used. Stir through the salt and pour the batter into a large jug. Set aside to rest for 30 minutes. If the batter is too thick, add a little extra milk. It needs to pour easily to achieve a thin crepe consistency.

While the batter is resting, make the chocolate sauce. Place the chocolate in a heatproof bowl. Place the cream in a saucepan over medium–low heat and bring to a simmer. Once simmering, pour the hot cream over the chocolate and stir gently until melted and smooth. Whisk in the butter and continue to whisk until smooth. Set aside.

To make the crepes, heat a non-stick crepe pan over medium heat. Add a small piece of butter and swirl to coat the base of the pan. Pour a ladleful of batter into the pan, just enough to coat the base, and swirl the pan to make an even layer. Cook for 1–3 minutes or until the batter is set. Using an egg slide, lift one side of the crepe to check it's golden underneath. If golden, flip and cook for a further 1 minute or until golden. Slide onto a plate and cover with a cloth to keep warm. Repeat with remaining batter and butter.

Fold crepes in half and spread with the caramel sauce, scatter banana and crushed peanuts on one side and drizzle with chocolate sauce to cover. Enclose filling and dust with icing sugar to serve.

Baked Vanilla Custard GF, V

Lagan nu kastar is a Parsi dessert with iconic status. It's obligatory to serve at a wedding feast (laden with nuts and sultanas) and is a popular treat at home for family gatherings. Incredibly rich, eggy and creamy in true Parsi tradition, this dessert is best served in small portions. Eggs play an important role in the savoury and sweet preparations of India. To flavour, a few drops of rose essence can be substituted for the vanilla, if you prefer. When peaches or nectarines are in season, I poach them in a light sugar syrup, then peel and slice to serve with the baked custard.

Serves 4

2 cups (500 ml) full-cream milk
125 g caster sugar
½ vanilla bean, split lengthwise
4 eggs
½ cup (125 ml) pouring cream
2 tablespoons blanched almond meal
1 teaspoon freshly ground nutmeg
2 teaspoons unsalted butter
2 tablespoons flaked almonds, lightly toasted

Place the milk, sugar and vanilla in a heavy-based saucepan over medium heat and stir to dissolve the sugar. Bring to the boil, reduce heat to medium–low and simmer until the milk has reduced by half. Remove from heat and discard the vanilla bean. Place the eggs in a large bowl and whisk until pale. Add the cream and whisk to combine. Stir in the almond meal and nutmeg.

Preheat oven to 160°C. Grease a 24 cm-wide x 5 cm-deep baking dish with the butter and pour the custard into the dish. Place the baking dish inside a larger dish and pour in enough boiling water to come halfway up the sides of the baking dish. Bake for 45 minutes or until the custard is just set. Remove from oven and set aside to settle for 15 minutes before serving. Garnish with flaked almonds to serve.

Bombay Mess GF, V

This is an Indian-inspired adaption of the classic English dessert Eton mess, which is basically a deconstructed pavlova loved for its textural contrast of soft and crunchy elements. It's a treat to make this when mangoes are in season. There's no better time to be in Mumbai than when the Alphonso mango is plentiful in April and May, a precursor to the monsoons. This dessert honours the city and its beloved mangoes.

Serves 6

100 ml pouring cream
100 ml creme fraiche
1 tablespoon caster sugar
2 mangoes, peeled and diced
3 passionfruit, pulp removed

MERINGUES
3 eggwhites
150 g pure icing sugar, sifted

LIME CURD
3 large egg yolks
60 g caster sugar
65 ml lime juice, strained
1 teaspoon minced lime zest
75 g cold unsalted butter, cubed

To make the meringues, preheat oven to 90°C and line 2 baking trays with baking paper. Place the eggwhites in a stand mixer fitted with the whisk attachment and whisk on high speed until soft peaks form. Reduce speed to medium and add half the sugar. Increase speed to high and continue to whisk for 2 minutes or until stiff peaks form. Reduce speed to medium, add the remaining sugar, increase speed to high again and beat for a further 10 minutes or until meringue is thick and glossy.

Drop dessertspoonfuls of meringue onto the prepared trays, making sure to leave enough space between each spoonful to allow for spreading, and flatten slightly with the back of the spoon. Bake for 2 hours or until meringue is crisp. The low temperature sets the meringue without changing its colour – you want the meringues to remain white. Remove from oven and allow to cool completely. Store in an airtight container until ready to serve. The meringues will keep in an airtight container for 2 days.

To make the lime curd, place the yolks and sugar in a bowl and whisk for 4 minutes or until light and fluffy. Add the lime juice and zest and whisk to combine. Place the bowl over a bain-marie (water bath) over medium heat and cook, stirring constantly, for 4 minutes or until thickened. Add the butter, one cube at a time, stirring each piece to incorporate before adding the next. The mixture should have thickened by the time the last piece of butter has been added. You're looking for a thick custard consistency. Remove bowl from the heat and stand over ice to cool. Store the curd in a sealed container in the refrigerator until ready to serve.

Place the cream, creme fraiche and sugar in a bowl and beat until thick and holding its shape. Break the meringues in half (the shapes are meant to be haphazard, not uniform). Gently layer the chopped mango, passionfruit pulp, meringue, lime curd and cream in bowls to serve.

Ginger Spiced Pears, Gingerbread and Yoghurt Sorbet v

I like the tangy flavour of either sheep or goat's milk yoghurt to make this sorbet. The gingerbread recipe makes a 24 cm-round cake and serves 12, but if you're not using the lot while it's fresh (within a few days), cut the cake in half, wrap and freeze for another use. If you aren't up for making the sorbet, simply serve the pears with thick plain yoghurt.

Serves 6

GINGER SPICED PEARS
1 litre sugar syrup, see Glossary
1 tablespoon minced ginger
1 cinnamon stick
6 whole allspice
4 cloves
2 teaspoons whole mace
½ cup (125 ml) green ginger wine
½ cup (125 ml) Poire Williams eau de vie
6 ripe Beurre Bosc pears, peeled, halved and cored

GINGERBREAD
2⅓ cups (350 g) self-raising flour
1 tablespoon ground ginger
½ teaspoon freshly grated nutmeg
2 teaspoons ground cinnamon
250 g brown sugar
200 g unsalted butter
100 ml golden syrup
3 large eggs, beaten
350 ml full-cream milk

YOGHURT SORBET
120 g liquid glucose
150 g caster sugar
500 g thick plain yoghurt
700 ml full-cream milk
2 tablespoons lime juice

To make the yoghurt sorbet, place the glucose in a bowl over a bain-marie (water bath) over medium heat for 5 minutes or until softened to a pouring consistency. Remove from heat, add the sugar and yoghurt and mix until combined. Add the milk and lime juice and stir until smooth. Place in an ice-cream machine and churn, according to manufacturer's instructions, until firm. Transfer to a tray large enough to ensure the sorbet is 1.5 cm-thick. Cover with plastic wrap and freeze until required.

Remove from the freezer 5 minutes before serving to allow it to soften slightly, making it easier to scoop.

To make the ginger spiced pears, place the sugar syrup, minced ginger, spices, green ginger wine and Poire Williams in a wide-based saucepan over medium–high heat and bring to the boil. Simmer gently for 15 minutes, reduce heat to low and add the pears. Cover with a sheet of baking paper and place a smaller plate on top to keep the pears submerged in the syrup while they cook. Cook for a further 15–20 minutes or until pears are softened. Remove from the liquid and set aside.

Continue to cook the poaching liquid over medium heat for 10 minutes or until thickened and syrupy. Pass through a fine mesh sieve and discard solids. Allow the syrup to cool. Pour over the poached pear halves and keep cool until ready to serve.

To make the gingerbread, preheat oven to 160°C. Grease and line a 24 cm-round cake tin with baking paper. Sift the flour, ginger, nutmeg, cinnamon and sugar into a bowl and set aside. Place the butter and golden syrup in a saucepan over medium heat and cook until melted and combined. Set aside to cool for 5 minutes. Place the eggs in a large bowl and whisk the cooled golden syrup mixture into the eggs with the milk until combined. Add to the flour mixture and stir until a smooth batter forms. Pour into the prepared tin and bake for 45 minutes. Allow to cool in the tin on a wire rack for 15 minutes before turning cake out onto a chopping board.

To serve, cut the cake crosswise into 3 cm-thick slices. Using a 9 cm-round pastry cutter, cut rounds from the cake slices and place in serving bowls. Arrange pears on top, drizzle with a little ginger syrup and top with a quenelle of sorbet.

Rosewater Yoghurt Cream and Black Pepper Strawberries GF

I love how each season is celebrated with fruit in India. During the hot summer months from April to June, juicy strawberries are sent down from the temperate Mahabaleshwar hills to food markets and street vendors. Introduced by the British during colonial rule, the fruit has become synonymous with many Indian desserts and sweet drinks.

Serves 4

410 ml pouring cream
110 g caster sugar
1 teaspoon dried rose petals, see Glossary
8 g gold strength gelatine leaves, softened in
  cold water and squeezed
3 teaspoons rosewater
225 g fresh curd (hung yoghurt), see Eggs
  and Dairy page 110
1 x 200 g punnet small ripe strawberries,
  halved lengthwise
¼ cup (60 ml) sugar syrup, see Glossary
½ teaspoon freshly ground black pepper
1 tablespoon snipped mint cress or tiny
  mint leaves

Place the cream, sugar and rose petals in a saucepan over low heat and cook for 4 minutes or until mixture reaches simmering point. Add the softened gelatine and cook, stirring, for 2 minutes or until dissolved. Remove from heat and stir through 2 teaspoons of the rosewater. Set aside to cool for 15 minutes before straining through a fine mesh sieve. Gently fold through the curd and stir until smooth, taking care not to overwork the mixture or it may separate. Divide between serving bowls (or stemless glasses), cover and refrigerate for 5 hours or overnight until set.

To serve, place the strawberries in a bowl with the sugar syrup, black pepper and remaining 1 teaspoon rosewater and gently toss to coat. Set aside for 10 minutes to macerate. Arrange strawberries on top of rosewater cream and sprinkle with the mint cress to serve.

Mango, Lime Curd and Ginger Crumble ᵥ

I created this dessert for the series of pop-up dinner feasts I hosted around Australia for the release of *Tasting India: Heirloom Family Recipes* in 2018. It's inspired by key ingredients associated with India – ginger, mango, lime – but is entirely Western in its method and presentation. Make sure the mango is not over-ripe, it needs to hold its shape when cut.

Serves 8

4 ripe mangoes
2 tablespoons candied ginger, finely diced

LIME CURD
300 g thick plain yoghurt, drained in a colander
    for 10 minutes to remove excess liquid
125 g ricotta, drained in a colander for 2 hours
    to remove excess whey
125 g creme fraiche or sour cream
½ cup (110 g) caster sugar
zest of 2 limes, minced
2 tablespoons lime juice
3 large eggs, lightly beaten
4 tablespoons finger lime pearls

GINGER CRUMBLE
⅔ cup (100 g) plain flour
100 g rolled oats
135 g light brown sugar
150 g unsalted butter, melted
1 teaspoon bicarbonate of soda
½ teaspoon sea salt flakes
2 teaspoons ground ginger

Cut the cheeks from mangoes, you'll need 1 cheek per serve. Scoop out the flesh with a large spoon, discard skin and cut mango into 1 cm dice. Cover the base of eight serving glasses with the diced mango and sprinkle with the candied ginger. Cover and refrigerate while you make the curd.

To make the lime curd, place the drained yoghurt and ricotta and remaining ingredients except the finger lime pearls in a food processor and blend briefly until just combined and smooth. Don't overwork the mixture or it will become too runny. Transfer to a bowl and stir through the finger lime pearls. Divide the lime curd between the serving glasses, making sure each glass is half-full. Cover and refrigerate for 5 hours or overnight.

To make the ginger crumble, preheat oven to 160°C and line a large baking tray with non-stick paper. Place all the crumble ingredients in a bowl and mix to form a coarse crumb. Spread onto the tray and bake for 15 minutes or until golden brown. Allow crumble to cool completely, then place in a blender or food processor and process to form a fine crumb. Cover the lime curd with a 1.5 mm-thick layer of ginger crumble to serve.

Fried Pancakes with Strawberries and Cream v

Malpuas are traditionally made with red millet flour in Karnataka and plain flour in Bengal. This is the Bengali version, which has a lighter, fluffier texture. However, using millet would make them gluten-free, so it's your call.

Serves 4

1 cup (150 g) plain flour
⅓ cup semolina
1 tablespoon caster sugar
1 teaspoon baking powder
½ teaspoon ground cardamom
1 teaspoon ground fennel seeds, plus extra
　　¼ teaspoon
½ teaspoon sea salt flakes
180 ml evaporated milk
¼ cup (60 ml) melted ghee
1 cup (250 ml) sugar syrup, see Glossary
½ cup whipped cream and sliced strawberries,
　　to serve

Place the flour, semolina, sugar, baking powder, cardamom, fennel and salt in a large bowl and stir in the evaporated milk to make a thick batter. It should have the same consistency as a pancake batter.

Melt the ghee in non-stick frying pan over medium heat. Drop tablespoonfuls of the batter into the pan, a few at a time, to make 5 cm-round pancakes (about the size of pikelets). Cook for 2 minutes or until golden and starting to crisp. Flip over and cook for a further 1 minute or until golden. Remove from pan and keep warm.

Combine the sugar syrup and extra ¼ teaspoon fennel and place in a saucepan over low heat until simmering. Remove from heat, add the cooked pancakes and set aside to soak for 2 minutes. Remove pancakes from pan with a slotted spoon and serve warm with strawberries and whipped cream.

Thank you

Thank you, most importantly, to my chief taste tester and life partner, Margie Harris, for your tireless support, critical eye, enduring love and loyalty.

To my dear friend and literary adviser and the Simon & Schuster publisher for this project, Julie Gibbs, who keeps me honest, on track and on time, and who has been by my side with every book I have published. Thanks for this opportunity to once again share my deep commitment and love for Indian food, a story retold in a different way.

Heartfelt thanks to Alan Benson, you have photographed these recipes so beautifully, it is so effortless working with you and sharing the same considered aesthetic. What a dream team!

To my editor Lara Picone, thanks for your astute editing and gentle wisdom, your fresh eyes that pick up the most minute error and your clever ability to be resourceful with words. Thanks for sharing this writing adventure with me. My appreciation also to the eagle-eyed Pru Engel for her proofreading.

Enormous thanks once again to my book designer Daniel New, for adding the wow factor and your contemporary, timeless design aesthetic to this tome. It's always a pleasure to work with you.

Dan Ruffino at Simon & Schuster, my appreciation for the opportunity and commitment to imagine this book, to celebrate a food culture close to my heart. Thank you also to production manager Anthea Bariamis for revisiting the specifications when the book grew – and grew!

Thanks to my crack publicity team Anna O'Grady and Angus Dalton who have made it their own mission to share the love for this book with a very broad audience.

A special thanks to Shelley Simpson for collaborating with me and providing your beautiful Mud Australia ceramics, whose dreamy colour palette transforms the food that rests on it. To Georgie Williams at Major & Tom, thanks for providing so many excellent background props, and to trusted courier Vlad for always being there and playing go-between for our busy work schedules.

Thank you Jamshyd Sethna and Lucy Davison of Banyan Tours in Delhi for always showing me the best time whenever I am in India and for being thoughtful and knowledgeable sounding boards for my India-related questions.

A very big thank you to those farmers and producers in northern New South Wales, who I am now lucky enough to have close at hand to source the very best bounty from the earth, the paddocks and the sea. Thank you for connecting me to community, in particular, Arabella Douglas and Currie Country who gifted me treasures from our coastal waters and rainforests; Palisa Anderson at Boon Luck Farm, your organic vegetables and herbs make my cooking sing; and John Picone, your tropical, exotic fruits add that special dimension and deep satisfying flavour. Indian cooking would not be possible without an array of fragrant spices in the pantry, so I'd like to thank Ian Hemphill at Herbie's Spices for supplying the freshest and best spices on the market.

About the author

As one of Australia's most celebrated and revered chefs, Christine Manfield has contributed enormously to the country's collective table. An inquisitive cook, avid traveller, and perfectionist, Christine is inspired by global flavours as well as local and sustainable produce that supports both communities and the environment.

Having penned the hugely successful and award-winning cookbooks *Tasting India*, *A Personal Guide to India and Bhutan*, *Dessert Divas*, *Fire*, *Spice*, *Stir*, *Paramount Cooking* and *Paramount Desserts,* Christine's influence has flavoured the kitchens of many keen home cooks for decades. One of Australia's leading culinary ambassadors, her life as a restaurateur culminated in three award-winning restaurants in Australia and abroad: Paramount in Sydney (1993–2000), East@West in London (2003–2005), and Sydney's Universal (2007–2013). She continues to collaborate with chefs and industry colleagues, hosting pop-up events across Australia, judging the *delicious.* Produce Awards, and is a mentor to Women in Hospitality (WOHO).

A true explorer who is endlessly fascinated with the food traditions of diverse cultures, over the past 20 years Christine has hosted bespoke culinary adventures to destinations both in Australia and overseas, including India, Italy, South America, Bhutan, France, South East Asia, Spain, Morocco and New Zealand. But it's her deep love and understanding of Indian cooking that she shares with readers here, in *Indian Cooking Class*. Drawing on her own extensive travels through the home, street and commercial kitchens of India's distinct regions, Christine hopes this collection of approachable recipes will empower everyone to confidently enter and enjoy the layered world of Indian cooking.

Glossary

Ajwain
In the same family as coriander, cumin and fennel, ajwain are tiny, pungent seeds with a flavour similar to a blend of thyme and anise. Ajwain is popular in North Indian cooking, where it is often paired with root vegetables and fried snacks. You can find ajwain seeds in Indian grocery stores.

Asafoetida
A resinous gum extracted from the sap of a fennel-like plant native to Iran and Afghanistan (related to mastic) and introduced to India by the Mughals. It's sold either as a resin (that needs to be pounded) or in powder form. Its characteristic pungent, sulphuric aroma is not dissimilar to fermented garlic (and used in place of garlic in Sattvic cooking of the high Brahmins). It's used as a flavour enhancer and to counterbalance acidity in Indian cooking and is commonly added when cooking dal to counter flatulence and respiratory ailments. Available from Indian grocers or spice suppliers.

Banana blossom
A popular vegetable in India and Asia, banana blossoms are the unopened tear-shaped purple flower of the banana plant. They hang beneath the cluster of bananas on a stem and are sold fresh in Asian and specialty food shops. Try to avoid ones that look wilted, as this means they have been cut from the plant too long ago. To store, keep the blossoms wrapped in a damp cloth in the fridge and to prepare, remove the outer leaves and the long, narrow yellow blossoms until you are left with the pale-coloured inner heart. Cut into quarters lengthwise, then cut crosswise into thin slices. The blossoms oxidise quickly, so have a bowl of cold water acidulated with a few slices of lemon ready to plunge the slices into. I suggest not cutting the flower until you are ready to cook. The blossoms can be eaten raw or simmered in boiling water for 10 minutes until tender.

Banana leaves
Fresh leaves can be purchased from Asian fresh produce stores and some markets. Or you may find them in your backyard, if you live in a warm climate where banana trees grow. To store, cut out the hard central stem, roll the leaves, wrap in damp newspaper and keep refrigerated for 2–3 days. Cut away any discoloured sections before using to wrap food that is to be steamed or cooked over hot coals.

Black salt
A purple-coloured rock salt extracted from the earth with a sulphurous aroma that dissipates during cooking. Used in north Indian cooking, black salt (*kala namak*) has a pronounced earthy flavour and pungency. It is ground into a fine, pinkish powder and requires cooking during the seasoning of a dish. With a unique flavour profile, there really isn't a substitute for it, but it's readily available from Indian grocery stores.

Boondi
Small, crisp pellets of fried, puffed chickpea batter, Boondi is a popular chaat snack sold in small packets (just like potato chips) from Indian grocery stores. Look for the Haldiram brand at Indian grocers.

Chaat masala
A blend of ground spices with a characteristic sour flavour. Chaat masala is a mix of amchur (dried mango powder), ginger, black salt, asafoetida and ajwain and is sold pre-blended from Indian grocers or specialty spice shops.

Chickpea (besan) flour
Chana dal or split chickpeas are stone-ground to make a finely textured, gluten-free flour that has a multitude of uses in Indian cooking. It's readily available at Indian grocers, health food stores and some supermarkets.

Coconut
Grated fresh coconut is conveniently available frozen in bags at Indian and Asian food stores these days. With none of the flavour or texture lost as it thaws, it's such a time saver. However, if you'd like to grate fresh coconut yourself, crack a mature coconut (hard brown shell) in half, discard water and use a zester or a hand-held grater to shred the white flesh. Use within a day of grating, as it will quickly sour.

Crab stock

To make crab stock, firstly extract the meat from the shells. Place the shells in a baking dish with a few chopped tomatoes and lightly roast in a moderate oven for 20 minutes. Transfer to a large saucepan or stockpot, add a few slices of fresh ginger and green shallot, cracked black pepper and a split chilli. Cover the shells with a light fish or chicken stock and bring to a simmer over medium heat. Once it starts to bubble, reduce heat to low and simmer gently for 30 minutes. Strain the stock through a fine mesh sieve set over another large vessel and press firmly to extract all the liquid. Discard shells and solids. Cool stock completely before pouring into an airtight container. Store in the refrigerator for two days, otherwise, you can keep in the freezer for one month until ready to use.

Cream

Cream used in all recipes, unless otherwise specified, is regular pure or pouring cream with a 35 per cent fat content. It's also sometimes called single or whipping cream. Thickened cream has gelatine added and is only used in recipes that require it. Double cream has a higher fat content and shouldn't be used to replace single cream, as this will affect the texture of the recipe.

Curry leaves (fresh)

I recommend you only use fresh curry leaves. I find it's a complete waste of time using dried, as they have no flavour and have lost their colour. And, unfortunately, freezing curry leaves doesn't work so well, either. These days, fresh leaves are readily available from greengrocers and growing a small tree in a pot is easy in most parts of Australia. When a recipe asks for fried leaves, simply heat vegetable oil in a saucepan to 160°C and fry the leaves, in small batches, for 20 seconds or until crisp. Remove from the oil with a mesh spoon and drain on paper towel. Fried leaves are best used the same day they're made.

Dried rose petals

Edible dried rose petals are readily available from specialty food stores and supermarkets. Of Persian origin and linked to the exotic richness of Mughal royal cooking, they are used to perfume and flavour sweets and savoury dishes alike, or can simply be added as a garnish, yielding a heady fragrance.

Fried shallot slices

To make your own fried shallot slices, peel red or golden shallots and slice finely lengthwise. Heat vegetable oil in a wok or saucepan over medium-high heat to 170°C and fry the shallot slices in small batches until golden and crisp. Be careful not to put too many into the hot oil at once, as this will drop the temperature of the oil causing the shallots to steam rather than fry, giving a soggy result. Remove from the oil with a mesh spoon and drain on paper towel. Store in an airtight container for up to three days to keep crisp.

Ginger garlic paste

An essential component in many of the recipes in this book, and in Indian cooking in general, ginger garlic paste adds an essential fragrance and flavour. Roughly chop equal quantities of garlic cloves and peeled fresh ginger and blend in a food processor with a spoonful of water to form a smooth paste. Keep refrigerated in an airtight container and use within two days.

Ginger juice (fresh)

To make your own juice, chop peeled ginger and blend in a food processor with enough water to loosen until smooth. Press the juice through a fine mesh sieve or squeeze through muslin. You can use the pulp in cooking or to flavour a stock. Keep juice refrigerated until ready to use or make a large batch and freeze until needed.

Green onion

Green onions are also called 'scallions' and, confusingly, can be referred to as green shallots by some providores. Green onions are frequently mistaken for spring onions, however, unlike spring onions, green onions don't have a white bulb at the end of their stem. Rather, they have long, even stems that are white at the base and green at the tips. They're readily available from greengrocers and supermarkets.

Gunpowder spice mix

You'll find this heady spice blend in the food of Karnataka and Andhra Pradesh in southern India. The recipe differs slightly depending on who's making it, but it will include ground roasted lentils, coriander, cumin, Kashmiri chilli, black pepper, sesame seeds and *dagar phool* (a type of lichen). I recommend you use the blend made by Herbie's Spices, which can be ordered from their online shop and posted to you, if you can't find it at your local shop.

Kasoori methi

Giving a distinctive yet pleasant bitter taste, kasoori methi are dried fenugreek leaves.

Sold at Indian shops and some supermarkets, you can use in this form or crush to a finer powder before cooking. Kasoori methi can be used in the same way as any other leafy green herb and fresh fenugreek (*methi*) is quite easy to grow in a pot or garden at home.

Kokum
The sun-dried rind of the fruit from the kokum tree, which is native to India, kokum has an almost black appearance that transforms to a pink-purple colour when cooked. In the south, it's used to flavour coconut curries, juices and vegetable dishes and imparts a distinctive sour and fruity flavour. Used as a cooling agent, it's a key ingredient for counteracting heat in a dish. I remove the fruit after cooking, when its flavour has been spent. Kokum is available from Indian grocers.

Masala pastes
The blending of spices gives a dish its character and complexity. A masala paste is like an Asian-style curry paste, but with more spices. Masala denotes the blending of spices and different blends yield distinctive fragrant aromas and flavours. A paste means the dry spice blend has been mixed with ghee, oil, coconut milk, tamarind, vinegar, onion and other aromatics to make a wet paste, such as green or red masala. They're used for marinades when blended with yoghurt or as a base for spicy gravies and curries.

Oven-roasted tomatoes
To make, simply drizzle halved cherry or grape tomatoes with a little oil and season lightly with salt and pepper. Arrange in a single layer on a baking tray lined with baking paper and roast in a low 150°C oven for 20 minutes or until slightly caramelised and excess juices have reduced. This helps to intensify the flavour and inherent sweetness of the tomatoes.

Panch phoran
A Bengali five-spice mix used as a seasoning in the eastern regions of India. Equal quantities of whole black mustard seeds, nigella, cumin, fennel and fenugreek seeds are combined together to make this spice blend.

Pistachio paste
I buy this from The Essential Ingredient (*essentialingredient.com.au*) or other specialty pastry shops. You can also make it yourself by blending fresh, shelled green pistachio nuts with caster sugar and a little water to a fine paste.

Saffron butter
To make, soak ½ teaspoon saffron threads in 2 tablespoons warm water and set aside to infuse for 30 minutes. Cut 125 g unsalted butter into cubes and blend with the saffron and the water in a food processor or stick blender until combined. Store in an airtight container in the refrigerator until ready to use. Keeps for up to two weeks.

Sev
A Gujarati *farsan* (snack), these little crisp sticks of lentil batter are essential to many snack preparations as both a main ingredient and a garnish. Yellow in colour, they're a noodle-like crispy snack made from gram flour seasoned with turmeric and chilli. Available in small packets from Indian grocers.

Sugar syrup
To make, combine an equal quantity of caster sugar and water in a saucepan and bring to the boil. Simmer for 5 minutes, stirring, until sugar has completely dissolved. Cool and refrigerate until ready to use. As a guide, 250 g sugar and 1 cup (250 ml) water yields 400 ml sugar syrup.

Tadka
Tadka refers to the method of tempering whole spices and sometimes curry leaves in hot oil to pour over a finished dish as a final seasoning.

Tamarind puree
For convenience, you can buy tamarind puree ready-made (usually from Thai or Asian food shops), which you can keep on-hand in the fridge once opened. However, to make your own, break up a block of sun-dried tamarind pulp (sold in packets at Asian food stores and some supermarkets) and soak in twice the amount of hot water for 20 minutes. Use your hands to break down the pulp and extract. Pass through a regular chinois (cone-shaped) sieve, pushing down to extract as much puree as possible, and discard solids. Keep refrigerated for up to one month.

Urad flour
A fine lentil flour made with ground split white dal, used for making dosa, pancakes, idli and vada. Sold at Indian food shops.

Dairy Free, Gluten Free and Vegetarian

Dairy Free

Appams 394
Baked Sweet Potato, Ginger and
    Coriander 152
Banana Blossom Salad 84
Beef Dumplings 42
Bengali Mixed Vegetables 158
Bengali Sweet and Sour Eggplant 140
Black Pepper and Garlic Butter Crab 174
Black Pepper Chicken and Onion
    Curry 264
Black Pepper Prawns 171
Cabbage and Coconut Thoran 87
Cashew Pulao 305
Cauliflower Pakoras 32
Cauliflower Pickles 353
Chicken Khao Swe 66
Chicken Mulligatawny 65
Chicken Pepper Fry 200
Chilli Mango Pickle 350
Coconut Beetroot Curry 240
Coconut Chutney 358
Coconut Crab Pakoras 37
Coconut Duck Curry 261
Coriander Coconut Chutney 358
Crab, Ginger and Coconut Soup 63
Cucumber Peanut Salad 82
Curried Mussels 251
Curry Fish Salad 90
Date and Lime Pickle 354
Deep-fried Okra Sticks 33
Dosa 389
Dry Fried Beef and Coconut 225
Eggplant and Cherry Tomato Masala 144
Eggplant Pickle 346
Egg Roast 127
Fenugreek and Tomato Braised
    Mackerel 186
Fish in Coconut Milk 185
Fish Steamed in Banana Leaf 187
Fish, Coconut Clam Curry and Crab
    Salsa 259
Fried Lentil Patties 36
Fried Masala Fish 180
Fried Masala Prawns 172
Fried Mustard Greens 161
Roadside Chickpea Salad 78
Ginger Chutney 364
Ginger Crab Salad 91
Goan Prawn Curry 256
Green Bean, Pea and Coconut Poriyal 87
Green Chilli Chutney 364
Green Mango Chutney 361
Green Mango Rasam 55
Green Masala Eggs 128
Green Masala Pipis 179
Gujarati Spiced Dal 332

Hot and Spicy Lamb Ribs 219
Kachumber Salad 82
Kashmiri Tomato Salad 74
Kerala Fish Curry 254
Kerala Prawn Curry 255
Konkan Fish and Eggplant Curry 252
Lemon Rice 306
Lobster Curry 260
Masala Baked Cauliflower 158
Masala Broad Bean, Lentil and
    Asparagus Salad 85
Millet Roti 382
Minced Lamb, Tomato and Green Bean
    Dal 340
Mint Chutney 361
Mushroom Curry 242
Mustard Prawns 172
Okra Masala 138
Onion Bhajias 33
Panch Phoran Spiced Prawns 174
Pappadams 378
Parsi-style Sweet and Sour Chicken with
    Potato Straws 205
Pickled Mussels 355
Pickled Prawns 356
Pineapple Chutney 366
Pork Curry 270
Pork Vindaloo 269
Potato and Fenugreek Leaves 147
Potato and Tamarind Papdi 22
Potato Puri Puffs, Tamarind and Mint
    Water 26
Pumpkin and Coconut Dal 326
Rice and Egg Fritters 118
Rice Flour Bread 393
Rice Porridge 309
Sesame Potatoes 150
Slow-braised Kid in Cashew Coconut
    Gravy 221
Smoked Eggplant Salad 85
Spiced Green Tomatoes 74
Spiced Plum Chutney 365
Spicy Puffed Rice 24
Steamed Rice Cakes 394
Stir-fried Curry Mud Crab 176
Stir-fried Ginger and Coconut Prawns 170
Stir-fried Kohlrabi 146
Stuffed Eggplant with Green Mango and
    Beetroot Salsa 142
Stuffed Potato Chops 16
Sweet and Sour Beetroot Salad 81
Sweet and Sour Bitter Melon 139
Sweet Corn Fritters 31
Tamarind Chutney 362
Tamarind Eggplant 140
Tamarind Prawns 166
Tamarind Rice 307

Tamarind-glazed Sea Mullet 182
Tomato Chutney 365
Tomato Dal 330
Tomato Duck Curry 262
Tomato Kasundi Pickle 350
Tomato Rasam 52
Tomato Shorba 56
Turmeric and Mustard Fish Soup 64
Vegetable Avial 145
Vegetable Dal 333
Vegetable Noodle Soup 59
Vegetable Sambar 58
Watermelon, Turmeric Squid and Mint
    Salad 93
Yellow Dal and Coconut Yoghurt Soup 57

Gluten Free

Almond Lamb Curry 272
Appams 394
Assamese Fried Rice Cakes 410
Baked Curd 114
Baked Fish with Mustard Cashew
    Masala 193
Baked Sweet Potato, Ginger and
    Coriander 152
Baked Sweet Yoghurt and
    Pomegranate 410
Baked Vanilla Custard 423
Banana Blossom Salad 84
Barbecued Chicken Legs 207
Beetroot and Coconut Soup 55
Beetroot, Spinach and Cheese
    Parcels 28
Bengali Mixed Vegetables 158
Bengali Sweet and Sour Eggplant 140
Black Pepper and Cumin Brown Rice 286
Black Pepper and Garlic Butter Crab 174
Black Pepper Chicken and Onion
    Curry 264
Black Pepper Mushrooms 157
Black Pepper Prawns 171
Bombay Mess 424
Breakfast Dal 322
Butter Chicken 206
Buttermilk Sambar 48
Buttery Black Dal 318
Cabbage and Coconut Thoran 87
Cardamom and Onion Pulao 305
Cardamom Rice Pudding and Saffron
    Pears 413
Carrot Halwa, Coconut Yoghurt and
    Cashew Nougatine 402
Cashew Pulao 305
Cauliflower Dal 328
Cauliflower Pakoras 32
Cauliflower Pickles 353

Vegetarian

Index

CHRISTINE MANFIELD'S INDIAN COOKING CLASS
First published in Australia in 2021 by
Simon & Schuster (Australia) Pty Limited
Suite 19A, Level 1, Building C, 450 Miller Street,
Cammeray, NSW 2062

A JULIE GIBBS BOOK
for

SIMON & SCHUSTER
AUSTRALIA

10 9 8 7 6 5 4 3 2 1

Sydney New York London Toronto New Delhi
Visit our website at simonandschuster.com.au

NATIONAL
LIBRARY
OF AUSTRALIA

A catalogue record for this
book is available from the
National Library of Australia

ISBN: 9781760852436

Cover, internal design and illustration: Daniel New
Typesetting: Hannah Schubert and Daniel New
Photography: Alan Benson
Printed and bound in China by Asia Pacific Offset Limited

MIX
Paper from
responsible sources
FSC® C136333